NICKED!
Parking fines and how to avoid them

Brian Scovell, ex Daily Mail
sports writer and author of 29 books

His motoring statistics...
Passed driving test – 1958
Number of Penalty Charge Notices – 47
Unsuccessful appeals – 27
Successful appeals – 20
Prosecutions – 0
Crashes – 0

Grosvenor House
Publishing Limited

This book is published by
Grosvenor House Publishing Ltd
Link House
140 The Broadway, Tolworth, Surrey, KT6 7HT.
www.grosvenorhousepublishing.co.uk

A CIP record for this book
is available from the British Library

ISBN 978-1-80381-316-5
eBook ISBN 978-1-80381-317-2

ACKNOWLEDGEMENTS

My talented, hardworking, multi-skilled daughter, Louise, took the photograph for the front cover and I thank her. Also thanks to Kenneth Wiles-Manly, the cheery parking attendant who posed for it and kindly agreed to it being used on the cover of the book.

When "Nicked!" was underway, after taking three Covid jabs in as any months, I contacted bullous pemphigoid, an immune disease, in April 2020. And despite the magnificent efforts of more than a hundred consultants, nurses, porters, ambulance staff, chemists and daily carers, I'm still housebound, though slowly improving.

So it puts pressure on Louise, humping me in and out of cars for treatment in five different hospitals after having twelve falls. My son, Gavin, who mainly works abroad as a senior TV director of cricket, has helped with lifts, photographs and computer assistance. Sir Geoff Hurst of World Cup 1966 fame has the same problem using a computer in his 80s.

Thanks go to Melanie Bartle and the staff of Grosvenor House Publishing company. And a round of applause for the adjudicators who let me off and boos for those who penalized me unfairly. I thank Bromley's parking department for wading through my persistent stream of letters.

The title "Nicked!" came from my best friend, Gillian Treharne, former head mistress, who keeps me in order. As I haven't driven for eighteen months – SORN (unlicensed) – I haven't had a single PCN but I'm hoping to be back at the wheel next year.

PARKING QUOTE OF THE DAY

Jack Flavell (George Sanders), in the 1940 film *Rebecca*, tells a policeman who told him not to park there, "Nonsense, man. It's a pity that you haven't got better things to do." There was a real Jack Flavell (1929-2004), and he was the Worcestershire and England fast bowler who terrorised batsmen in the 1960s. Ruddy-faced and red-headed, he resented being told what to do. His job was to pitch the ball on a length to hit the top of the off stump, and he rarely strayed. Now and again he fired in a bouncer aimed for the batsman's head.

When he retired, he still had the remnants of the temperament of a tough car parking attendant, but that breed had yet to be invented. Instead he owned a café and then a hotel. I knew him when I became a young cricket reporter working for the *Daily Sketch* between 1960-1971, and he was an honest, upright Staffordshire man.

A BRUSH WITH THE LAW

I am guilty as charged, like most of the increasing number of pensioners who still drive to do their shopping and often exceed the two-hour limit and are fined. When you storm into Waitrose or Sainsburys to protest, they tell us it was nothing to do with them, it's a private parking company in Qatar or the Cayman Islands. "Take it up with them," they say. When they write back months later, we have difficulty in remembering the facts, so the matter is closed.

I've clocked up 50 or so parking offences, and as a man aged well over the three score and ten years, it will get worse. Yes, I'm a serial offender, and the authorities must be fed up with my appeals. I succeed in around one-third of the cases, but it is a tiresome affair wasting a day in stuffy rooms in central London when it is impossible to park your vehicle without being booked yet again.

The phrase about age comes from Psalm 90, verse 10 in the Bible, and now life expectation for a male is in the early eighties. A vast number of today's veterans are sports fanatics – playing golf in all weathers, bending to play bowls, taking part in over-70s or even over-80s cricket, and a new creation – walking football for slow coaches no longer able to "run" more than 3mph. They also forsake red meat and go for vegan, and some have moved into the ranks of teetotallers. And I am a lifelong member of non-drinking the hard stuff.

My only brush with the police came at 4am some 30 or so years ago while driving from Heathrow along the A4 into London, when a police car slowed down and drove about 30 yards behind my Honda Legend for some time. I observed the 40mph limit, only slowing to go round corners and roundabouts, and after a mile the policeman turned on his flashing lights signalling me to stop, which I did. He was of Indian or Pakistani origin, with a moustache, and was polite as he said, "Why are you driving so slowly?"

I said, "I had to slow to go round the roundabouts and corners, that's all."

He said, "Could you please step out of the car?"

I said, "I have been disabled since 1943, and as you can see I have a Blue Badge. You might notice my Press card. I work for the *Daily Mail*." I've never seen anyone react so submissively. "I'm terribly sorry, sir. Remain where you are. But if you don't mind, can I smell your breath, sir?"

"I have yet to clean my teeth," I said.

"Don't worry, sir," he said.

I turned my head towards him as he bent down, and I blew my nose vigorously. "I've never taken alcohol, as you can detect," I said.

He smiled, wished me a good day, and drove off. Some police officers, in my experience, were rather curt and unfriendly. Ditto with parking operatives of both sexes. There are, of course, many of them who are human and show respect, like this one.

So what do the local council parking clerks do in their offices? Instead of taking all aspects of a parking case, they send you a long-winded, jargon-loaded Penalty Charge Notice, and if you don't pay the £65 fine within a fortnight, it will be doubled to £130. By the time you remember your password, it is too late to check with the photographic evidence online. The authorities are ready to call up the bailiffs, and if you don't pay up you could be imprisoned in an already full cell without running water.

It gets worse if stubborn people keep objecting as a right. The iniquity of introducing PCNs was included in the Road Act of 1991, and it spread like a flu virus throughout Britain that winter, becoming impossible to avoid. With the nights closing in, more and more veterans became victims.

Nothing is being done by the police when we are half blinded by trying to avoid far-too-bright LED headlights coming towards us, but if we are a minute or two past the time when we first parked, they jump out of their vehicle and snatch photographs of the alleged "evidence".

I could go on, but we need to humour the parking officer who is younger these days and smarter. The answer is to give him a copy of this book, which sets out the best accounts of my number of PCNs. Read on, friends, and win confidence in trying to persuade the parking ticket officer to tear it up and say, "On your way, mate." Well, they used to.

WAS HER MAJESTY
THE QUEEN EVER BOOKED?

Unlikely, because in all her travelling in cars on public roads, other people took the wheel. We only saw pictures of her driving in the royal parks, and she has been a good driver.

As a *Daily Mail* cricket writer, I went sometimes to the holiest of the holy – the Lord's pavilion, built in the 1890s. Kings have inspected the two teams before a Test match, and Queen Elizabeth II visited on 27 occasions while inspecting the two teams in a male preserve.

At one Test – I can't remember the year – I was standing outside the Committee Room on the right on the first floor, when a man inside the room pushed open the door as the Queen came up to me. She looked up with a half smile and I noticed her blue eyes were beautiful. She didn't recognise me. The security man might have introduced me!

The other person who had fantastic blue eyes was Margaret Thatcher. Around the same time, I sat next to her at the Cabinet Room in 10 Downing Street, discussing curbing the growing volume of football hooliganism. I had been invited as the Chairman of the Football Writers' Association. She dominated the meeting, though she didn't know much about the failings of English football. She wanted fans to join a membership, but the police rejected the idea. I managed to correct a fact about Gary Lineker's transfer which she got wrong about where the money went. And the "wets" – Cabinet members who were bullied by her – provided hardly anything. It proved a futile exercise.

In 2010, our wandering social club, the Woodpeckers CC, played the Windsor Great Park CC – mainly servants working

5

at the Castle – and despite losing by nine wickets in a reduced 30 overs game, Stephan Lazarczuk, their Ukrainian secretary, wanted to keep us on his fixture list because we took them to the last over. Stephan's elders were forced to fight for the Russians in the WW2 and were classed as displaced persons afterwards, and his family migrated to England and finished up working in the Castle.

Our fixture in 2011 fell on the day of the 150th anniversary of their club, June 26, and Stephan said the Queen often went to the nearby church where the players and their wives and partners would be presented to her.

Suddenly we were gazumped by an old hard-bitten, Australian 82-year-old bat-maker known as Swan Richards, whose Crusaders CC have played five times at Great Windsor Park. On June 26, they were scheduled to play at Chester, but when Richards heard the news about the Queen, he cancelled the Chester fixture and contacted the Great Park chairman who agreed to make the Woodpeckers redundant. I made great efforts to change the new arrangements but without success. "Swan" isn't his real name, but after scoring eight ducks for the 6th X1 for Prospect CC in Adelaide, he said, "They were all gracefully performed and so they named me Swan." His real name is Robert Milton Richards.

It was incredible that this heroic, saintly, loved Queen was still working on stately affairs within a day or two before she died. I was extremely bucked when I watched the television coverage of the procession from Balmoral to Edinburgh as I saw the registration number of one of the cars: 'AES'. That is the Christian and surname of my wife Audrey Esther Scovell, who died from cancer of the liver on Christmas Day, 2000 aged 58. I don't look at every registration but key times, an 'AES' catches my eye. It is very uplifting.

HOW NOT TO DO IT!

As the lockdown was just about to happen in early July 2020, I wanted to park in Court Street off Widmore Road, in the centre of Bromley – one of the more orderly boroughs in London. It is a small road of 40 or so metres, running up to the fire station, and there are two disabled parking spaces which are usually occupied. At 10.49am I spotted that one was filled by a white Ford saloon. The other space was empty.

Another vehicle, a Toyota C-HR saloon, was parked on double yellow lines. Both cars had Bromley Blue Badges. I found it difficult to park between them – a mere two feet away from both cars.

After each attempt to get closer to the kerb, I checked my Honda and it was still three feet away, but having a right leg, which hasn't bent since 1943, I needed to swing my leg without being blocked by the door or tripped on the kerb. If the car is less than a foot away, I find it difficult to try to stand up.

Suddenly a grey-suited parking officer in his twenties, without a "Good morning, sir", appeared, waved an arm dismissively, and shouted, "You are illegally parked!"

I said, "I am disabled."

He shouted, "I know, but you are illegally parked."

Before I could explain about my leg, he made off. I resumed my attempts to park legally – driving forwards and back five or six times with the wheel spinning round one way and the other. In going into reverse, I now have a piece of equipment which shows the lines, and a noise is sounded if the wheels are over the white lanes. I noticed that my offside wheels were marginally up to the white line.

Bromley has plenty of CCTV cameras, and I needed VAR which they use in football. The wheel might be a millimetre over: could be costly. Fortunately it wasn't. The driver of the Toyota had his time of arrival on his Blue Badge and it showed 10.50, which was inaccurate because he'd parked much earlier. Two offences then!

I left the scene and tried to find the Vodafone shop in The Glades Mall to find out why my monthly bill for my mobile had risen to £194.69 in April. There was a notice saying the shop was closed and said to ring 191. Back home, I tried 191: it was "not recognised". You need to speak to these people, but it's nigh impossible! Two months later, when I went to the Vodafone shop, it was still closed – despite having seen online that they were opened at 9am until 6pm.

I managed to get through to Vodafone GHQ after 40 minutes of listening to unwanted music and hearing countless repeats of "your call is important and we have experienced a high number of calls", and was told the nearest Vodafone shop was Eltham High Street – four miles away. I set off, only to discover those new plastic, red obstructions indicating no parking and only one disabled space near the shop, which was occupied. It required a long walk after finding a parking space. When I eventually arrived, there were three young employees who were trying to help costumers who were speaking in loud voices. When it was my turn, I could hardly hear the young man who was explaining why my account had reached a record high for an over-80. I signed up for a new account with 280 free calls. A month later they sent me a reminder I was £11 in debt and my cheapo mobile had been suspended.

More abortive calls to Vodafone GHQ proved fruitless, and I set off on the trek to their Eltham store. I spotted a parking space 50 metres from the shop and U-turned to move into it. Suddenly a white Ford saloon beat me to it. I did another U-turn at a junction, upsetting several drivers, and saw another driver leaving right outside the store. It was a "disabled" space, so I nipped into it.

Another piece of luck was being the only customer, and an employee – a young, smart, tattooed lady from Eastern Europe – quizzed me in perfect English. Tattoos started in the Neolithic times more than 40,000 years ago, and spread to Britain from 1671 onwards. Sailors and criminals were favourite customers, and two English kings went for it. Not long ago, the House of Lords called for it to be banned at a young age, but the idea was dropped. More and more tattoo shops have been opened in recent years, and a growing number of females are joining in. One wonders whether their skin can take any more when they reach the menopause.

Ben Stokes is probably the most tattooed English cricketer and had physical and mental problems. Are they related?

The young lady tried to call an administrator from behind a plastic anti-virus shield to ask why my mobile was "restricted", and after 20 minutes an automated answer came up: "This service is unable to deal with this matter at the moment and we thank you for contacting us." She dialled again several times, and after a delay she succeeded in speaking to a human being, who came up with the same answer.

I had my Visa card ready to pay the tiny £11 debt, but further delays occurred before I was able to have the bill paid and leave. After sitting on an uncomfortable tall chair for 90 minutes, I thanked her and added, "As someone disabled, these chairs are very awkward to sit on."

"I agree," she said. "We've ordered better ones, but they have yet to arrive."

Half an hour later, sitting in a traffic jam, my mobile sent a text: "Are you satisfied with Vodafone?"

What could I say? I didn't want to blame the patient girl who had dealt with me. I didn't bother to reply.

A SHORT HISTORY
OF MY RIGHT KNEE

The Scovell family moved into 5, Kimber Cottages, Ocean View Road, Ventnor (named after vents) overlooking the English Channel in, after our nearby house started to crack up. I read online about 20-year-old William Duggan, who lived three doors away from our terraced house, and died on November 15, 1915, in the Battle of the Somme. It made me think. Rudyard Kipling thought up the idea of putting up memorials for the war dead, but someone ought to have followed up by putting plaques on the walls outside their homes as a permanent reminder of the horrors of war.

The family Scovell – my mum, Maude, my father, Percy, my brother Allan, seven years older than me, and me – all took turns in a tin bath, using the same water poured in by bowls heated by the cast iron Aga oven, and placed on the stone floor of the kitchen each Saturday night. A Swedish physicist Gustaf Dalen invented the Aga in 1922, and when he was working on a new model, it blew up and he became blind. The sturdy Agas had a life span of 50 years or longer, with no more being made after 2017.

Our family was ready to take on Hermann Goering's Luftwaffe and Adolf Hitler's Wehrmacht, after WW2 was declared on September 3, 1939, and Prime Minister Neville Chamberlain finished his soulful speech by saying: "Now may God bless you all and may He defend the right, for it is evil things that we shall be fighting against – brute force, bad faith, injustice, oppression, and persecution – and against them I am certain that the right will prevail.'

British convoys, mostly from the Dominions, were carrying food, materials, and armaments, and were continually attacked by Stuka bombers, Heinkels, Messerschmitts, and Junkers. Allan found a large, round mirror, and we used to take it to the top of our garden and flash the rays of the sun onto the sea on sunny days while we watched the dogfights between RAF's Spitfires, Hurricanes, and other, slower aircraft against Luftwaffe's superior forces.

We listened to the BBC to hear the latest reports on how many more German aircraft were shot down against ours. Winston Churchill and his great friend Lord Beaverbrook, who was given a Cabinet job in charge of mass production of Britain's aircraft, ordered the BBC to tell blatant lies about losses. The facts about losses in the Isle of Wight were that 46 RAF aircraft were shot down, while the Luftwaffe's total was just 20. The fake news was to keep morale up at a sticky time, which was understandable.

Churchill and his mother often stayed at Flint Cottage, where his nurse's sister lived in Steephill Cove in his youth. It is overlooked by Ventnor's cricket ground, where my cricket first started in 1946. I met their first team captain Jack "Dooley" Rogers, and he invited me to take part in the nets. Each year the club organised a fair to raise money, and my friend Ged Steele and I would queue up to try to bowl out the left-handed opener Frank Cowley. Frank put a 5p on the off stump, and every time we bowled him out, he would hand over the money.

I started out bowling Chinamen – the left-hand slow delivery bowled with a leg break turning away from the off to a left-hander. Peter Mabey, the star all-rounder, showed me how to bowl quicker, to swing the ball late. Four years later, my confidence in bowling was shattered at a charity match at Shanklin against a Hampshire XI, when the great West Indian batsman Roy Marshall slashed 20 runs off my first over.

I asked Denis Cuthill, Shanklin's captain, if he ought to take me off. He said, "No, try your Chinamen instead." He kept me on for an hour and a half, and my figures were 3-132, all caught on the boundary in 15 overs and obviously no maidens. The crowd was shouting, "Take him off!"

My victims were the great medium bowler, Derek Shackleton, off-break bowler Mervyn Burden, and Alan Rayment, who scored 86. I met him in 2010 at the Dorset Cricket Society, and he said, "I can't remember that." Well, he was in his nineties and died not long after.

In one of Churchill's visits, he claimed he'd seen the wreck of the troop carrier *Euridyce* offshore at Bembridge, with the loss of 365 lives in WWI. The victims were mainly destitute coloured South Africans who wanted to join the British army.

Ventnor, population of around 5,500, has attracted many famous people for its temperate climate, including Karl Marx, Haile Selassie, George Bernard Shaw, Edward Elgar, Charles Dickens, Joachim Von Ribbentrop – the then German Ambassador to Britain – and Reichsmarschall Hermann Goering, about to be Commander in Chief of the Luftwaffe, the man who ordered the bombing raids in Britain.

Our mum, Maude Janet Scovell, known as Poppy or Kitty, once told us, "One of these days the Germans will see that mirror shining and drop a bomb on us." Lo and behold, she was almost right.

In the autumn of 1943, in one of the last German tip and run raids, two Focke-Wulfe 190s strafed and bombed where we lived under the 241ms high St Boniface Down – the highest point of the island, and where one of the chain of radar stations was built along the South Coast.

Percy John Scovell, my father, was a jobbing carpenter and worked on the building of it for several months in 1937. He never told us what he was doing, because the authorities ordered the workers to sign the Official Secrets Act. Anyone blabbing could be arrested and imprisoned for a long time. Or even been hanged as a traitor. The talkative Percy, known as "Pud", went to his grave, aged 87, without giving any hints about his war work.

He also worked on the underground, smaller radar station close to where I was born at The Toll House, built in 1830 in the village of St Lawrence (population 400) on The Undercliff, perched on blue slipper clay. One hundred and sixty years or more years later, the blue slipper started to slip, and huge holes appeared in the main A3055 road in February 2014. It connected St Lawrence to Niton, where Perce was born, and the council blocked the road before spending a large sum of EU funds to restore it. The closure meant that for some time the residents had to use a four-mile detour up a steep, narrow road past the defunct railway station, and you had to turn sharp left to Niton – if you were lucky. Alfred Noyes, who wrote the poem "The Highwayman", lived there and some of his literary friends often stayed with him.

William Spindler, a rich German chemist, visited St Lawrence in the 1880s and fell in love with the area, particularly one of the bays, Binnel Bay. He set about building elegant Victorian mansions to outdo those in nearby Ventnor. The venture flopped, and thereafter William's properties were known as "Spindler's Follies".

Karl Marx stayed in a Victorian house close to Bonchurch between 1881-3, but except for a small blue plaque on the wall, there is no memorial to commemorate the bearded, blinkered man who cocked up a sixth of the world. After the Russian Revolution in 1917, his followers Lenin and Stalin subsequently ordered over 20 million deaths. The followers of the extremists want Communism brought back. No chance!

Since 1810, there were seven more occasions when blue slipper brought about more collapses in the south of the Isle of Wight. In Luccombe, a village overlooking Shanklin and Sandown Bay, there were similar blue slipper avalanches.

Allan worked on Uffa Fox's Flying Fifteen yachts at Cowes before becoming a builder. He bought a house there, despite insurance companies not being keen to insure it. It still stands proudly on a hillock, catching all the wind from all sides, but as he used to say, "It has great views." Parking was easy, but you risked losing your car to a hole in the roadway any time.

On the night of 15 August, 1943, a German U-boat dropped a dozen or so armed storm troopers in two dinghies, and after paddling a short distance, they disembarked in Woody Bay. It was a favourite haunt of our family, and we spent most of our Sundays there every summer. The Jerries, as they were called in those days, scaled the 100 feet high cliff and were undetected as they raced along the rounded pathway to the radar station. The alarm was set off, and soldiers from a nearby barracks appeared and exchanged fire with them.

A book, written by the Ryde historian Adam Searle, was published in the autumn of 2019 claiming the Germans entered the building and made off with cathode-ray direction-finding equipment which they took back to Alderney where they were based. John Arlott spent his final years at Alderney, on the heavily armed island. Thousands of slaves captured by the Germans did all the work on building sheltered gun emplacements, and many of them died there.

Searle quoted a German survivor, who went on the raid to St Lawrence, as saying, "We were shocked to be met by regular British soldiers rather than the Home Guard. It is unclear whether any British soldiers were killed or wounded. This incident was wiped from the war history within hours of it happening, with witnesses made to sign the Official Secrets Act."

When I wrote my book *Thank You, Hermann Goering – the Life of a Sports Writer*, which was published in 2010, I interviewed the owner of the Old Park Hotel not far from the radar station. A fellow pupil at my private school Ventnor College, his name was Rob Thornton. He said, "The raid definitely took place, and there was a fire fight between the Germans and regular British soldiers. The Germans got away with a piece of equipment, and none of them died. Young educated young ladies who were in the Women's Auxiliary

Air Force worked in the radar station, and I think one of them was killed.

"Around this time, another one spotted the German battleship *Scharnhorst* passing through the English Channel, but her superiors said it wasn't the sister ship of the *Bismarck,* which was commissioned in 1939. Later, it was proved that she was right, and she was promoted and moved to Bletchley. *Scharnhorst* and its accompanying destroyers were sunk by a British force at North Cape on Boxing Day in 1943. Only 36 survivors from *Scharnhorst,* out of a crew of 1,943, were picked up by British vessels."

Another witness I interviewed was an active 95-year-old sheep shearer, who confirmed the validity of the story. Searle reported that the Air Raid Precautions Service wrote in a log book, saying, "Special Report, police report two dinghies full of Germans in the sea. Seen at 2.18 hours, reported to police through Navy."

Both British and German official war diaries never mentioned the Woody Bay raid – the first and only time when Germans invaded Britain in WW11.

Not having a John Anderson-reinforced air raid shelter, we took refuge in a cupboard under the stairs as the siren went off, when a couple of Focke-Wulfe 190s were detected by the staff at the main radar station at the St Boniface Down – famous for its Bronze Age burial ground. The 190s were looked on as superior to the Spitfires at the time, and their 30mm cannon did immense amount of damage, as well as dropping two bombs.

In 1940, a squadron of German bombers attacked the underground bunker at the radar station, which was protected by ten feet of concrete. No-one died, and the station was back functioning the following day. Most of the RAF spotters were teenagers straight from leaving school and eager to pick up a girl at a dance on Saturday night. An entrepreneur bought the site and turned it into a historic museum-cum-hotel which has one of the best views of Southern England and the Channel.

The Isle of Wight's official wartime records say there were 1,594 alerts, 125 bombing attacks, 1,592 explosives and oil bombs were dropped, thousands of incendiary bombs, six V1s (Doodlebugs), and that there were 10,873 instances of property being damaged, and 92 men, 90 women, and 32 children, died.

On that day, we heard an explosion then the all-clear was sounded, and there was no sign of our row of cottages being damaged. Next day, we were at the top of the garden wielding our mirror again, when my mum called us to come in for lunch. I started running down the path, but tripped and fell headlong. I got up and didn't see any injuries so went down the steps past the outside toilet and into the kitchen, which had a stone floor with no carpets or lino. My mum pointed to my right leg and said, "What's that sticking out from your knee?"

I looked down and realised that was my knee bone was sticking out from a gaping hole. There was hardly any blood and it didn't hurt, but I soon burst into tears brought on by the shock. She said, "I think the glass was blown out from the greenhouse next door, and you landed on a piece of glass."

Many years later, I spoke at a primary school in Carisbrooke, and a nine-year-old boy asked, "Was there any blood?"

I laughed and replied, "That was a good question. The skin on the patella is very thin and, yes, you are nearly right. There wasn't much blood." The children were very relieved.

We didn't have a telephone, a computer, a mobile, or an iPad, but there was a red telephone box opposite our house. My mum crossed the road, went into the red telephone box, put in four pennies, and pressed the red button to get through to the number of the surgery of our new doctor, J. Bruce Williamson. He was a 6ft 3 Scot who was married to an actress. Our first doctor, Professor Carl Prausnitz, had been briefly interned at the start of 1939 under the Defence

Regulations, because he was born in Germany, but he was soon released. Pity he had been detained, because he might well have been a better stitcher than Williamson.

Searle is a diligent researcher, and he revealed that Prausnitz was a well respected, world renowned immunology expert. If he were alive, no doubt he would be helpful in finding the right vaccine to eliminate Coronavirus-19.

Prausnitz was born on October 11, 1876, in Hamburg, of mixed German-English parentage, and he often visited English relatives in the Isle of Wight. In 1935 he made up his mind that the Nazis were ruining Germany and settled down as a GP in Bonchurch, a pretty village adjoining Ventnor. His mother's maiden name was Giles, and he then came known as Prausnitz-Giles.

Bonchurch has a famous 11th century church, and across the road Charles Dickens wrote a slab of *Great Expectations* when he stayed at a house called Winterbourne in 1849. Apparently, he used the extraordinary story of the jilted Margaret Dick, and the called her Miss Havisham. Half of the building was later to become an exclusive restaurant called Peacock Vane. Audrey and I dined there when we visited the Island, but in 2005 the building was turned in two prime houses.

When I visited the church, I was introduced to an elderly worshipper, aged 88, who claimed that she knew all about the German invasion in 1943. She also told me a fascinating tale about Hermann Goering, the Deputy to Hitler, who stayed in Godshill to see the speedboat races in the Solent in 1935 and then went to see Lord Jellicoe about appeasement talks at his home at St Lawrence Hall. A few months later, the Hall was destroyed by fire, though Admiral of the Fleet Earl Jellicoe of The Battle of Jutland in WW1 luckily wasn't present. The destructive battle of the British and German battleships was credited as a win by Britain, because the surviving German dreadnoughts never came out of their docks afterwards for the rest of the war.

Prausnitz was awarded the Iron Cross 1st class in WW1 and served as a captain in the Home Guard in Ventnor in WW11. Our family thought he was a nice, friendly man. He lived to 97. The World Health Organisation – mainly financed by former USA President Donald Trump until he pulled the plug in 2020 – said the average life expectancy in the population of 140,200 in the Isle of Wight has risen to the mid-80s and will continue faster than most parts of the UK, because of its equable climate.

Back at 5, Kimber Cottages, Dr Williamson's secretary took the message about my knee injury, and he was soon driving up the well named Zigzag Road towards Lowtherville, where the vents happen. A few months earlier, the telephone kiosk had been put out of action when a German aircraft, firing indiscriminately, sent a bullet through one of the glass panes and killed a man who was standing while making a call. That wasn't on the BBC news! That telephone box was fated, though. Some years later, the green painted seat next to it suddenly disappeared down from a vent. The seat was eventually found, but no bodies were discovered.

Forty-two-year-old Dorothy O'Grady from Sandown was the first person in the Island to be charged under the Treachery Act, and after a two-day trial in 1940, she was found guilty and sentenced to death. Her offence was passing on information about the Island's defences and possible landing details, while taking her dog out. She would have been the first woman to be hanged in Britain for the offence, but she appealed and the decision was commuted to a sentence of 14 years.

She was released in 1955 and, when asked about her feelings, said, "I'd be happy just to stay on at Holloway Prison." The last woman who was hanged was Ruth Ellis, in the same year. The Tower of London was one of the favoured places for executions, and the last one took place in 1941 when a German spy, Josef Jakobs, met his end by a firing squad.

Doctor Williamson lived in a secluded detached house overlooking the Esplanade, and as a heavy smoker he had a square hole in his surgery to let the smoke escape. He was a heavy drinker as well. He parked his car outside our house without being penalised and knocked at the door. Today, that road would have double yellow lines and he would have been sent a PCN.

"What's happening, you bonny lad?" he said. Bonny would have been the last word I would use in the circumstances. "Does it hurt?" he asked.

I said, "A bit."

He picked me up and put me on a white bathroom towel on the kitchen table, poured some iodine from a bottle on cotton wool and put it on the cut. Whoa, that stung! He'd asked for a bowl with boiling water to put a needle in the water to kill any germs. He then pulled together the skin either side of the patella and started to insert seven stitches. That was really painful.

"Within a week you will right as rain," he said.

The ugly stitching remains with a scar, after 78 years. No respected surgeon would want to redo it, although one suggested a full replacement of the joint. I demurred. My hardy right knee has lasted a lifetime and it might have complications after surgery.

Within a few days, my temperature shot up to 105F, and my mum rang the doctor and asked him to call in as soon as possible. When he arrived and took my temperature – with the old glass phial under the tongue – he said, "I'll ring for an ambulance. He needs to go to the Royal Ryde Infirmary Hospital as soon as possible."

The homely hospital was visited in the 1930s by Prince Edward, Prince of Wales, who became, very briefly, King Edward V111. He was reputed to have had to stay with the Duchess of Windsor and her entourage at the Beach Hotel on the Esplanade, close to our doctor's house. It is now established that the Duchess had an affair with Joachim von Rippentrop, the English-speaking German Ambassador in the 1930s, who was sentenced to be hanged after the Nuremburg trials in 1946.

A Channel 4 programme on Edward and his voracious Wallis described how the pair cavorted with Hitler and his cohorts. In one document sent to Berlin, Edward suggested "heavy bombing of Britain would cause surrender". No wonder they were exiled and despised by the royal family.

There was an open fire in the Ryde hospital ward, and debris from the smoke landed on the open wound of a boy next to me. Alexander Fleming, who had a second home in Shanklin, Isle of Wight, was the first to bring out penicillin in Britain. My best friend at the time, David Prior, and I were the first boys to be given it in the island. In my case, aged eight, hairs appeared on my legs and the nurses would whip off the bed clothes to see how they were progressing. The normal attire was a white smock and no pants. Invading our privacy was normal then; today it would lead to a disciplinary case.

The hospital was pulled down in 1991, leaving only one hospital in the island – St. Mary's in Newport. In those days, my illness was known as septic arthritis, and there was no cure for it. Today it is called sepsis. I spent six months in the hospital, mainly with my leg in plaster, which caused continual itching. I was then transferred to the Lord Mayor Treloar Cripples (Sic) Orthopaedic Hospital, named after a Lord Mayor of London.

After the war, the hospital concentrated on long-term orthopaedic cases of young boys. Block 5, where I spent another 18 months, had a huge balcony, and once the temperature was over 60F, the glass doors opened and we were wheeled out. We had great suntans. When the plaster was eventually hacked off, rather painfully, I couldn't straighten my right leg, so they put me in an extension – a weight attached to my foot with the aim of straightening my leg. That didn't work either. I had three manipulative operations – someone jumping on the knee to break the adhesions. No joy from that either. I was eventually discharged with a five-degree movement of a permanently stiff leg, and it is still holding up now – just about.

When I was 11, I went on train trips on my own to attend a physiotherapy unit in the Newport Hospital three times week. On one occasion, I was the only passenger in a compartment when a middle-aged man got in and sat next to me. I was wearing shorts, and he looked at my scar on my knee and asked, "How did that happen?"

I began to explain, and he started rubbing his hand up and down on my knee. Suddenly he shoved his hand in an attempt to touch my privates. I yelled out, but it wasn't a through train, and no-one heard me. So I jumped up and rushed to the door. Luckily, the train was about to stop.

I got out and, not seeing anyone, I ran to the next empty carriage. I told my mother, and she complimented me, but she didn't ring the police. With CCTV everywhere now, the police would put out the man's photograph online and call for a prosecution.

Another piece of luck was when we moved to St. Alban's Road, overlooking St Albans Church. We were seldom attendees at the church, but the Reverend Andrew Rumball asked if I wanted to join the choir. I declined. Some time later, he was sentenced to 11 years for abusing children.

Boys are cruel; no-one would contest that. Back at school, fellow pupils would taunt me with taunts of "Hopalong", or "Hoppity", and using various other demeaning words like "you cripple", but I ignored them. When someone brought along a tennis ball for a kickabout, I was able to get around better than most of them.

My mum had experienced similar insults in her school days, and she recited that old rhyme first used in the US Christian Recorder addressed to young black children in 1862: "Sticks and stones might break my bones, but words will never hurt."

In a past generation, racist or demoniac shouts at a football match were looked on as banter, and George Cohen – the nicest of the players in the 1966 World Cup – has one of the best anecdotes about Fulham's Jimmy Hill. "Jim was always baited because of his beard and appearance, and on one occasion he was going mad calling for the ball, which was always going to Johnny Haynes and not to him. One fan yelled, 'For God's sake, give it the Rabbi!' Afterwards, he was always called the Rabbi."

I was present at the same, haunted ground in Sofia on November 2, 1983, when Watford beat Spartak Levski 3-1, and there were no Nazi salutes nor racist abuse despite Watford having a black player, the popular Luther Blissett, in their team. My family had just finished a week's half term break at Val de Lobo in Portugal. Unbeknown to us, the *Daily Express* had a front-page story about a Tory Minister nearly drowning on that beach, and if the *Mail* news editor had known that I'd stayed in the same hotel, I would have been reprimanded for missing the scoop.

Shortly afterwards, I drove to Luton airport and parked, ready to join the Watford party to fly off to Sofia. Elton John was chairman at the time, and he sat up the front of the Monarch aircraft while the journalists sat at the rear. After we flew off, he defied the warning sign about seat belts and stood up and introduced himself. He began cracking jokes and teasing us as he poured out the champagne. I thought he was very excitable and, having read extracts from his 2019 book about his career, I can now understand how he behaved. In one extract in the *Mail*, he confessed that he took cocaine. He said, "Cocaine made me a monster."

Eddie Plumley, probably the most liked secretary of any English club at that time, explained that Elton was upset at the reporting about his hair transplant. In June, Watford played a friendly against Ipswich in front of 60,000 fans in Beijing, and lost 3-1 in a three-match pioneering tour. Elton proved a big hit there, and Sofia was tame in comparison. We were billeted on the 19th floor of our hotel, and it took some time to get down to the ground floor. I was short of the local currency, and a local told me, "Don't go to a bank, they never give you the proper rate. People will come up to you with a far better rate."

Foolishly, I allowed myself to be approached by a man flourishing notes out in the street, and he offered me a small wad of notes in exchange for a £20 note. "It is ten times better than the official rate," he said.

Back in the hotel lobby, I asked a Bulgarian journalist how much it was in English money, and he said, "It's worth 50 pence... in Greek drachmas."

When Elton and the players heard about it, they chided me. Elton joked, "You're in the wrong country!"

The 30-odd media people travelled to the ground in a bus behind the team coach, with a police escort. And up in the open-air press box, we soon discovered it was extremely difficult to ring our offices, and no-one was unable to find a remedy. The journalists were cursing, and when the match went into extra time, most of them were panicking. One or two calls got through from their sports desks, and we had to ad lib our stories to copywriters – just in time.

After the match, our aircraft was waiting at the airport and had to depart on time, otherwise the airport had to be closed. It was a close-run thing and my report arrived just in time for the last edition of the *Daily Mail,* courtesy of my *Daily Mirror* friend Harry Miller, who passed his open telephone line to me. Someone on the *Mirror*'s switchboard transferred the call to the *Daily Mail.*

Elton cheered us up when we flew off, pouring out the last of the champagne. Nearing the English Channel, the pilot announced that there was heavy fog at Luton, and we would be re-routed to Manchester. Curses all round. Coaches then took us to Luton, where we arrived at 5am. I was relieved to see my Honda Legend was unclamped with no PCN on the windscreen.

On another Euro football trip, in 1967 with West Ham, the opponents were Magdeburg in East Germany, and we were delayed for more than an hour at Checkpoint Charlie. Armed, grim looking soldiers kept checking our passports and travel documents. We passed the time by competing with our colleagues to name footballing Charlies. I came up with only two: Charlie Cooke, one of the most intelligent footballers I've known; and Charlie Hurley, the Sunderland centre half.

When I arrived at Heathrow afterwards, I travelled on the Underground to Upton Park to collect my car, but I couldn't remember the name of the road. It took me some time to find it, and when I did, I noticed my keys had been left hanging from the driver's side. That area was renowned for stealing cars, so it was a remarkable let off.

Elton went on all three foreign trips during Watford's cup run, and he was the life and soul of the party. The first one was to the German club Kaiserslautern, where Watford won through in the half full Fritz Walter stadium. The third one was at the more lively Sparta Prague ground, where the Czechs won 4-0. On the way back, Elton ribbed manager Graham Taylor all the time, and if laughs are the best remedy to cheer people up, Watford were top of the range. Taylor was much loved in Watford and its environs, as evidenced by the fact that a statue of him now stands proudly outside Vicarage Road.

HIATUS ABOUT MY BLUE BADGE

Yes, my mother was a very brave, determined lady, who made every effort to have a normal life with her disability. But in later life when she moved to a bungalow in Lake, the shops were too far away, so she needed a car. She failed her first four driving tests but succeeded with the fifth. In 1970, the Government brought in the Chronically Sick and Disabled Persons Act and introduced the Orange Badges as a right for people if a person met statutory requirements. One was that you couldn't walk for 100 yards. She applied and said she had difficulty in walking too far, but could manage 100 yards. The local council department rejected her application, and it took some time with letters flying backwards and forwards before they relented.

Soon she found it difficult getting in and out of the car, so she stopped driving. A kind neighbour used to collect her weekly order, and she gave her Orange Badge, which had no name on it, to me.

I was living in Beckenham, a cricketer's long throw from Dave Bowie's property. Fortunately we never mixed with him and his mates, because he flouted normal conventions and probably had a pile of PCNs lying in his car. In 1991, the Blue Badge took over and I applied to the Council and was given one. Early in 2002, I had a stringent test, and a friendly, middle-aged lady passed me as suitable for a renewal.

Then a member of staff in the same department wrote to me on June 23 – Audrey would have been 60 on that day – saying they had changed their minds and that my badge had been cancelled. I think a whistle-blower might have told them that I was still playing social cricket for my wandering side, the Woodpeckers. As captain and organizer, I was an automatic selection each Sunday, fielding at first slip which didn't require running, and also between the wickets because I'd perfected a hobble of around 6/7 mph. My much used "shot" was the snick through the slips which didn't necessarily need leaving my crease.

When you run with a stiff right leg, you have to swing your leg out like a Paralympic runner. In the Harrogate match between the English cricket writers and the Australian press team, which included the infamous Kerry Packer and former Australian captain Ian Chappell in 1978, the late and respected John Thicknesse of the *Evening Standard* came up with a hilarious description of my "running": he said, "It swings as it sweeps."

The Bromley parking people ordered another physical check into my condition. This time, a stern looking, older lady decided that I had failed the test again. I was too fit, according to her. I wrote to the man in charge – his name was Trevor Browne – and he responded with a rude letter of rejection. I asked for a retrial, and they sent a much younger lady who was much more friendly and seemed to be rather sympathetic. A few days later, though, I opened the envelope and the answer was still no.

I had previously written to the fiery, red-headed Labour MP for Blackburn, Mrs Barbara Castle, who was Minister of Transport, suggesting that having a Blue Badge should cover the whole country, not just the area controlled by the council where you live. Meanwhile, I'd been nicked by the Kensington Council and been served with a PCN. I hoped that my letter to the MP could be used in my appeal. She sympathised, but some unknown civil servant pointed out the main objections and finished up saying, "This matter, after further investigation, may change." Eventually, it was made law.

It was a brilliantly sunny day on February 24 when my appeal was heard in a room overlooking Kensington Palace, close to Audrey's sweet chestnut conker tree dedicated to her. That was a cheering aspect, but it soon ebbed away in front of a three-man panel which included a bilious Tory and a Labour supporter who was anti *Daily Mail*. Three girls from social services gave evidence, dissecting my submission and reducing it to just one: compassionate grounds. I'd forgotten to bring up supermarkets and how I couldn't open the door of my car because of my stiff leg. The cost of the 90-minute hearing must have been rather expensive.

Just in case I'd won, I went over the road to the baroque Orangery, built in 1704-5 behind Kensington Palace, and had a pre-celebratory high tea. The building, which has been expensively renovated, was commissioned by Dutch-born William the Third of Orange (1650-1702). Born at The Hague and married to Mary, daughter of Charles 1, he was invited to become King of England by the country's ruling elite because they feared a Catholic would be appointed.

Nowadays, it is a haunt for tourists, particularly Americans who love talking about England's royalty through the ages.

Three days later, a letter from the chairperson Lesley Braithwaite arrived, saying that my appeal had been rejected because my case was flawed – only on compassionate grounds. Silly me!

Undaunted, I contacted Alison Graves at the Anerley department handling PCNs, and provided evidence that when I try to park in supermarkets and multi-storey car parks, I am prevented from opening on the driving side because of my unbending leg – particularly when hemmed in by diesel-thirsty 4x4s. My height then was 5ft 10½, but these days I may have lost an inch or two. Anyway, she agreed. The case was dismissed, and since then I have been able to claim exemption anywhere, except Camden and Kensington and a few other councils around the land.

In April 2006, my Blue Badge was about to expire. I filled in the necessary documents on the same day I was sent a reminder from the Congestion GHQ in Coventry telling me my exemption for entering central London had been refused because my Blue Badge had expired. It hadn't: the expiry date was May 11. I called in to see BATH, who run the Blue Badge operation in Bromley, to clarify this and was told there would be a 6-8 week delay in processing applications for renewal. As I needed my car almost every day, I was naturally very upset – firstly, because the London Borough of Bromley never send reminders about Blue Badges; and secondly, I was concerned that I may have to go through the same painful procedure inflicted on me between 2001-3 when my badge had been wrongly taken off me.

The letter arrived after my wife died suddenly of cancer of the liver, and I felt I should lodge an official protest, but decided against it. After months of correspondence and assessments (I have a file bulging with paperwork in front of me), my badge was finally reinstated with profuse apologies.

An ally, Mrs Margaret Howard, Assistant Director (Adults) of Bromley Council, came to my aid after I wrote a detailed letter to the Council's leader Steve Carr. Unlike some of his staff, his signature is clearly legible – not a squiggle. In my letter to Mrs Howard, I listed five reasons why my badge should be renewed: "Firstly, in my view, the medical report I submitted to the Council wholly justifies the continuance of my badge. Any new criteria should take into account the willpower and mental strength of potential applicants. I put up with a lot of pain because I am determined to try to live a reasonably normal life. One of the failings of the NHS and the private sector is that they rarely advise patients to work on their muscles to alleviate arthritis after surgery. Luckily, I met a lady physio at Orpington Hospital who told me 'you should keep exercising after your hip replacement', and I am still doing that now, many years later. I carry out an exercising programme at breakfast time lasting almost an hour, on the knees, hips, the back, shoulders, and ankles, while watching the BBC TV News.

"I visit Beckenham Spa once a week, and undergo self-imposed hydrotherapy. As a long-term heart sufferer, I find that the best way to keep the circulation going is to keep exercising. Incidentally, I park close to the BATH offices. I could sit at home and rest, and probably would have qualified for the use of an electric car by now, supplied by the authority.

"Secondly, I have to rely on my car more than ever now, because most of the knocks and bruises I collect these days are from travelling on buses when drivers are inconsiderate or on packed trains. Since then, I see a growing number who now offer up their seats to people like me, which is reassuring.

"Thirdly, is the fairness or otherwise of imposing a new criteria for badges. I think it is grossly unfair to be told I cannot qualify for one at the age of 67, when I have had one for more than 35 years. I was thinking to take legal advice about the Disability Discrimination Act and how it affects my case.

"Fourthly, I can understand the Council needing to reduce the numbers of badges, but their campaign should be aimed at the cheats, not someone who has been incapacitated for almost 60 years and has tried hard to cope with his physical problems.

"Why did the Council remove pictures of the holders of badges to enable wardens to see if the person at the wheel is actually the disabled person? The head of social services said there were egalitarian reasons to do with privacy. How many prosecutions are served in Bromley on drivers who cheat? Not many. I asked the Kensington staffer, and he said he couldn't remember any. But for those who cheat, the fine was £1,000 for wrongful use. A purge on them would bring far more money from fines than from parking tickets.

"Fifthly, intend to keep battling on in this long, drawn out saga. I will not concede, and if Bromley deny me a badge, I will persist with my complaint and may well have to finish up in court."

After a further postponement, Margaret Hodge wrote, "I have seen the letter from Mrs Graves and am very pleased that the new guidelines for the interpretation of the Blue Badge Criteria have enabled us to allocate you a new badge. I am sorry that this has taken so long and caused you so much distress. I do know Mrs Graves has always had a great deal of sympathy with your particular circumstances and has worked hard to find a resolution. Please accept my best wishes for the future."

I thanked both ladies for their forbearance and that common sense had eventually prevailed.

MY FIGHT AGAINST
OFFICIALESE (JARGON)

When Boris Johnson became Prime Minister, he told his Cabinet colleagues and their advisors to cut out the jargon and write their speeches, emails, and documents in plain English, in brief. My letter to Blackburn MP Barbara Castle, when she was Minister for Transport between 1965-8, was succinct, and I asked her why, if someone with a Disabled Badge is able to park without charge where he or she lives, they then have to pay to park in another borough. "They are still disabled."

Some weeks later, I received a lengthy two-page letter, dated 13 March, 1968, written by C.J. Hadley, one of her team of civil servants. He was very understanding. He wrote, "Let me first assure you that the Minister is very conscious that everything possible should be done to help the disabled. Already, a great deal has been done."

In the 16 months before becoming Minister for Employment, she introduced the breathalyser test, made the 70mph limit permanent all over the UK, announced that all new cars had to be given seat belts, presided over the closure of 2,050 miles of railways to encourage more use of vehicles in rural areas, and was first to suggest a congestion charge. Small, red-haired, and a fiery, inspiring speaker, she said, "Hitler didn't manage to kill as many civilians in Britain as have been killed in our roads since WW2. Between 1945-65, some 150,000 people were killed and several million injured on our roads." Later, she introduced an allowance for the severely disabled, but declined to act on disabled parking badges.

Mr Hadley, who signed his letter very legibly, went on, "It is the Greater London Council, as the traffic authority, who are responsible for the designation of Controlled Parking Zones within Greater London. We know that, like us, they are aware of the very real problems facing severely disabled drivers in such areas and are anxious to do all they can to help them. But, as I am sure you will appreciate, in the Central London area where the demand for on-street parking space by far exceeds the supply, it is just not possible for the GLC to grant all road users all the concessions they seek. For this reason, the Council have recently been studying all the traffic and transport problems facing the disabled to see what new steps, if any, can be taken to ease this great problem that exists in London."

He finished up, "In the last analysis, it is for the GLC to decide who is exempt from the traffic regulations and parking restrictions they impose. I am therefore passing a copy of your letter to the GLC with the request that they look into the points you raise and let you have their comments direct." So the buck was passed, and I heard no more.

Ironically, Mrs Castle never drove and had a chauffeur while attending functions. She was born in 1910 into a Socialist family, and her father Frank was a tax inspector who moved house on a regular basis. She forged ahead at the Girls' Grammar School at Bradford and finished up Head Girl, then went on to graduate with a third-class BA in Philosophy, Politics, and Economics at Oxford University. In 1945 she was elected to Parliament for Blackburn East, and within days she was appointed Parliamentary Private Secretary to Sir Stafford Cripps, President of the Board of Trade.

One of the many improvements she introduced was legislation for equal pay for women, brought to peace in the Ford sewing machinists' strike of 1968. In 2010 a film about it, called *Made in Dagenham*, proved popular. For many years she was the longest serving woman in Parliament, and in 1990 she was made a Baroness. She died at Hell Corner Farm in

Ibstone, Buckinghamshire, on 3 May, 2002, after suffering lung disease. It was fitting that this remarkable, controversial woman fell out with Harold Wilson, James Callaghan, and many others, and she gave them all hell.

'LIKE AN OLYMPIC CHAMPION'

In 1992, I drew into one of the four disabled spaces outside of Northcliffe House – the home of the *Daily Mail*. As I got out and changed my card clock, I noticed a youngish man, who also had a Blue Badge displayed, running off down the road. A lady parking attendant was nearby, and I said, "You ought to book him. He's like an Olympic sprinter."

She replied, "He could be mentally ill."

At that time, mental illness wasn't considered a reason for dispensation of mental sufferers, but in 2019 it changed and swelled the number of the existing 6m badge holders.

A letter to the *Daily Mail* on October 16, 2019

UNFAIR BLUE BADGE

I have difficulty in walking due to arthritis in both knees. I use a stick, so I applied for a Blue Badge, but was rejected because I was deemed not to be disabled enough.

Imagine my surprise when my neighbour was given a Blue Badge for her eight-year-old son. He has mild autism but otherwise is a fit, happy child who runs everywhere and goes to the local school. I thought disabled access to disabled parking was to benefit those with mobility issues.

BRIAN CONSUL, Leeds

CHELSEA'S SET A PRECEDENT

Chelsea's former captain John Terry was fined a modest £60 for parking his Bentley in a disabled space outside a Pizza Hut restaurant in Esher in 2008, and seven years later he committed a similar offence, leaving his Range Rover outside The Kebab and Burger House in Esher. This time the fine was upped to £70. As he was earning up to £110,000 a week at the time and lived in Oxshott, one of the richest parts of Britain, he could have donated a week's salary to a local hospital to pay for NHS staff to park their vehicles free until the money ran out.

In 2020, the year of lockdowns, a Government minister wanted the fine for this offence to be £1,000, but abuse continued – as I know too well. In 2016, the Department of Transport discovered that 61 out of 152 authorities didn't have a policy of prosecuting drivers. The number of cases in the previous year was less than 1000. It's a scandal that so many people flout the law when they deny a fully disabled person use of these spaces.

I spoke at the Probus Club at Oxshott in 2012, and sat next to a member who owned a house with surplus land close to John Terry's house. Apparently Terry wanted to buy the land to build another expensive property. "Looks like you'll win the equivalent of a National Lottery handout," I said to the man.

Probus means in favour of business, and their members are mainly retired business people, most of them past retiring age. The organizer warned me to speak up because some in the meeting had hearing problems. After my hour's oration, a man wearing two hearing aids approached, and I asked him if he enjoyed it. "Didn't hear a word," he said.

Terry was involved with one of Britain's most publicized foul language cases in 2011 when he clashed with QPR's defender Anton Ferdinand – younger brother of Rio – and was alleged to have used the F...... and C... words in the same sentence addressed to Anton. He was charged at Westminster Court and managed to get off, but the FA suspended him for four matches, fined him two weeks' wages, £220,000, and he was stripped of the England captaincy.

In December 2020, the BBC devoted a whole hour to the matter, during which Gary Lineker said, "I'm not a lip reader, but you could see the words coming out."

Anton claimed afterwards that his mental stress and the ensuing vile social media comments ruined his career. The answer, surely, would have been to cancel his social media and accept that stones may hurt you, but words don't. Not easy to accept in today's world.

The FA was in a tricky position, because it never publicised what Anton said to Terry to cause his offensive outburst. But the Westminster magistrates took a note of it, and the case was dismissed.

Sledging is dying out in cricket, but in football it is rampant. And with no crowds during the pandemic, everyone could hear it and the broadcasters had to apologise. A simple solution would be to tell the managers that their players need to stop swearing or be heavily fined. But most managers curse as well!

Someone of stronger fibre, Colin Valdar – injured in WW1 – was the editor when I first joined the *Daily Sketch* in 1960, and he had an artificial leg and limped. He had the common touch.

Another high-flying former managing editor of the *Daily Mail* was Marmaduke Hussey, known as Duke, who had the same problem. As a Grenadier Guards officer, he landed on the Anzio beaches in Italy in 1944, and was cut down with a hail of bullets and had to have one leg amputated. The Germans must have admired his courage and his extrovert character, because they had him repatriated back to England. One bullet was lodged in his spine, and he spent the next five years in hospital.

To shock one of his irritating critics, he once unstrapped his wooden leg and threatened to hit him with it. That story might, however, be fake news. You know what happens in bars where journalists gather – they go in for embellishments!

Duke was headhunted by Roy Thomson, the billionaire Canadian newspaper magnet who bought Times Newspapers, and he was a key man in smashing the unions by changing ways of producing newspapers at a much lower cost. Many of the printers would sign in as "Mickey Mouse" or "King Kong" and other names, and then go home. Then on Fridays they would turn up on time to collect their bulky pay packets.

His next job was as chairman of the BBC. He married a young debutante who was 16 years younger, and she became a Lady in Waiting to the Queen. He died in 2007 – a great, brave man.

Lord Alfred Northcliffe, who launched the *Daily Mail* as a women's newspaper in 1896, never lost a leg, but he died of syphilis. He was married to a lady who couldn't have children, and he sired four children from two-long term mistresses. He was one of the pioneers who financed the exciting, new motor racing in streets in Bexhill. He died in 1922 at the age of 57 – a volatile but brilliant communicator.

I sat close to his relative, Vere, Lord Harmsworth, who was chairman of the *Daily Mail*, at a lunch for my friend Ian Wooldridge on becoming the Sports Writer of the Year. And to liven up the conversation, I said to Vere (everyone called him that), "I've just read about your uncle, and is it true that he died of syphilis?"

Vere turned to Sir David English, editor of the *Sketch* and later the *Mail*, and said, "Who is this young man?"

Sir David replied, "He's one of our enthusiastic young men in the sports department."

Vere then turned to me and said, "You're right. He did die of syphilis."

Nigel Dempster, the renowned *Mail* gossip writer, loved telling that story.

Vere's wife, a former J. Arthur Rank film starlet, Patricia Brooks, was universally known as "Bubbles", and they had three children. When she died, Vere married his mistress, Maiko Jeong Shun Lee. Audrey and I met "Bubbles" at a *Daily Mail* function at the Grosvenor Hotel, Park Lane. She was perched on a high stool at the entrance of the Grand Hall, and as the Toastmaster read out our names, she looked at us, sniffed, looked to one side, and held out her hand. We took her manicured right hand in turn, and a minute or two later we burst out laughing.

PETER FOSTER, THE INFAMOUS AUSSIE CONMAN, FOLLOWED TERRY'S LEAD

Quentin Letts, the *Daily Mail*'s hugely entertaining Parliamentary sketch writer, now with *The Times*, described how Peter Foster, the Australian conman who starred in a scandal in 2002, defrauded a council by parking in a disabled space. Quentin said, "That orange parking disc did it for me. That was the moment in last night's Cheriegate film when it became copper-bottom clear that Peter Foster was not some megadeal global tycoon who deserved his comeuppance. The bloke was a small-fry con. A whitebait villain.

"A man who sticks a disabled permit in his car window to avoid paying 50p to the pay-and-display is obviously nothing more than a bit-part, frontier-hopping, Aussie Del Boy Trotter who somehow stumbled into the Blair family and found the whole thing too good to resist."

That embarrassing film was possibly the low point of Tony Blair's premiership of ten years. Late night telephone calls to 10 Downing Street between Blair and his wife Cherie, the QC, with Foster and his lady friend Carole Caplin, kicked off with a major scandal. Foster's mother Louise was an estate agent in Australia, and Foster volunteered to help the Blairs to buy two flats in Bristol for their son Euan, who was a student at the university in the city. The owner of the flats wanted up to £300,000 for each of them, but the deal went through at an overall cost of £540,000. The gregarious Caplan was reckoned to be Cherie's guru, advising her about her appearance and dress. Once the story appeared, the Blairs broke off their relationship with the conman and girlfriend.

Foster was born on 29 September, 1962, on the Gold Coast, and as a teenager tricked people by selling dud projects. For the rest of his life, he ran up a vast number of convictions for breaches of trade practices and the Trade Descriptions Act, forgery, fraud, money laundering, immigration offences, contempt of court, assaulting police officers, and resisting arrest. In 2018, he figured in a murder investigation. He operated in Australia, Britain, Ireland, the USA, and Vanuatu – a French island in the Pacific.

Sam Fox, the English sex symbol, was one of his victims. She was thinking of marrying the fantasist but soon found out the truth about him. Between 1993 and 1997, he acted as a police informant for the Australian Federal Police.

Cherie's heroine and mentor was Dame Rose Heilbron (1914-2005), the first woman to become a Queen's Counsel. She worked with my friend Lord Learie Constantine, the man who won the High Court action in 1944 when he was awarded damages from the Imperial Hotel owners in Russell Square. Learie had booked a room there, but white GI officers and soldiers objected to seeing a black man, and he and his family had been ordered out. Later, Learie – a qualified barrister and a great, all-round cricketer – helped the drafting of the Race Relations Acts. He became the first Afro-Caribbean Lord in 1969, and today he is finally being recognized as someone who did a Dr Martin Luther King – standing up for deprived black people.

In the 1960s, I ghost-wrote Learie's pungent comments on cricket in the *Daily Sketch*, and he and his wife Norma were godparents to our daughter Louise. Learie died in 1971, and Norma departed a few weeks later, possibly from a broken heart as well as cancer.

THE EVIL ROBERT MAXWELL

Peter Foster was small-time. But Jan Ludvik Hyman Binyamin Maxwell was big-time, the biggest fraudster of his time (1923-1991). A huge man of 6ft 4, weighing 18 stone, and with dyed black hair, he was a terrible bully.

He professed to be an Arsenal fan, as he told my friend Harry Harris when we worked together in the sports department of the *Daily Mail* off Fleet Street, one of the most polluted streets in London. Maxwell told us that when he was a teenager, he had climbed over a wall to get into Highbury. If that was true, he would have needed a ladder, as the wall at the ground was around 18 feet. We didn't believe he was a true supporter.

After he took over a number of big companies, he told us he wanted to take over Manchester United. He would ring us and give us "tips" to blacken the reputation of their directors – unsuccessfully.

The first club he took over was the destitute Oxford United and he lived in Headington Hall on the outskirts of the city in 1982. He was intent on joining with Reading to form a new club, Thames Valley United, but both clubs soon scotched his idea.

Jim Smith, one of my nicest coterie of managers, achieved a major success when Oxford beat Everton in the semi-final of the Milk Cup, and I was standing outside of the home dressing room with a group of fellow journalists to interview him. Suddenly the door opened, and Maxwell blocked Jim Smith then proceeded to claim all the credit.

An hour later, I was standing outside to put another question to Maxwell. His Rolls Royce was parked there, and a young radio reporter was keeping me company. Maxwell came out and started to get in his vehicle as the young man tried to put his question. Maxwell said, "I'm late, but get in. I can do the interview."

He drove off, and ten minutes later they arrived at Maxwell's home, where he got out and rushed inside, calling, "Good night." The youngster had to walk back two miles in the dark. At least he could have offered him a lift!

On another occasion, Harry and I were inviting managers, directors, or players, to our table at the Football Writers' Association annual dinner in May. Harry invited Maxwell, and I invited Ernie Clay, the volatile chairman of Fulham. Maxwell arrived an hour early and insisted on sitting in the empty dining room and ordering the most expensive bottles of wine.

When dinner was served, Ernie shouted, "Have you been banned as a director yet, Robert?"

Maxwell spluttered into his soup and didn't reply. So, Ernie repeated the question twice as loud. Maxwell got up and left.

Early in April 2022, the BBC2 aired a programme on Maxwell's mysterious death. It was poor quality, trying to use his words to his patient French wife Betty – they had nine children together –- about his predicaments, accompanied by frequent shots of swirling seawater as he slipped off the back of a luxury yacht off the Canary Islands. He was 68, and left 30,000 *Mirror* pensioners bereft of their entitlement.

THIS IS A LETTER FROM LORD SHINKWIN IN THE DAIILY TELEGRAPH ON DECEMBER 30, 2020

" Sir, In the three months since Blue Badges eligibility rules were extended, 12,299 new badges – around 130 a day – were granted to people who cannot walk as part of a journey without 'considerable psychological distress' or risk of 'serious harm'.

"I live in central London with a severe mobility disability, and often cannot park outside my home because the disabled bay is taken by other Blue Badge holders. I have two questions: Are 130 new bays being created every day to meet the increased demand? If not, it's obvious that, whatever the merits of the eligibility extension, limited access to disabled parking is only going to get worse. That must be exactly the opposite of what was intended, so what is the Government proposing to do about it?

Lord Kevin Joseph Maximilian Shinkwin, Balham, SW1."

Lord Shinkwin was made a Conservative Peer for his voluntary work aiding disabled people. He suffers from osteogenesis imperfecta.

He had a good point. In Bromley, they have reduced the number of disabled spaces. Across at the well attended St Joseph's Catholic Church, there is a disabled space, but the word "disabled" has virtually disappeared, and in the autumn it is covered with soggy leaves and non-disabled people park in it.

ONE MINUTE I WAS ACCIDENTALLY LET OFF AND TWO MONTHS LATER I WAS CHARGED WITH THE SAME 'OFFENCE' AND FIVE MONTHS LATER I WAS REPRIEVED

Confusion reigned after BY16151675 arrived at my residence in August 2019. It was one of those pesky ones of mistakenly parking on a "Loading" space, but I was sure the evidence would win a reprieve. This is the letter I sent to Bromley Parking HQ:

"Dear Parking CEO,

Your follow-up later dated October 3, 2019, now says the appeal of Penalty Notice BY16151675 from you has been rejected. However, several days after the offence happened, I received a letter signed by Cathy Suckling saying the PCN has been cancelled because she was satisfied I was loading my Apple. At the moment I have yet to find her letter, but you must have a record of it. My files of PCNs is too heavy to lift, and finding the letter in my study will demand a lot of wasteful time!"

This is my original letter:

"Dear Manager, I wish to appeal against this notice. The circumstances were that I needed to take my Apple to their store in the Mall and now, having difficulty in walking – I might need a third right hip replacement, and carry an

Anticoagulant Alert (Heart) Card –I needed to park nearby. After several circuits, there were no parking spaces, but turning left from the High Street there were two Disabled spaces occupied. I noticed a vehicle parked in the first one, and two able-bodied boys of around 15 or 16 got out without any physical impediments. Thinking they were dropped off by the middle-aged, blonde lady who was the driver, I drew alongside her car and intimated, 'Are you going?' As she got out, she gestured with two fingers as though she was signalling they would return in two minutes. So I sat there for around 15 minutes in vain, and no-one showed up. A bespectacled, around five feet tall female CEO, aged in her early 20s, approached and said, 'If you stay here, I will book you.' I explained what had happened, and I saw the other vehicle had a notice saying 'Not apparently disabled'.

"Well, I have been disabled for more than 70 years.

"She then said, 'You can park on double yellow lines opposite.' I thanked her and proceeded to park on double yellow lines on the left side of the narrow road. When I returned an hour later, another CEO had stuck a PCN on my windscreen. The officer said two lines indicated 'no parking because of loading'. I said, 'I was told to park up that road, which I did.' It was still parked, with no-one in it, and I realised the driver's two fingered gesture was really 'Up you!'.

"If the lady CEO had told me I ought to have parked at the top of Churchill Way and not at the bottom, I could have been excused, because there were no loading restrictions there."

Two days later, Bromley Parking department sent a letter – must be a record! – saying they accepted my appeal, adding, "Thank you for providing a copy of the receipts which adequately confirm that loading/unloading was carried out at the time in question. The PCN has therefore been cancelled on this occasion."

Signed Cathy Suckling, Parking Support Officer.

Clearly a compassionate lady!

Almost two months later, my discharge was dismissed, and apparently I was guilty. If G. Tippett – the person who wrote the letter – insisted on fining me £65, I would appeal and spend a day at the Independent Tribunal in London. I would use the Churchillian spirit. However, I hoped common sense would prevail!

SORRY, IT'S MY FAULT THEN!

On November 19, 2019, Andy Smith, Park Support Officer. wrote a curt letter, Ref BY16151675, saying:

"Dear Mr Scovell,

"Thank you for your correspondence. Having reviewed your case, our decision not to cancel your PCN remains the same. The letter that you referred to from Cathy Suckling is for a completely different PCN (BY14951579). The decision made with regard to this PCN has no bearing on our decision made regarding the above PCN, which was issued correctly and has not been cancelled. If you are unhappy with our decision not to cancel your PCN, please do not write to us again. Wait for the Notice to be sent to the registered owner who can then make formal representations."

Three months after the alleged offence, they were telling me to wait a month or two, and I was tempted to reply commenting on the delay. I refrained. But seven weeks later, one of the staff of Bromley Parking department sent me a letter, dated January 28, 2020, with joyous news:

"Having considered the contents of your letter, we have decided to close the case and no further action will be taken due to the delay in responding to you. Please be aware this is not because the contravention didn't occur. Therefore, it may not be possible to cancel a future penalty charge in similar circumstances. Yours sincerely, Sarah Fox."

All's well at last. Though I doubt circumstances will happen again.

I put this circuitous case down as one of my greatest parking let-off achievements and, as they say, time is the best healer.

DONE LIKE A KIPPER!

I used to ghost-write the articles of the great Surrey and England cricketer Ken Barrington in the *Daily Mail*, and one of his favourite phrases was "done like a kipper" when he was charging down the wicket and was stumped against a tricky slow bowler. He also used malaprops – using the wrong words. Three were typical examples:

Talking about the menacing West Indian fast bowler Charlie Griffith, he said, "The ball came at me like a high philosophy bullet."

In a comment to Mike Brearley after a torrid day against the Aussie fast bowlers, he said, "Look at them, they're like a plague of lotuses."

And when discussing crowd trouble in Bangalore, he said, "It was all right, though, because the police were sent in to mingle with the crowd, with 200 plain-clothed protectives."

Ken died of a massive heart attack, aged 50, in the Holiday Inn in Bridgetown, Barbados, where we loved sitting next to the Barbados Yacht Club. A nervous type, he was much loved by all.

I WAS DONE LIKE A KIPPER

On November 8, 2019, at 3.32pm, I became a victim of a conman and his associates 40 metres away from the Bromley Police Station.

This is the report I made to the police:

REPORT ON BEING DEFRAUDED BY A CRIMINAL WHO STOLE £1045 FROM MY BARCLAYS ACCOUNT AND MADE A SUCKER ON NOVEMBER 8, 2018

I am now 83 and have been disabled since 1943 but still, luckily, have a reasonable active life as a sportswriter and author. On this day, I arrived to have a blood test at the Bromley Dysart Clinic at 13, Ravensbourne Road, and parked my car LV18 VLS Honda, and didn't see my offside front tyre being flat. I was on a single yellow line, half blocking an entry to a yard. Realising a parking attendant was about to pull out his camera to take pictures of this heinous offence, I beat him on the draw. I started the engine and moved ten metres further down the hill and started to occupy one of the four parking spaces in front of the surgery. As I manoeuvred my vehicle into the space, a large Volvo 4x4 squeezed in next to it, and if my car had a flat tyre, I would have spotted it. Or should have seen it. The distance between the two cars was six inches, and with having a stiff right leg I wouldn't have been able to get into my car afterwards.

I asked a receptionist to put a tannoy message for the owner to move it to enable me to leave. The owner turned out to be a friendly lady doctor and was very helpful in shifting her car into the road. Another BMW black 4x4 was half parked across my path, and it wasn't easy to back out, so I intimated to the driver could he move it back. Rather oddly, he didn't react. The doctor then said to me, "You have a flat tyre."

I tried to drive to the local Kwik Fit half a mile away, but realised it was too far and I was in danger of damaging the wheel, so I parked on a pavement near the Police Station in St. Martin's Road around 2.30.

I had left my mobile at home, and as I got out, a man aged about early 40s came up and said, "I'm in the tyre business and I do all the police work. I've done four already today." I told him I rented my car from Honda in Orpington, and I had a Honda Care agreement with breakdowns.

He was very persuasive and said he could change it on the spot for £120. He was slim built, about 5ft feet 10, with greying, flat hair, and a woman approached who he said was his wife. She had greying hair and was smiling. "I'll get you a cup of tea from Waitrose while you wait," she said. "You must be cold." She brought the tea in a plastic cup with a cap.

By this time, I'd opened my boot to check whether I had a spare wheel, and the man moved the boxes of unsold books – all authors carry spare unsold works of art, and I'm one of them. After rummaging around, the man said there wasn't a spare wheel.

He chatted away jovially, and after a while he persuaded me to go to the nearest ATM to withdraw the money to pay for a new tyre. He seemed so genuine I thought it would be the answer to my problem, because I planned to attend a prestigious cricketing dinner that night.

I said to him, "What's your name?" He said, "Joe Walker and that's my wife, Wendy." The woman had gone. I asked him where he lived and he said, "Close by, and my work is also round corner." It should have rung alarm bells, because I didn't know any other local tyre company other than Kwik Fit.

I've never used an ATM, because I've been a victim of scammers and never gave my pin numbers to anyone. When I pay in cheques at the Barclays Bank in the Bromley High

Street, I ask young members of the staff to do it. I have a rather bad limp, and he gave me the impression of someone acting like a Good Samaritan.

'Joe Walker' asked the man selling the flowers outside Bromley Police Station, "Where is the nearest ATM?" And the man said, "Inside in the rail station on the right."

The time was around 3pm, and I assumed there were CCTV cameras filming our actions when the £160 emerged – eight twenties. Not familiar to using a plastic shield to prevent people seeing one's pin number, I had to lift it to press the right buttons, and the numbers well have been spotted by the criminal. Significantly, he was the person to collect the notes. He said, "I'll pick up a jack with the tyre, and I'll be a few minutes."

Ten minutes later, he came back and said, "The tyre cost £225. You need another £65."

As I struggled out of my car, he volunteered to go back to the ATM. I pulled out my debit card to check whether it was the right one, and he said, "Let me save you going back to the station," and he took it from me. I hadn't given him permission, but I should have called him back. "I'll only be a minute or two," he said.

Parking on most pavements in Bromley is an offence, and I was anxious not to collect another PCN.

Then he went off, and I returned to where I had parked on the pavement. Ten minutes later, a red Kia unmarked saloon stopped next to my car, and a bespectacled stocky lady in her thirties, about 5ft feet 2, said she was a police officer and got out and said, "Someone round the corner is saying you are having trouble. Can I help?"

Rather foolishly, I said, "No thank you."

How did she know about my predicament? Was she in with the con man? There was a man who drove the car off and I couldn't see his face, but he could have been a member of a gang. They would have been checking up whether they needed more time to go to ATMs to draw out the limit of £200.

A few minutes later, I realised I'd been duped. I walked to the Police Station at around 3.45 and managed to speak to an amiable, light-skinned man in a mauve coloured top behind the glass. There was just enough to pass a telephone through the gap to enable me to ring Barclays and cancel my debit card. That took some time to speak to a lady, who said the criminal had taken out four payments of £200, all from Sainsbury's, and £245 in other shops. The total money stolen was £1045, not including the extra £165 for the tyre.

I also rang Honda, and Ben, the manager, said he wouldn't be able to do the tyre that evening but called up the AA on my behalf. The AA driver arrived ten minutes later and exchanged my wheel with one of his to take my car to Kwik Fit. I was given a receipt of £181 for the tyre and fitting. Later, Barclays refunded the money for that, and the amount was taken out from my account.

One consolation was that I wasn't attacked by hooded moped drivers with a knife. That reminds me that the suspect who made off with my debit card claimed someone was stabbed the day before at Bromley Station. I didn't see any reports about it. The con-man is a dastardly liar and a villain of the worst kind.

A PECULIAR HAPPENING

Around 2am on November 20, 2019, I had just woken up with itchy feet and various parts of the body, and applied E45 ointment on the affected areas, when someone rang the front door bell. This has been happening for several years, and up to now we've done nothing about it. Obviously, it was a nut case.

But a month or so ago, our damaged green box for unused food in green bags was replaced by Bromley Refuse Department, and every week when we put it out for collection someone took the bulky green bags. Jeremy Corbyn was speaking earlier in the day in his one-to-one General Election contest with Boris Johnson on ITV, about starving homeless people needing to go to food banks. Surely no-one would be such in a desperate state to take out the remains of our unwanted leftovers?

Not having heard the promised visit of someone from Bromley Police department about the theft of my debit card, my daughter rang to report this incident, and a lady was very helpful and arranged to visit us six days later. She said an officer who had my report on my theft would question me about that and also about the phantom night bell ringer. She wondered if he or she might have stuck a sharp pin into my tyre which led to a slow puncture before it finally collapsed.

The officer was very diligent and spent more than an hour interviewing me in the police station. There were one or two rough looking characters trying to get in, and she said, "We get all sorts here, and you have to be careful." She promised another officer would call round to see me.

Three days later, PC Steve Bale arrived and wanted more details, like more detailed descriptions of the crooks. I said the incident when the criminal and I had gone to the ATM at

Bromley South was around 2.47, because I noticed that was the time on my bank statement with the first £200 withdrawal. He was quite excited.

"We can put round a description," he said.

I still await the result.

SAVED ON THE BELL
AT RAVENSBOURNE ROAD

On July 14, Bastille Day, 2016, I bought two tickets for a Russell Watson operatic evening at the Churchill Theatre. Gill, my best friend and confidante, was unable to attend, so I invited my good friend Steph, who does an amazing job cleaning and upgrading my massive mansion. Churchill Theatre is in the High Street, and Ravensbourne Road is about 150 feet below, in parkland next to a bandstand and tennis courts. There is a limited amount of parking spaces, nearly all for residents. It was 7.45pm when we arrived, just in time for an 8pm kick off, and I noticed a driver was about to move out of it.

A parking attendant was standing there, and as the other car moved off, I started occupying the space. Most roads in Bromley only charge for parking until 6.30pm, but I was unaware you had to pay in a residents' space at that time. As I got out, the attendant didn't tell me that my Disabled Badge wasn't valid, and he disappeared. Later on, he came back and made out a PCN and left it on my windscreen – with a demand to pay the £60 penalty within a fortnight.

I appealed and explained the facts, and Charlotte Webb from the Bromley Parking Department wrote, "We are aware that some Local Authority ("ies" in place of the "y") allow Blue Badges holders may park in bays reserved in resident bays. However, the London Borough of Bromley does not. I have withdrawn the charge on this occasion, but I may be unable to withdraw further PCNs issued in similar circumstances." Well done, Charlotte!

The concert was sensational, and at the end 800 mainly elderly women were on their feet cheering and clapping.

A woman in the front row jumped up waving a piece of paper suggesting that Russell ought to do another song. It turned out to be the most popular one from *Les Miserables*, quickly followed by the tear-jerker, *Raise Me Up*. That Bette Midler song was played at the funeral of Professor John Treharne, Gill's husband, an eminent eye surgeon. He was 58 when he died, the same age as my Audrey, and both had cancer of the liver.

Back home, I switched on to the TV BBC News and heard the news about the 84 people who had been massacred that evening in Nice, where Audrey's twin sister Lucy and her husband, Czuk, had a flat. They have twin sons, and one is married to a French lady. They lived in Nice but luckily none of them was at the Bastille Parade. The woman in the front row with her message must have been texted by a relative or friend, and that was why Russell extended his performance in a tribute to La France.

BY *DAILY MAIL'S* STEVE DOUGHTY, SOCIAL AFFAIRS CORRESPONDENT

WEDNESDAY, NOVEMBER 13, 2019

COUNCIL PARKING CHARGES SOAR BY 90% AS POTHOLE CASH PLUMMETS

The squeeze on drivers can be pinned on council chiefs trying to replace revenue through Treasury cutbacks, according to the Institute for Fiscal Studies. Town halls have also hiked the costs of burials and cremation and slashed spending on sports pitches, leisure centres, and parks.

They are being forced to focus on the services they are legally required to provide – especially social services for troubled children, and care for vulnerable and elderly adults. The value of parking charges to councils is now approaching £1billion a year. Since 2010, it has gone up 88%, from £490m to £920million.

Money spent on regeneration on private housing went down by 70% for each resident over the decade, but spending on homelessness went up by 72%.

Hugh Bladon of the Association of British Drivers said, "Shocking amounts of money have been taken from motorists. Things are at the point where it is almost a crime to drive a car these days. The neglect of the roads is bad enough for people who use four wheels. For those on two wheels, cyclists and motor cyclists, it is seriously dangerous.

STAKANOVIC WORKERS NEEDED

Both Conservative and Labour promised extra billions would be spent on improving the state of roads and social housing before Boris Johnson's unexpected Brexit landslide in the General Election a month later. I give credit to the Brexit man who stood outside Parliament holding up signs behind TV experts being interviewed on the green, like "Get Brexit Done" and "Don't take notice of Labour's lies". Six weeks of that was the most pro-Tory advertising of all. And he did it without pay, working a 16-hour day. A real Stakanovic (not a footballer, but someone who works at a frantic pace).

My latest appeal against an £80 fine was troubling me, but mercifully they wrote back cancelling it.

There was an amusing sequel to my Honda CR-V car. Some months later, a gruff Yorkshireman from the Dales rang asking about the vehicle. I asked him how he got my number.

"I've checked the garage where I bought it from, and it's making funny noises." "Well," I said, 'I didn't hear any noises when I had it. Must be caused by those narrow bending roads in the Dales."

He put the phone down. At least he doesn't have trouble with a Congestion Charge fine.

A FIVE-MONTH BATTLE
WHICH ENDED IN DEFEAT

On March 3, 2017, my car was under attack by a parking attendant armed with a camera and a notebook at 11.48 in the lower High Street in Bromley, outside Wetherspoons, named after the oddly christened Richman Crompton Lamburn (1890-1969) who wrote 41 "Just William" books and even more plays on the same mischievous, 11-year-old boy.

Her books are still being bought today, but the last time I was at the Wetherspoons establishment, there were no copies to be seen. But Bromley Library, which is close by, had some. One suspects that most of the present generation have never heard of the prolific unmarried suffragette who volunteered to serve in the Fire Service in WW2. She was born in 1890, daughter of a clergyman, and taught in schools in Lancashire. At the age of 33 she contacted polio, and her right leg had to be amputated. She then had cancer of the breast, but managed to survive. In her latter years she lived in a house in Cherry Orchard Road in Bromley Common, along with her mother, and when her mother died, she was confined to a wheelchair. She died aged 78, of a heart attack. Clearly a very brave lady.

My car was parked opposite Bromley Police Station and Bromley South station, and it was raining heavily at the time. There used to be two disabled spaces, which I used infrequently. I wanted to buy a return railway ticket to Watford with my Senior card to watch a Premiership match at Vicarage Road, which I did next day.

There was no queue at the station – unusually – and the cheap return was duly issued, so within four minutes I was back at my vehicle. There was no attendant in sight, but I noticed a PCN on the windscreen. I had parked on the second space, not noticing that "Disabled" had changed to "Car Club". This is a commercial deal between the Car Club Enterprise Company and Bromley Council in an effort to bring in money to pay their burgeoning outgoings. In the past around London. I had noticed that Enterprise spaces were now being occupied in spaces previously designated for the disabled. The company has now 1,200 locations with on-road access and is now sponsoring the Rachael Heyhoe Flint women's cricket trophy and European Cup football matches in 2020-1.

There was a law brought in saying that 6% of car parks and certain roads should be given over to the disabled, but Waitrose, which I used often, only has five disabled spaces out of 206, and I pointed out to one of their seniors that they were 12 short of the complement. He said the car park was run by another company.

The chances of getting more parking in that area is almost nil, because a massive tower block of flats was constructed next to the Police Station and the station. Most of the flats recently built across the road have a limited amount of parking, because the developers say, "The householders don't need cars. They are living right next to Bromley Station, and the road is serviced by half a dozen bus routes. Shopping at Waitrose is within 60 metres." Good business for Messrs Wait and Rose, the founders.

Next day, I typed out a letter to the parking GHQ at Rochester Road, saying, "Dear Parking Manager, Oh dear, another PCN (BY 01222781A)! I plead inadvertence. I haven't parked there for some time, but there were two disabled spaces, and in a crowded road I thought one was available for a Blue Badge holder to use.

"My purpose was to buy an advanced ticket at Bromley South station, and when I arrived there was no queue, and the lady in the ticket office issued my ticket without delay and returned to my car.

"I thought that parking attendants were supposed to give a few minutes leeway when a Blue Badge holder is found in a wrong space, but apparently not. The enclosed receipt for my train ticket is timed 11.52, exactly the same time when he or she put the notice on my windscreen. He or she must have disappeared quickly, because I didn't spot him. In view of this, I wish to appeal. Your sincerely."

On June 9, the Bromley Parking people sent me the Notice to Owner, saying the original £65 had been doubled to £130. On the bottom of the letter, they explained how to appeal. Next day, I delivered my letter of appeal, giving five reasons:

1 The clock next to my Blue Badge hasn't been photographed (no sign of it in seven pictures by the Council).
2 I remember I had it marked on just after 11am, roughly the same time the CEO stuck on the PCN on my windscreen.
3 I was buying a rail ticket 30ms from Bromley South Station, which took only a few minutes, and I inadvertently failed to notice that "Car Club" was painted on the particular space, not the old sign "Disabled". Neither was easy to see on a rainy day.
4 I've been living in Bromley since 1968, and when parking bays were laid out years later at that part of the road, there were two disabled spaces. One has been sold to Car Club for a meagre £25 each year! There is no law about having to provide bays for Car Club bays. It is merely a commercial action between Bromley Council and the Car Club, enabling their members to park by booking in advance. Every time I go past, the same car is often parked there all day. Disabled drivers used to be allowed to park for only three hours.
5 With 100s of flats being built near Bromley Station, it is impossible for the disabled to park anywhere near the station. The high-rise car park now has fewer spaces.

I finished up by detailing my medical history, saying, "I am NOT a Car Club member, though."

With unusual speed, the Parking Department fired back this letter, dated July 25, saying that a Charge Certificate surcharge of £65 had been added onto the £130 penalty, taking it to £195. They gave four reasons. The first was "no representations were made in response to the Notice of Owner". I did make representations!

The second reason – We issued a Notice of Rejection of representations made against the Notice to Owner, and we have not been informed of an appeal having made to the adjudicator. But I did ask them to appeal in a letter to their offices in the City of London.

They gave me 14 days to pay up, and if not, they would apply to Northampton County Court to recover the money by using bailiffs which would add to their costs "which may significantly increase the amount that will need to be paid".

MY REPLY:

August 1, 2017

"Dear Mr Suckling,

"I have been on holiday, and I'm now horrified to receive your latest letter indicating that I have to pay £195 or be visited by bailiffs.

"When this PEN (BY0122781A) was issued on March 16, I wrote back next day saying I would like to appeal. A month later, I answered your next letter, setting out the reasons why I wanted to attend an Adjudication in the City of London.

"You replied, saying I would receive a Notice to Owner form for an appeal. In your letter of May 24, it said, "The form will offer you the chance to formally challenge your PCN or pay the £130."

"I did not receive the Notice to Owner. I then received a letter doubling the charge to £130.

"Each time I sent these letters, I brought them round to your offices, making sure they would arrive.

"I enclose a copy of my reasons, which I previously sent you for an appeal, and a copy of my receipt from South-eastern railway company indicating that it was timed 11.52 when the parking attendant issued the PEN. By the time I got to my car, he had disappeared. I also enclose my latest medical report.

"All this hassle about a minor parking "offence" is causing me a lot of distress. I've lived in the borough since 1968, paid all my dues, and a few years ago the Council charged me an extra £3,000 on top of my yearly rates by mistake. I did not ask for compensation, but the rates department repaid me the added-on money which should have been charged to another ratepayer in Chislehurst.

I have met Mr Patterson at one of those community meetings, and I intend to write to him and say "This is NOT on!" Bromley Council has a good reputation in dealing with pensioners, not persecuting them.

Yours sincerely."

Twenty-nine days later, Ms Sarah Cox, Parking Support Officer, wrote:

"Thank you for writing to us. It is now too late for you to challenge or continue challenging your PCN. The Notice to Owner we sent you gave you 28 days to challenge your PCN, but this this time has now passed.

"There is a sign where you parked that explains that the bay you parked in is for people with a car club permit. You were given a PCN for parking without a car club permit that was both valid and clearly displayed. Even if you have a car club permit, you have to display it so that a Civil Enforcement Officer can see all its details."

She listed the way I needed to pay within 14 days, or the force of law would take over, making me a felon with a criminal record.

My final letter, dated August 31, started:

"Dear Madam, I did NOT see a Notice to Owner, and that is the reason why I keep saying – in my various letters delivered in person and dated shortly afterwards when your letters arrive – that I wanted to appeal. A normal response from your department ought to send another one to me, not hike up my 'fine'. Any lawyer could see a reason for appealing in this case. It is common sense.

"I am arranging to have my daughter take pictures of my car parked on the Car Club space when it is not filled. The signage is a dull grey colour (in the past, they were white). It was raining when the attendant took his or her pictures, and it was not easy to see 'Car Club'. This will, I hope, be part of my appeal when I face an independent adjudicator.

"I enclose a post-dated cheque for £130, in case I incur court cases and am visited by a bailiff – hoping that my long requested (from April) appeal is heard by an adjudicator.

Yours Exasperatedly."

There was no answer, and one of my longest cases finally ended with a creditable defeat. They kept my £130, but knocked off the £65 surcharge. When I see anv Enterprise vehicle, supposedly members of the Car Club, I blow a raspberry at it.

A QUICK VICTORY IN THE TOWN OF COLONELS, TUNBRIDGE WELLS

The genteel Royal Tunbridge Wells is one of my favourite towns in Britain, and that rake King Edward V11 granted the town its title in recognition of royal visits, mainly made by Queen Victoria. In 1606, Lord North discovered the chalybeate spring there, and it attracted the hoi polloi. Beau Nash, the builder of Bath, lived there from 1735 until his death in 1762, and he designed the two major projects – The Pantiles, 160ms of posh shops and flats known earlier as The Walks and Calverley Crescent, full of elegant, expensive houses.

Two cricketing friends – Ron Hart, who owned two flats in The Pantiles, and Carl Openshaw, former chairman of Kent CCC – still live in Calverley Crescent. Less than half a mile up Nevill Road, the county cricket ground is partially surrounded by rhododendrons, and former Indian captain Kapil Dev made it known worldwide when he scored 175 in the World Cup in 1983. I knew Kapil, and unlike the current Indian captain Virat Kohli earlier, he could be a bit peppery. Virat has become so as well when he toured here in 2021.

Adolf Hitler had Tunbridge Wells on his WW2 bombing hit list, and 3,800 properties were damaged, but only 15 people died. They must have been one of the first towns to build Anderson shelters. The population is around 60,000 and 97% are white. The number of colonels has dropped considerably, but they do still have some.

On January 14, 2016, at around 8.20am, I parked in the covered Great Hall car park to be interviewed by BBC Radio Kent, whose offices are 200ms down the hill. I was there to promote one of my books and was keen to arrive early, but most of the spaces were occupied.

Like older journalists, I always advised young journalists to arrive at least a quarter of an hour early for appointments. As mine was at 8.30, I just made it on time. After spending an hour in the studio, I returned to my car to find that a Civil Enforcement Officer, TW 107, had put a PCN on my windscreen, timed at 8.42. My offence was parking in a space marked "Motor Cycle". The light in the Great Hall was murky, and I hadn't seen the offending words. The fine was £70, but if paid within 14 days, it would be £35.

The same day, I wrote to the Tunbridge Wells Parking Department, starting off with my experience with the Luftwaffe in 1943, then detailed my stiff right leg, two hip replacements, one knee replacement, two heart attacks, and now, thanks to the NHS, I have a pacemaker. I've no complaints about the NHS, none at all.

I said, "On the day I was served a PCN, I was making my first visit to the Great Hall car park to be interviewed by BBC Radio Kent's staff man Phil Harrison. When I arrived, the light was rather dim and I thought all the space in that area was designated 'Disabled'. However, I now learn that the space where my vehicle was parked had another purpose.

"On leaving, I stopped at the machine and checked that disabled people are not charged, and an angry woman whose vehicle was behind mine shouted, 'You're blocking the entrance, get out of the way!'

"I said, 'Sorry, I am disabled.'

"'Doesn't matter, you are blocking me,' she said. Not the kind of behaviour one would expect in a genteel county town where Queen Victoria stayed on many occasions!

"Not familiar with this part of Kent's parking areas, I ask for leniency and, hopefully, the cancellation of the PCN."

I signed and added (Formerly sports writer for the *Daily Mail* 1971-2000, and author of 27 books).

Glen Walker, TW Parking Administration Officer, wrote on January 27: "Thank you for writing to us. Although your PCN was correctly given, we have cancelled it on this occasion. You were issued a PCN for parking in a motorcycle bay. The enclosed photo helps to show why your PCN was issued. If you get another one, we may not be able to cancel it. I hope this has been of help."

Very relieved, I wrote back to him on February 3, saying, "Dear Mr Walker, Many thanks for your letter. It was good to see a Council showing some compassion. Where I live in Bromley, they adopt a Trumpian attitude, and I have been forced to take many appeals in Archway! Best wishes."

ANOTHER WIN AT CHANCERY LANE ENGINEERED BY "WG"

The reason this PCN was inflicted on me was because of Dr. William Gilbert Grace, universally known as "WG", who was buried in the Elmers End Crematorium in the Borough of Bromley on October 23, 1915, aged 67. I've been a member of the Forty Club since 1987, and it was founded in 1936 by the lawyer and cricketer Henry Grierson. His cricketing days were fading, so he started the club for ailing players over the age of 40 to take on mainly public schools, to show youngsters how to play the game in the right way – in a sporting manner.

"WG" was the hero of the previous generation and didn't figure in all Grierson's objectives – like his unsportsmanlike behaviour – but after WW11 ended, someone noticed that his massive gravestone was tumbling down and was surrounded by foliage. The MCC took over the remedial work and paid the bills. Then the Forty Club donated money each year, and one of their members, Harold Smith, was appointed as Curator to maintain the memorial. He lives in close proximity.

"WG" wasn't a good model to young players in one way – he was renowned for his cheating and for bullying umpires. On one occasion, when his off stump was knocked, he should have walked to the pavilion but instead picked up the ball, put it back in its place, and said to the baffled umpire, "Very windy day today," and resumed his innings. He played between 1864–1915, a record as a first-class cricketer, and scored 54,896 runs and took 2864 wickets. At 6ft 2, he dominated the sport, and as an amateur he picked up more money than any other cricketer of his time.

MCC put on a centenary dinner at Lord's on October 23 to honour him, and beforehand, a well attended service took place at St. George's Church in Beckenham. I attended both events and was also present when the priest spoke at the grave in mid-afternoon.

One wonders how "WG" would fare today against super fit, sleek men, throwing themselves down to stop a boundary, and batsmen reverse sweeping sixes. Not too successfully, one thinks, and today's rulers would have punished him for his excesses. But in his time, he was looked on as a hero, and a century later he deserved recognition.

Sir Jack Hobbs, an outstanding sportsman throughout his long career, receives similar recognition, and Surrey CCC started a Masters' Club of which I am a member. They stage two dinners – one in the summer, and one on Jack's birthday on December 16 – and the menu is always the same: roast lamb, and apple pie with custard – his favourite meal.

Football is less enthusiastic at honouring their heroes. It took years of persuasion by my *Daily Mail* colleague Jeff Powell and his friends before a statue was put up at Wembley for Bobby Moore. I started another campaign to pay for a statue there to Sir Walter Winterbottom – the first and longest serving England manager, and the first FA Director of Coaching. A highly self-educated man with a ready smile, Walter was born in humble circumstances in Oldham. He coached a generation of England managers, and most of the time he paid his own expenses while travelling all around Britain.

The campaign target fell well short, and instead of a statue of him, the FA commissioned a bust which is on display at their 330-acre National Training Centre in St. George's Park near Burton on Trent, opened by the Duke and Duchess of Gloucester in 2012.

When I arrived for the WG service at the municipality-owned car park opposite St. George's Church, not far from where David Bowie lived, it was pouring with rain. I drove to the disabled area – two bays each side of an entrance bays where I last went. The street lights were obscured by the drooping boughs of the trees, and it wasn't easy to read the signage on the concrete, especially as it was covered by rotting leaves. As a result, I failed to see that two disabled bays on the right had been altered to charging up electric cars. Enid Blyton, who lived in Beckenham, might have written a short children's story about the 12th century church, or Julie Andrews, also a Beckenhamian, might have sung in it. Another eminent lady who migrated from Trinidad to Beckenham, Baroness Floella Benjamin, the Blue Peter actress and TV presenter, started her career moving into the nearby Mackenzie Road.

When she spoke at the unveiling of a bust of the great Trinidadian cricketer and politician Lord Learie Constantine in the House of Lords on May 1, 2019, she said, "It almost caused a riot in Beckenham. People were objecting to seeing black people moving in, and the police was called." She also spoke passionately about the Windrush affair in the 1960s at the unveiling ceremony. Around that time, she was appointed the chairperson of the £1m Windrush Museum, which might include some of Learie's memorabilia. For her charitable work, she was made a Dame in the 2020 New Year's Honours.

Learie was highly critical of a number of great English batsmen like Peter May, Sir Colin Cowdrey, Ken Barrington, Sir Geoff Boycott, and Mike Smith, in the Tory supporting *Daily Sketch*. "They use their pads rather than their bats," he said. "Their first move is to defend."

When I went to the 80th birthday of Sir Garfield Sobers – I wrote his first autobiography in 1988 – I asked the former England captain Mike Smith, known as MJK, if he felt Learie was right.

"Yes," he said. "We were too cautious and put the West Indian bowlers on top, like Wes Hall, Charlie Griffith, Sonny Ramadhin, and Alf Valentine. That gave the initiative to them. We should have played more shots."

Sir Gary agreed.

Sonny was a very popular, shy Trinidadian, who kept a pub for many years in the North, and died in 2022, aged 92.

A distinguished Trinidadian, Learie broke the colour bar in 1944 when he became a qualified barrister in his late forties, and he went on to help draft the Race Relations Acts. He also counselled a vast number of Jamaicans who had been persuaded to live in Lancashire in WW2 to fill the gaps in armament factories caused by locals being called up to the armed services. When he was the first High Commissioner of Trinidad in London, he undertook a similar role for Windrush survivors.

If anyone should be selected for a statue in Parliament, it is him, and I am still pressing for one. I wrote to Theresa May when she was Prime Minister, and Sadiq Khan when he was Mayor of London. Both thought it was a worthy idea and passed it to their civil servants, who shamefully derailed it by sending me undecipherable jargon in letters. With Andrew Stephenson, MP of Nelson, and the Tory Whip, I am still campaigning for a statue of Learie on the Parliament Estate, to join the black statues numbering just three people –- Mahatma Gandhi, who never lived in England; Nelson Mandela, ditto; and Millicent Fawcett, the comparative obscure suffragette. None of them matched the revolutionary diversity work of Learie, who lived in England for 29 years. Incidentally, Learie was proud to call himself black, and made jokes about it.

His friend, Trinidadian C.L.R. James (1901-1989), the political activist and author of *A Life Beyond a Boundary* – acknowledged to be one of the best cricket books of all time – stayed with the Constantines in Nelson. I disagree about his book, though – it's too much about unknown Trinidad cricketers and himself.

Learie arranged a part-time job for him, reporting on cricket at Old Trafford in the *Manchester Guardian* before moving to London. I met him in his tiny flat near the Oval just before he died, and I noticed that his cup of tea was spilt in the saucer before he started to drink. I said to a friend, "He's got the shakes."

She said, "He's always had the shakes."

What we need is a Sir Alec Douglas Home, who played ten first class cricket matches and briefly became Prime Minister in 1963-4, after Harold Macmillan was rejected following the Profumo affair. Had he stayed in the job, he might have made Learie a Lord earlier than 1969, when he was finally given the ermine.

But another Harold – Wilson – whom I interviewed in 1969 about football hooliganism, regained his position as Prime Minister for a second time. Wilson didn't give me any exciting news, but I thought my scoop was worthy of a mention.

Next morning, I picked up my copy of the *Sketch* and there was no sign of it. Bob Findlay, the sports editor, said, "Lord Vere Rothermere, the owner, didn't want to see the left winger Wilson on the front page."

His father, Rothermere, supported Sir Oswald Ernald Mosley (1896-1980), the leader of the British Fascists in the 1930s. I went to one of Oswald's rallies in 1958, and he was a very convincing orator. He was interned for his political pro-Hitler views in 1940, and went to live in Paris after his release.

RUN OUT!

My PCN BY0513578A appeal was abruptly run out by M. Jones, a Parking Support Officer, but he offered a smidgeon of sympathy by saying, "I am sorry to hear of the problems you have, however they are not grounds for withdrawing a PCN. It is the responsibility of the motorists to check the signs to ensure that their vehicle is parked correctly. I have looked into your case and read the previous letters (yours to us and ours to yours). I can see you are raising a point that we answered in our previous letter. Although I understand that you feel strongly about this point, I do not have anything new to add to the answer we gave in our previous letter.

"You have 28 days from the date of this letter being served (delivered) to: pay £110 or appeal to the Parking Adjudicator.

I certainly did appeal.

AN HONEST AND
CONVINCING SERIAL APPEALER

Here I was at my D-Day Adjudication hearing at the London Tribunal in Chancery Exchange, Furnival Road, EC4 IAB on February 16, 2016. With little or no parking nearby, I went by Underground and walked from Blackfriars. This is familiar territory, round the corner from Fleet Street. There were half a dozen nervous people all waiting to be interviewed by trained lawyers. After reading the sports section of the *Daily Telegraph,* my name was called to go to a small room. Mr Teber was very attentive, unlike one or two adjudicators in the past who were abrupt and were keen to go off for lunch.

My case might have been helped by Bromley's submission, because it contained several mistakes, like "License" instead of "Licence". They made six clangers in this paragraph: "The Local Authority acknowledges the extensive problems OUTLINMED by the appellant, which meant he would not have been paying full attention when parking (no full stop!) Given, however, that parking is part and parcel of using a vehicle and it would seem the appellant felt sufficiently FOCUSED to drive, the Local AUTHORUTY do not consider the problems compelling RAESON to withdraw the Notice (no full stop)"

Mr Teber flashed up some pictures of my case and said, "They don't look too clear. I'll see if there are other, clearer ones."

I pointed out that it was dark at the time, and it was hard to read the notices. After a second look, he said, "The signage is poor. I am dismissing the case." It took just 12 minutes. And I was elated.

Three days later, I received another amazingly quick letter from Bromley Parking Department, signed by Sally Jacobs, PATAS (?) Officer, who ended it, "Yours sincerely".

It said: "Having received the decision on your parking appeal, the Local Authority is exercising it's (sic!) right to request a review on the following basis:

"The EA (who?) requests a review on the basis of a factual inaccuracy as the Adjudicator stated the EA did not provide anything to rebut the appellant's comments about the inadequacy of the markings and signage. Yet as indicated on the Form K, evidence checklist and summary there were Officer's photos showing the markings and signage, which were to be viewed on the EA website via the URL (?) already supplied to the Adjudicators and also DVD (?) footage showing the location. It appears that the Adjudicator did not view any of this evidence which has prejudiced the EA's case. Once the review is received you will be advised accordingly."

On February 21, I replied, "I realise you had the right to pursue these matters, but I am saddened to see that you are now appealing against my appeal. I took the DVD footage with me to give it to the Adjudicator and, not having seen it myself, he spent five minutes looking at it. He said, 'Is that your car?' I said, 'No. It was someone else.' Then part of my vehicle showed up, and only half the registration could be seen. He then said the signage wasn't clear and decided to grant my appeal.

"In his letter to me, he described me as 'an honest, convincing, and consistent witness', and I think he also took into account my evidence about my personal situation. I had five days in the King's College Hospital fitting a pacemaker in mid-December, and a further five days there two weeks ago, and the last thing I want is to be involved with a PEN, having apologised for making an understandable mistake.

"I explained to Mr Teber that I was a sports writer for the *Daily Mail*, and I'm still writing books and articles about football and cricket and have built up a lot of experience writing about referees and their actions on the field. When a player commits a foul and when he holds up his hand and says sorry, he doesn't expect to be shown the yellow card or be sent off, unless it is a serious offence. The player is invariably warned not to repeat the offence. This is a fair and reasonable approach which seems totally absent in your set-up. In any court of the land, magistrates and judges will always take into account the circumstances of the person's life, and I suspected Mr Teber followed that course.

"At the moment, I have weekly blood tests to assess my low blood pressure, and the doctors have yet to settle on the best treatment. My 'offence' took place at 7pm, and I can't imagine someone owning an electric vehicle would turn out on a wet night to recharge his or her car and be denied by me parking in one of the two bays.

"Yours sincerely."

On March 18, Miss Jacobs wrote again, saying, "Further to your letter of 19 February, I write to advise you that Mr Stephens has arranged for a recent review on your parking appeal to be withdrawn and the Notice closed. Accordingly, I confirm that your liability as been cancelled. Yours Sincerely."

Thankfully Ms Jacobs gave me a yellow card!

Next day, I celebrated by buying a new lawnmower. I bought a discounted £110 model. The old one was unusable.

ON A WINNING STREAK

This one – PCN BY14951579 – was straightforward. Was I loading or not loading, that is the question? Bromley has reinvigorated the north side of the High Street, and nearby roads and shut up premises have, in the main, been re-opened to business. Parking attendant Y471 booked my car between 15.58 pm to16.02 on June 21, while I nipped into a Brazilian-owned art shop. Next day, I sent this letter to the Parking Authority:

"I wish to appeal against this Notice. The alleged offence was 'parked in a loading place during restricted hours without loading'. Well, I was loading – picking up an etching from the Frames and Art shop 30ms from where I parked in the High Street, which is almost devoid of any disabled spaces. I paid for the etching on June 12, and on the 21st I arrived at 3.50pm at the shop. Having been disabled since 1943, and now aged 83, I am no condition to walk too far. I may well be having a third hip replacement and have a long-term heart condition.

"The staff had trouble to find the etching, and I had to wait for about 15 minuets before they found it. When I explained I was loading it into my vehicle, the officer said he couldn't cancel it, and I told him I would appeal. The etching has a sentimental history. It was one of the many etchings designed by my late wife Audrey, who died on Christmas Day 2000, aged 58, and my current lady companion Mrs Gillian Treharne, a former headmistress, was born on June 17, six days before Audrey's birthday. Audrey had six sisters, and Gill has five sisters, and Audrey is buried at Chislehurst Cemetery 300ms from Gillian's cottage.

"I was giving the etching as a birthday present to Gillian, and now I have a fine of £65 to contend with. I hope it is cancelled. I attach the shop's receipts as evidence.

"Next year, the Government is going to give Blue Badges to mental patients, almost doubling the overall total. In Bromley, the number of disabled spaces has been reduced to accommodate a car company (opposite Bromley South Station, and other places). The law indicates 6% of parking spaces should be devoted to the Blue Badge holders. Where are the new patients going to park?"

On August 13, Cathy Suckling, their PSO, sent a heart-warming missive, saying, "Thank you for providing a copy of the receipts, which adequately confirms that loading/unloading was being carried out at the time in question. The PCN has therefore been cancelled on this occasion."

Hallelujah! But she didn't say where the disabled spaces are coming from!

H.G. WELLS WAS BORN THERE

Herbert George Wells, one of the biggest selling authors of countless futuristic books and novels, was born in Bromley on September 21, 1866, and this is commemorated by the plaque and a futuristic large figure in the Market Square, which today's generation hardly notice. And round the corner is another plaque, on the wall at number 9 on a terraced house in South Street, saying, "Mrs Knott's Dame School. H.G. Wells was a pupil there, born 21 September, 1866." Next door is a shop and workplace named "Marbles", specialising in gravestones, and which was owned for some years by Graham Simpson, my neighbour on my left at Widmore Road. His company built my wife's gravestone in Chislehurst Cemetery, which was designed by my daughter.

South Street is a nondescript, little road, and I often park on a single yellow line there. And on June 23, 2011, I jousted with my friends at Bromley's parking people about it, and lost. The amount of traffic is spasmodic, and Uber and other taxi drivers park there, but when they see a parking attendant, they start their engines up and drive off. There are a small number of residential parking spaces, invariably occupied by the householders. Bromley Fire Station faces the council offices, and one of the fire engines has a registration "AEO", Audrey's maiden name. I find it a welcome reminder of her, an exemplary driver who had an almost faultless record at the wheel – no PCNs, and only a Conditional Discharge for backing into a one-way road.

But on June 23, my Honda Accord GF56VMY was booked by CEO 187, who supplied photographs of it straying over to a double yellow line designated as "Loading Only". I used to park on the left in Court Road without penalty, but it was soon designated "Loading Only". Behind my parked Honda, there were two cars with engines running, and they were giving out harmful emissions. Neither had Disabled Badges.

I pointed this out in my letter, dated June 24, and added, "In most of the road there is no chance of loading; on one side there is a small car park, and the other side a derelict Council building was empty. At the time of writing, the Council are planning to turn it into a hotel."

Very frustrated, I started my letter, "On the day, I received a letter from you acknowledging that I have paid £120 to settle a PEN, and another PEN 85022626 was stuck on my windscreen saying I would have to pay £130. On May 26, I was given yet another one from Enfield Council, claiming £130. I am appealing against the Enfield one, because a CEO gave me permission to drop a book into Waterstone's for only a minute or two, and I have high hopes that it will be annulled. However, in less than a month, I have run up a bill of £380 in parking 'offences', and it seems the authorities want me to be confined without use of my vehicle."

The two-page letter from Enfield's Borough Treasurer's Department, on behalf of the Parking Department, explained all about "loading", and I was given a receipt for the £65 fine. It was signed by "JB" Josh – Ben of The Progressive and Representation Team of Parking Services.

Not a good use of simplicity!

H.G. Wells was known as "Bertie", and he was the fourth child of Sarah Neal, a domestic cleaner, and Joseph Wells, an odd job man, later head gardener, and a poorly paid cricketer who played only eight games for the Kent CCC. He scored only 48 runs at an average of 4.30, and 15 wickets at 9.14, bowling round arm. He didn't have a contract but relied on handouts from supporters who gave extra "nobbins" for his achievement, becoming the first County payer to take four Sussex wickets in four balls. One of his victims was Spencer Leigh, a great nephew of Jane Austen.

Joseph was born at Penshurst Place in 1828, and his uncle Timothy Duke had a business making cricket balls and bats. "Bertie" was born in Atlas House, 46 High Street, Bromley. When he was seven, he broke a leg and spent several months in hospital, during which time he became an avid book reader. His favourite authors were Charles Dickens and Washington Irving.

When I was seven, I was recuperating in hospitals, and I also read many works of the classical authors. My mother won a full set of Charles Dickens works from a competition in the *Daily Herald*, and I still have them – not all read, though. "Bertie" left school and worked as a teacher before concentrating on writing books and articles. He never made a fortune in his life, and married twice – once to his cousin – and had a child from Rebecca West, the author, outside of wedlock. His work is still being reprinted.

He died at Regent's Park on August 13, 1946, after a tangled love life, aged 79. *The War of the Worlds*, one of his finest works, was shown on TV in 2019. One of his many sayings was, "When you take a fall, stand next day." I agree you have to try, but in my illness between May and March 2021-2, I had 11 falls!

MY FIRST AND LAST
MY VISIT TO ENFIELD

It was on May 26, 2011, when I parked outside Waterstone's bookstore where the manager John Chater, a sports lover, wanted me to put on a signing session for my book about the local hero Bill Nicholson. I brought a copy to give to John, and he was delighted. However, he warned me that there was no parking outside, even for the disabled.

I said, "I've just spoken to an attendant and explained I wouldn't spend more than a few minutes, and he said okay."

I had a convivial chat with John then in came the late Peter Baker, the Tottenham Hotspur right back who played 344 first team games until 1965, including in the Double season 1960-1, and was the longest serving right back for the club before Cyril Knowles took over. Born locally in 1931, the clean-cut Baker was one of three home-produced players in the Double team: the rest of them were Scots, Welsh, and Irish.

Not wanting to be relegated to the reserves, he signed for Durban United in South Africa, and later became manager for a period before returning to Hampstead. Most players of that era took pubs, but he owned a stationery shop before retiring to play golf. Our pleasant chat, reviving memories of when I used to interview him in his prime, delayed me, and when I went to my car a PCN was affixed.

Enfield has a long list of advice to the disabled, and one caught my eye: "You can appeal if you think you have been treated unfairly."

I used that as my explanation: the actual words of the attendant giving me a few minutes' waiting time, and I finished up by saying, "I live in London, and I am reluctant to go to an appeal, but if I have to, I will. People who have spent more than 50 years and cope well without seeking allowances from the Government, as I do, should be treated with sympathy and understanding."

From 1958, when I first worked in Fleet Street as a sports writer, I used to pass through Enfield to the Tottenham training ground in Cheshunt, seeking interviews with Jimmy Anderson, Bill Nicholson, and a list of successive managers. The superbly articulate Danny Blanchflower hogged most of the interview time, whereas many of the others would duck out and speed off home.

Like most London boroughs, Enfield has many links with famous politicians, including Benjamin Disraeli, William Pitt the Elder, Norman Tebbitt, Michael Portillo – the former Tory Minister who wears colourful clothing in a TV programme on railways – and others of distinction, including Mike Gatting, the former England cricket skipper; Joseph Bazalgette, who created a sewer system under London; Boris Karloff, John Keats, Bruce Forsyth, Bernard Bresslaw, Adele, and Amy Winehouse. Bernard (1934-1993), who was 6ft 7, towered over all of them.

Enfield started out as a market town at the time of the Domesday Book, and firstly the Danes and then the Romans invaded before the Normans arrived. There was no Border Authority in those days. It is 315 square miles, abutting a forest, and the population was 333,869 in 2018. Enfield played a big part in WW1 when the Lee-Enfield rifle was built in a local armaments factory. Millions of Lee-Enfields were made, and if the Germans had bombed the factory early in the war, the result might have brought about a win for the Kaiser.

The British Army stopped using the venerable Lee-Enfield in 1957 and went on to make Bren and Sten guns. When Mihir Bose's Fleet Street cricket team was invited to tour India in 1995 after 52 people died of a bubonic plague and the number of tourists from Britain fell alarmingly, the Indian

Government gave Bose's players armed escorts wherever they went, to assure potential British holidaymakers not to cancel their holidays.

I was the senior player, and my son Gavin was the all-rounder star. No cricket team had better protection in the sub-Continent – soldiers with Lee-Enfields WW1 rifles! We were strongly represented by Roland Watson, political correspondent of *The Times;* Mike Evans, who was defence correspondent; and Nick Wood, political editor of the same newspaper; Peter Oborne of the *Telegraph;* Tim Jotischky of the *Daily Mail;* George Pascoe-Watson, the political editor of Sky; and Charlie Thomas of Sky Sport. Nick Hewer, Sir Alan Sugar's PR advisor on "The Apprentice", didn't fancy playing cricket at the age of 61, and wrote our touring brochure as a spectator and cheerleader. Asked how he avoided Delhi belly, he said, "Kept swigging whisky." And no-one picked up any kind of fever or sickness.

Before we set off, Prime Minister John Major invited the party to a reception at the House of Commons, and he said to the political correspondents, "I hope you are so successful that you don't come back for several years."

But some might have caught the first sign of cancer through breathing the foul air of New Delhi. The fixture against the British Embassy team had to be moved to another ground ten miles out, to avoid the clinging smog.

Bose lost the toss, and our athletes were soon exhausted in the 40-degree heat. He asked their skipper about drinks and lunch, and was told they hadn't catered for the visitors, only the Embassy team. Bose proceeded to ring the 5-star Hyatt Hotel, where we were staying, and ordered copious drinks and pre-packed lunches. An hour later, a coach arrived with the goods, with the bill being handed over to the Embassy treasurer.

A week after we returned home, I found myself sitting next to Douglas Hurd, the then Foreign Secretary, at a promotional lunch. I told him about how our Fleet Street survivors had been treated, and he said to one of his aides, "That's extraordinary. What a way to carry on! I'll see that this is looked into. We can't upset the political writers." Years later, we still haven't heard from the Foreign Office, but we did have a fine feast at a smog-less day.

After my sole experience with ATMs, when a smooth-talking man conned me and plundered money from my current account of Barclays Bank in Bromley in 2019, I steer clear of them. But on my visit to Enfield I learned that the first ATM in the world was used at the Barclays Bank opened there by the actor Reg Varney, famous for appearing in the TV programme, "On the Buses". The ATM was invented by a Scotsman, John Shepherd-Barron, and now there are 70,000 in Britain and an estimated 3m in the rest of the world. Barclays laid on a red carpet at the opening, and if I ever go the town again, I'll check to find that out it is still there! Nowadays, we don't need money any more.

After leaving Waterstones, I called in at Haileybury College – one of the world's finest public schools, originally funded by the East India Company in 1806 – to write an article in the Forty Club Year Book about a cricket match between the school's first XI and the Forty Club. Viscount Allenby, the Field Marshall, and Labour Prime Minister Clement Attlee were both educated there, and 17 of the pupils were awarded VCs. The impressive Cross of Sacrifice at the entrance commemorates the 1,436 former pupils killed in various wars. The school occupies 500 acres and has ample parking facilities. The racquets court, built in 1908, was destroyed when it was hit by a V11 doodlebug, but was rebuilt in 1952.

The visit gave me the chance to interview an old mate, Geoff Howarth OBE, the former New Zealand cricket captain who is similar in personality to the current skipper Kane Williamson. He had an outstanding record in his 47 Tests, and played for Surrey between 1971-1985 before retiring to become cricket coach at the school for 16 years, up until 2017.

He made a very good point. "There's far too much sledging in schools' cricket," he said. "I don't mind encouraging their colleagues, but I don't like hearing these inane comments all the time. And sledging is definitely out here."

As I was typing this, I heard Kevin Pietersen, now living in his native South Africa, commenting on the Newlands Test in 2020 on Sky and saying it was good to hear the sledging of the South African top order from Jos Buttler and the close fielders. Buttler's comments were picked up on the Sky mic and broadcast from one of the stumps, and he was reprimanded and fined 15% of his match fee – a lenient penalty, but his previous good conduct was taken into account. Adjudicators and parking departments should copy.

SPEEDING ALONG THE A127
ARTERIAL ROAD AT LEIGH-ON-SEA

VAR, short for Video Assistant Referee, was introduced in football by the International FA Board in 2018, to help referees come up with the right decisions in matches. Up until then, many British referees had a 95% success rate with their decisions, but the Board wanted 100%. Previously, the benefit of the doubt was given to the attackers, because the owners wanted more goals and more excitement to keep the interest of the public. The same thing happened in cricket, when batsmen were given the benefit of lbws and questionable catches.

With one sweep, the Board – half of which comes from the four home countries: England, Wales, Scotland, and Northern Ireland – wiped out leniency, and virtually all football writers, broadcasters, and presenters agreed. VAR officials, based in Stockley near Hayes, Middlesex, were ordered to stick to the laws and not deviate. The nondescript business park had been used as a tip by barge owners before it was built over.

On offside decisions, if a big toe was just a millimetre over the line, or even a nose, the flag was raised to signal offside. In the 2020-1 season, there was uproar, with dozens of instances of penalised Premiership clubs contesting VAR interpretations. The old precept of "in the opinion of the referee on the field" was replaced by VAR – less experienced referees sitting miles away from the grounds. It was similar to seeing drones armed with missiles being controlled by CIA officers sitting in bunkers in Nebraska thousands of miles away.

So far, VAR is making far too many wrong judgments, and the authorities have still haven't achieved 100% success. Needs more tinkering.

This thought process happened to me on the A127 Arterial Road at 21.58pm on May 21, 2005, when I was driving home to Bromley after reporting on a football match at Roots Park, Southend, when the home side lost 0-1 to Northampton. It was a dreary game, and after I phoned my copy, I reckoned my 12 ordered paragraphs would be pruned it was, and reduced to just one par.

As I was driving along the dual carriageway, I didn't pay much notice to the 40mph signs. Travelling west at the junction of Bellhouse Lane at 49mph, the red light appeared as I sped over the junction.

Shortly afterwards, Essex Police sent me a "Particulars of the Offence", saying, "The time into red was one seconds (sic!). The amber light having previously been on three seconds." It was signed with an undecipherable squiggle from PC S.D. Langdon 698, Camera Enforcement Officer at Billericay.

I wrote back in a jocular manner on June 1, saying, "I am a football reporter for the *Daily Telegraph* and was thinking about how to write my intro on the Southend v Northampton game on the day in question, when I suddenly realised I should have braked sooner. There was no traffic in front or behind, and I accelerated to avoid the dreaded red. Unfortunately, I missed the mark by one second. I can't remember having been charged with this offence in 47 years. I blamed Kevin, the Southend captain, because I was thinking about a par or two about him missing his brother's wedding on the day of the play-off! Please be merciful!"

They weren't. I was fined £60 and given three points on my unblemished record. The maximum could have been £1,000. Now I have a more sophisticated Honda, and when I reach 30mph a noise is sounded, right up to higher limits of up to 70 mph. Luckily, I haven't erred a second time.

FOXED BY THE DOUBLE YELLOW

In the spring of 2014, I was hit with a run of PENS. Fed up with it, I took the matter to the executive level at Bromley Council. One offence was to stray over a disabled space designated as "Motor Cyclists".

I wrote to a Mr Bowen: "I've attended Beckenham Spa since it opened for hydrotherapy exercising to keep my muscles toned, and I've never seen a motor cycle in that part of the car park. I arrived at 14.05, and one of the wardens might have seen my vehicle and said, or put a warning on my windscreen and said, 'Excuse me, sir, you have parked too far over.' That would be the common-sense, compassionate way of dealing with it. No, it's straight in with the PEN – another £110!

"I noticed the Civil Enforcement Officer's alleged signature on it looked like a fallen 'Z' (with racist intones!). In a court of law, that would not be admissible.

On my previous letter to you, I forgot to mention another matter which reflected badly on Bromley Council. In 2012, I wanted to reduce the amount I pay for rates, and spoke to Alan Smith, manager of my Barclays Bank – no relation to my friend of the same name, who is now a football commentator after a distinguished career with Arsenal. I showed my monthly statements to the manager, and he said, 'You seem to be paying a lot of money to the Council.'

"I took the matter up with the rates department, and someone wrote back apologising, and they had put another ratepayer's charge on top of mine – a man living in Chislehurst. Eventually, I was paid £3,235.94 which was put back into my account. In normal circumstances, I would have asked for a payment to recompense me, but I wrote back, 'Don't bother. I know the Council needs every penny.'

"I hope Mr Davies or Mr Pattinson, the CEO, will look into my recent PEN cases and respond with the same spirit of goodwill."

Regrettably, they rejected my appeal.

In the past, I've parked on a single yellow at the eastern end of South Street, opposite the small park which is now closed. On this occasion, I parked there, and a parking attendant put a PEN on my windscreen.

He explained, "You haven't seen those foot-long double yellow lines on the pavement facing the road that means it is illegal to park because it is designated as 'loading'."

Instead of painting long yellow lines, this may have been part of the Council's austerity campaign, saving money on paint. Round the corner into Court Street, lots of unaware drivers must have been fined for not noticing the new 'Loading Only' signs.

In another one, I parked in a residents' space across the road in Freelands Road, not seeing the grubby sign under a tree. The name "Freelands" should be altered to "Costly Road". But a Mrs Dot Shergold, a Parking Support Officer, wrote: 'We have considered what you have said, but regret we have decided not to cancel your parking ticket."

In one letter from the Council, it was addressed to "Scorell", which I said lacked competency. It was also unsigned. But some time ago, I did write to the CEO, and he cancelled it.

THE CASE OF THE CAR ALARM
THAT KEPT BLARING AWAY

It started at 9.22am on Saturday, July 31, 2010, and ended on April 1, 2011, when a second adjudicator ruled against me. I put up stiff resistance and based my case on the lack of community spirit in Bromley – one of the most affluent parts of Britain and where the teenage tennis star, Emma Raducanu was brought up and educated. Voted the Best Young Women's winner of 2021, the young lady is a great advert for the Borough.

Normally I go to the magnificent Beckenham Spa three miles away, either around 2pm on a Friday or early on a Saturday. On this particular day, I started my car, and the alarm came on. I tried various ways of stopping it but failed, so I set off, hoping it would cease. As I approached Market Square, it was still blaring away, and I pulled into the 2.8ms long loading section opposite McDonalds.

I got out, raised the bonnet, and looked around, hoping some Good Samaritan would come to my aid. None did. I had a film to hand into the photograph shop round the corner and they were short-handed, so I had to wait for ten minutes or more before someone gave me a ticket to collect my photos. I then returned to my Honda Accord and the alarm was still making a loud noise. I was duly booked.

In their refuting letter from Bromley Parking and Traffic Appeals Service, Anju Kaler, an adjudicator, wrote on December 15: "Mr Scovell says that the vehicle alarm started sounding off suddenly, and he was not sure what to do about it. Why he chose to park in the loading bay instead of driving onto another location is not explained. His manner of parking and his movements on the DVD do not indicate that he was distressed or panicking. The explanation amounts at most to mitigation and does not provide an exemption to the contravention. The Council may exercise discretion and decide not to enforce payment in such circumstances. I have noted the circumstances described by Mr Scovell, but do not consider that they amount to compelling reasons warranting a recommendation that the authority cancels the Notice to Owner."

Well, Anju, I am not someone who has been distressed or experienced panic attacks after seeing several bombing raids near a radar station on St. Boniface Down in the Isle of Wight in WW2 and spending two years in hospitals recovering from septic arthritis – latterly known as sepsis – caused by a piece of flying piece of glass. Our family, like everyone else's in those circumstances, got on with it, employing humour to cheer us up. We didn't call for counselling.

Some years later, I might have found Good Samaritans, because more people – particularly migrants now with British passports – are kinder since years of austerity. There are now instances when people in trains see me limping and get up and let me have their seat.

The best example was in mid-summer 2019, when I tripped over a foot-high chain and landed painfully on my left shoulder. Not being able to get up, a lady of around 30 stopped her car and rushed over to help. Another, younger, woman did the same. A young man joined in, and the three of them hauled me up. The first lady laughed and said, "You've got fantastic eye lashes," and we all roared with laughter.

The other one said, "Where were you going?"

I said, "I was about to drive to my girlfriend."

She said to the other girl, "He's one of those!" More uproarious laughter.

Before WW2, many of the population were hard on young people. Rich people sent their children to board at public schools, and some people had the strap or a cane available to whack youngsters' bottoms when they misbehaved. When peace came, the pendulum started to swing the other way. Too many parents indulged their children, and you now see toddlers pointing out which sweets and chocolates they want in supermarkets all over the country.

Not many youngsters are self-disciplined enough to succeed in life. Others look to their hard-working grandparents to contribute money to their mortgages. Richard Littleton of the *Daily Mail*, an old footballing mate of mine, might put this over more expressively than me.

Anju claimed I should have parked further into nearby Church Road, which I normally take going to the Spa, rather than in a loading bay. The answer for that is to explain that the four disabled spaces opposite the church have been reduced to three, and they are filled by 9.22am, and the other parking spaces were also occupied. Several girls walked to the shops where they work, and I didn't bother to ask them to try and silence my alarm. Another mistake she made in her judgement mentioned the siren going off in Market Street. It didn't; it went off at the Chinese garage which is currently being turned into flats.

There was one consolation: the Council reduced my fine from £120 to £60. I thanked them and told them I intended to appeal to the Independent Tribunal for Parking and Penalties in London in City Road.

In Angel Square, directly above the Hearing Centre on April 1, All Fools' Day, Bromley Council supplied a 20-page summary of the case. The sanitised, quiet second floor was occupied by several booths manned by legal trained officers, and there were no signs of security men or police officers.

My adjudicator was Paul Wright, and one of the points I included in my submission was that some years before, my Blue Badge had been taken away for 18 months because I failed to meet the criteria of not being able to walk 50 metres unaided in front of a stern looking, middle-aged tester. I could walk much longer distances. I appealed, and a second lady, more friendly, assessed me and gave me the impression that my appeal would be granted. Alas, that was also turned down. It overlooked the fact that, having a stiff right leg, I often can't get the door open to get out of my car, especially in supermarket car parks. I appealed a third time, and someone at Anerley agreed with me and my Blue Badge was reinstated – with no apologies.

Mr Wright squashed my faint hopes with his Adjudicator's Reasons: "I can now confirm that I am of the view that the decision reached by the previous Adjudicator was one at which she was reasonably able to arrive on the evidence which was before her. Her decision shows that she had appropriately weighed the evidence and her conclusion is such that I do not regard the decision as an error of law.

"An adjudicator, contemplating an application for review, will not interfere with another adjudicator's findings of fact or law unless the applicant can show that the findings are ones that the adjudicator could not have reasonably arrived at on the evidence, so much so that the applicant is able to establish that the adjudicator erred in law. Only then would it be in the interests of justice to review the decision. Otherwise a finding of fact or law will generally be viewed as final. This is the position in your case for the above reasons. There are no grounds for a review. Your application for review is therefore refused."

Somewhat repetitive jargon of the worst type!

WE NOW GO INTO ART

Hans Holbein the Younger was known as one of the greatest portrait painters and printmakers of the sixteenth century, and a photograph of his last self portrait before he died from an infection, aged 45, in 1543. Born in Augsburg, Germany, in 1497 he followed his father The Elder and worked in Basel, Lucerne, France, England (1526-28), Basel again, and England (1532-40). He experienced painfully slow transportation in horse-drawn coaches and costly overnights, and ran up lots of debts. In England, Anne Boleyn and Thomas Cromwell were among his patrons before Henry VIII gave the order to execute the promiscuous Ms Boleyn. Another patron, Sir Thomas More, also had his head summarily removed. However, Henry VIII sat for portraits for Hans, and the portly king commended him on the likeness, which he thought was uncanny.

Hans lived for a while in Aldgate, but one of his patrons must have lived in Belgravia, and after he died a street near Sloane Square was named after him.

On December 28, 2013, I made the mistake of driving to the *Poule au Pot* French restaurant near Victoria Coach Station for a family post-Christmas lunch. I should have gone by train and walked the three-quarters of a mile from Victoria Station. Although most of the population was still on holiday, it was impossible to find any parking spaces, particularly disabled ones. Driving round and round fruitlessly, I spotted an empty space and managed to reverse into it, behind a blue Bentley. When I returned two hours later, a Royal Borough of Kensington and Chelsea's Enforcement Officer KC 1413 – do they now have a full regiment of 1413 of all sexes? – had whacked a PCN under my windscreen wipers. The penalty was £80, but if paid within a fortnight it would be £40.

Remember, I had a Kensington Council exemption for a disabled person while I wound up my final 12 years (1988-2000), and I often parked right outside the New Northcliffe House next to the old store Barker's, close to where Diana, Princess of Wales, used to rendezvous with my friend *Daily Mail* writer Richard Kay. In my letter of mitigation, I wrote: "While I was driving around, I saw one of your officers and asked him where were the disabled spaces, and he said, 'There are two further up the road, both vacant.' I drove off, only to find the bays were occupied. I made another abortive circuit and saw several free 'pay' spaces in Holbein Place, as distinct from 'Residents' Only' and, knowing that most councils penalise the drivers, I took a risk.

"There were no indications on any signs saying disabled drivers had to pay. I realise there is an acute shortage of spaces for the disabled in Belgravia, but in supermarkets particularly, and other parking areas, anyone of my height – almost 6ft – I find myself in a position where I can't get out of my car, hence the necessity to have a Blue Badge. Making me pay is a form of discrimination against the disabled.

"I am thinking of appealing but, having suffered two heart attacks, in 1997 and 2013, I am reluctant to take that course. I hope someone might show the Christmas spirit and show leniency in this case."

Good try! However, no Christmas spirit was shown, so I sent off my cheque for £40. Lo and behold (an unused description nowadays, but it was common in my youth), Bryan Picoto, Kensington and Chelsea's Notice Processing Officer, wrote to me on January 15, letting me off! What class!

To quote him: "Thank you for your letter, and I apologise for the delay in my response. The council receives comments about the lack of different types of spaces including disabled bay parking spaces. But unfortunately, little can be done to alleviate the problems due to limitations of space within the Borough.

"The European Blue Badge (EBB) scheme does not fully operate within the Royal Borough of Kensington and Chelsea. For future reference, concessions have been arranged for visitors who hold an EBB (European Blue Badge) and special EBB parking bays have been provided near to places of interest in the Royal Borough. (BS: one thinks of Audrey's tree outside Kensington Palace).

"On this occasion I have decided to cancel the PCN, due to the circumstances. The case is closed. Now that you are aware of the regulations concerning the proper display of Disabled Badges in the Borough, any subsequent PCNs issued for contraventions of this nature will be enforced. Accordingly, we are arranging for a payment of £40 to be refunded to the payee as soon as possible."

This has to be my most successful appeal, and sincere thanks to Mr Picoto and his department.

NO SUCH LUCK AT BROMLEY'S
ETHELBERT ROAD

My defence against a PCN 15333658 missile which landed on my doormat on November 14, 2007, was probably more detailed, but it was rejected. Here it is:

"I wish to appeal against this notice. From my records you will know that I have been disabled more than 65 years, and since the main Post Office was closed in East Street (which was just accessible through using two nearby disabled bays), the opportunity of going to it now is denied. I was one of the 1617 people who signed a petition against the closure.

"On the day in question, I was trying to park in Ethelbert Road to go to the new Post Office on the first floor in WHSmith's and noticed that the almost vacant disabled bay of the three was partially filled by a car. I could have parked there with part of my car overlapping but, having been booked on a previous occasion in those circumstances, I proceeded down the hill and, with a troublesome two-year-old grandson and a fraught mother, I parked on the left, inadvertently filling a residents' space.

"When I came back a few minutes later, I noticed the warden (137, I think) was absolving a woman in a car with a Disabled Badge parking on a double yellow line on the other side. My daughter and I had a laugh about it, but that soon changed when I was driving off, seeing a PCN on my windscreen. I caught up with the warden in Kentish Way and I said, 'Why is that woman let off while I have been booked?' He offered no explanation other than I had parked in the wrong space (the same applied to her). I don't want to spend another day attending another appeal, and urge common sense to be used. I am not a serial breaker of the law. I think a warning would be sufficient."

Bromley Parking Services wrote back saying, "Our records indicate that we have responded to your initial appeal. If you are unhappy with the decision (BS: to knock it back!) not to withdraw the penalty, you may make use of the formal appeals procedure." (BS: yes, I want to appeal!)."

On February 5, they sent me a Notice to Owner which had this menacing threat: "THE PENALTY CHARGE HAS NOT BEEN PAID. PAYMENT OF £120 IS NOW DUE."

On April 1 – this wasn't the first April Fool's Day I've been served a PCN, but the second – they wrote again with a Notice of Rejection. David Thompson, of The Processing and Representation Team, wrote: "I have read your representations and taken into consideration the points you have raised. I have also fully investigated the circumstances surrounding the issue of the PCN and assessed the pocket notes and any photographs taken by the Parking Attendant when the penalty was issued. However, for the reasons outlined below, I am unable to withdraw the PCN. While the scheme offers many concessions, Blue Badge Holders may not park in bays reserved for specific users, including residents and permit holders, unless the signs at the location indicate that they may do so."

Well, I have been a resident of Bromley since 1978!

In 2007, I went to a residents' meeting with the senior officers of Bromley Council and outlined my dissatisfaction about being harshly treated as a lifelong disabled person. Stephen Carr, the then chairman, and the CEO were amenable and helpful, and I left reassured. After being given another knockback, I wrote to another Bromley Processing and Representation member, Maureen Paris, with this plea:

"Last year I wrote to Stephen Carr, and he assured me that his council would be taking a more common-sense approach to the subject of parking in the Borough. The Government sent the same message to councils, but still the Parking Services in Bromley fail to exercise common sense. Especially in my case, when an innocent mistake, parking at a residents' bay for less than ten minutes, has led to a demand for £60, rising to £120.

"I was disabled in 1943, and in 2002 BATH (Bromley Association of People with Disabilities) withdrew my Blue Badge and, despite several appeals, they failed to reinstate it until April 23, 2003. My wife Audrey had died on Christmas Day, and their cruel, uncaring decision further aggravated my stress. I should have sued them. Now my other arthritic leg is causing problems and I might need a knee replacement. Do I have to go through yet another appeal to New Zealand House? If I have to, I will, but it isn't a fair and reasonable way this matter should be dealt with."

On August 1, my independent adjudicator sent me his damning verdict – the equivalent of a boxing points decision over 15 rounds: "The Adjudicator, having considered the evidence from the Appellant and the Authority, has refused the appeal."

I had to pay £120. But ten months earlier they sent me a dreaded pink CHARGE CERTIFICATE saying the fine was now £180. At least I managed to reduce it back by £60.

WINNY WOULD HAVE BEEN ENRAGED

My worst experience of minor bumps took place outside one of our favourite tea shops in Westerham, near the statue of Churchill, some years ago. A woman came out of an antique shop, looked at a small mark on her vehicle, and said, "You'll have to pay for that, and it's an expensive 4 by 4. It'll cost you."

A week later, she sent me the bill – £330 for an inch-long scratch. I didn't argue. My equally small scratch was part of a service, and the whole bill for my car was no more than £100. The last time I visited Westerham the shop was on sale.

The north side of Murray Avenue running into Widmore Road, the main road from Chislehurst to Bromley, has a chequered history. The Ashgrove private school is only 50ms from it, and the young children used to play there after leaving school, until the council put up a "No Ball Games" sign.

That sign erected all over the country, particularly in the inner cities, has done more harm to the chances of English-born children being picked for the England squad than anything. Instead of Trevor Brooking learning the mastery of using a small ball in small stretches of land or in quiet cul de sacs, the main composition of Premiership clubs is costly foreigners, and the fittest and fastest ones come from Africa where they picked up the art of using the ball with natural skill on bumpy, sandy surfaces. By lacking finesse and having played on beautiful, well drained pitches, the home-grown players are heavily coached and told "give it and go". Hardly any of them can beat opponents at speed.

In the hot summer of June 2005, I wrote to Peter Sibley, the Safe Bromley partnership of Bromley Council, complaining about the appalling behaviour of teenagers annoying residents, including me. I wrote that my neighbours in Widmore Road, next to my house and adjacent to Murray Avenue, had been "alarmed to see a gang of teenagers of both sexes causing mayhem, damaging the trees and shrubs, and vandalising the bungalow which was being built at the bottom of my garden".

The next night, a small number of smartly attired hooligans started upsetting the residents. After suffering a heart attack in 1997, I decided it would not be advisable to take these people on, so I drove to the police station to wait to see a clerk. "We are very busy," she said. I gave her my mobile phone number and asked the duty officer to ring me. No-one rang me.

Later, I saw two Community Officers walking near The Glades and told them about it. It took a long time to convince them this was a potentially serious problem in the heart of Bromley. Eventually they took details, promised they would pass the information on, and started to leave.

I said, "Murray Avenue is 400ms away, why don't you go in person?"

One said, "It is out of our area."

I told them I worked for national newspapers including the *Daily Mail*, and I could write an article about Bromley being invaded by well heeled, disruptive, rude, and aggressive hooligans who seem to do what they like without check.

Just saying "We'll come round and watch things" is not good enough. If there are any disturbances, the police should apprehend them and charge them under the Public Order Act.

Mr Sibley wrote back on June 12 with a three-line letter: "I shall ensure that your comments are passed to the local Police Officers for the area. Should you have any further problems, please do not hesitate to contact me."

I never heard back, but later in the year the hooligans went elsewhere. Except for isolated sessions of pot smoking, Murray Avenue is now a safe area. A year before, I wrote to Norwich police about hooligans causing trouble in the Prince of Wales Road close to the Nelson Hotel, where I often stayed reporting on matches at Carrow Road. I was the chairman of the

Football Writers' Association Facilities Committee. Also, I was a regular when Ipswich's David Sheepshanks and the Cobbold family were in charge.

Norwich FC is the most pleasant club to report on, and they and Ipswich were amazingly helpful in building modern press facilities. When Delia Smith took over the Canaries, I gave her some ideas about a new press working room, and for the following season she sanctioned a glitzy room better than five-star hotels in London or on Cunard liners.

But the previous chairman Robert Chase let the side down by putting up metal, swivel seats known as "knee crushers" in the press box when people got up. I was blamed for that.

My letter to the police brought a two-page response from Inspector Gavin Tempest, Central Area Licensing Inspector of Norfolk Constabulary, who explained that an 'Operation Enterprise' in the Fine City – it is known as that, deservedly – had started a 12-month initiative targeting violent crime, drug misuse, and alcohol-related disorder on weekend evenings, in that part of the centre of the city. It worked.

WRONG TRAIN COMPANY!

I was a frequent traveller to Ipswich, Colchester, and Norwich, to report on football matches, and just before Christmas 2003 I wrote a letter of complaint about hooliganism on a trip to Colchester. Melita Withers, Customer Relations of Anglia, wrote back saying, "I'm afraid I am not able to answer you, as we do not run the train service you are writing about. That service is run by First Great Eastern!"

"DOCTORED" BY AN UNTHINKING
WHITE VAN DRIVER

One of my favourite parking experiences was leaving my vehicles in Finsbury Square – probably the finest square in that part in the City of London. When Bobby Robson was manager of Ipswich Town FC, his team was rivalling the Liverpool squad in the First Division in the 1970-1980s, and he had exceptional players like the Dutch pair of Frans Thyssen and Arnold Muhren – one of the most skilful midfield players ever to appear in the English game – and outstanding defenders in Mick Mills, Allan Hunter, and the sadly late Kevin Beattie.

In one season I reported on 28 of the 58 matches, which meant I often left my car in Finsbury Square on a Saturday to catch the 11.30 train from nearby Liverpool Street to Ipswich station, which was half a mile from the Portman Road ground.

In 1981-2, as chairman of the Football Writers' Association I had the pleasurable task of presenting Frans Thyssen with the Stanley Matthews-inscribed trophy for the Footballer of the Year. He spoke immaculate English, and his modesty shone through in his short speech. Neither he – nor Muhren – was mobbed by his frenzied colleagues and charged into the crowd after scoring a goal, which is common now. They were gents; a handshake sufficed.

In the speech, I also had to mention the 20-odd guests at the top table, including several eminent previous winners of the trophy. And I was told to make it short without any wisecracks, which I did. As I sat down, there was mild applause, then the uniformed MC announced a comfort break of ten minutes.

I was one of the first into the male toilet room and heard a middle-aged man say to his friend, "Listening to that Scovell is worse than spending four years in a Japanese prisoner of war camp." I shouted, "Hear, hear."

I knew E.W. Swanton (1907-2000) – known as Jim – who was imprisoned in 18 Japanese camps during the building of the Thailand-Burma Railway between 1942-5, having been captured in Singapore. When WW2 started, he had volunteered to join the Bedfordshire Yeomanry along with his great friend Ian Peebles, the Middlesex and England leg spinner and author.

As a Major, he was given a Not Subversive classification by the Japanese, meaning he had certain privileges, and many of his colleagues resented this. During his imprisonment, he gave lectures on religion, life, and cricket, and he had a battered copy of the 1939 Wisden Almanac, which he often quoted from. That was the only piece of memorabilia he brought back from the camps.

The only food for the prisoners was rice served in a small bowl three times a day. When he was captured, he weighed 16 stone, but by the end he looked like a skeleton. Mahatma Gandhi was imprisoned at the same time in 1942-4 for campaigning on the behalf of the Quit India Movement, and in early January 2021, a purchaser bought Gandhi's tiny, tin bowl for £60,000.

Many of the internees with Swanton died of malnutrition or disease. Halfway through his imprisonment, he contracted polio and although his strong constitution saved him, he was left with a withered arm. On arrival at Waterloo after his long trip home, his father walked right past him as he didn't recognise him.

Swanton's stockbroker father was a club cricketer for Forest Hill CC, where Jim started his career as a rather stodgy opening batsman and a leg spin bowler. His mother, Lillian Emily Wouters, was the daughter of a German merchant who changed her name from Wouters to Walters. Jim was born in

Forest Hill in 1907, where WG Grace lived, and his parents gave him the nickname of Jumbo to indicate he was rather heavy. Soon they changed it to Jim.

He claimed he attended a match at Forest Hill in which WG played in, and the infant watched a Zeppelin – a slow moving barrage balloon – fly over the ground. His father was able to pay for him to be taught at Dulwich and Cranleigh Schools, but his educational successes were modest and his handwriting was awful. Despite these handicaps, his persistence enabled him to become a great man of cricket, an outstanding broadcaster on BBC radio, the highly valued cricket writer of the *Daily Telegraph*, and author of 16 books including the monumental *World of Cricket,* which he edited. His last work, *Cricketers of His Time*, was published in 1999 a few months before he died, aged 92, of a stopped heart.

I first met him at the Oval in 1958, when I worked for the Press Association. Back to his normal weight of around 16 stone, he had a reserved seat on one of the long benches, but it was usually filled by a succession of assistants – like John Thicknesse who went on to become the cricket correspondent of the *Evening Standard*, and Daphne Surfleet, who became the wife of Richie Benaud. Jim sat mainly in the BBC studio above, and the likes of Brian Johnston, John Arlott, and Jack Fingleton took the mick out of him unmercifully, but he loved the attention.

Another Major, the anarchist cricket writer and historian Rowland Francis Bowen (1916-1978), described Swanton as the "Pomporius Ego". I met Bowen a number of times before he cut his right leg off at the age of 52. Most people thought he was completely mad, but during his time serving in the Indian Army in 1942-5 he learned a lot about self-amputations of limbs. In my three cricket tours in India, I encountered a lot of beggars who had cut their own arm off to attract sympathy. It was the only way of picking up money living on the streets and with no chance of finding a proper job.

Bowen lived in Eastbourne at the time of his amputation. He used a hacksaw, a hammer, and a chisel, and clearly defied the pain. The art of self-amputation was recognised as apotemnophilia. Bowen had many feuds with most of the leading cricket writers after he produced several masterpieces on the history of cricket to correct some of their works.

One of the best stories of Jim Swanton was the occasion when I was at the St Lawrence ground when Kent opener Peter Richardson (1931-2017) stopped play and told the umpires that he had been distracted by hearing a loud booming sound in the top of the pavilion. He was a great prankster and wit, and the 'noise' he was referring to was Jim's booming voice. Richardson had a habit of writing spurious letters to Jim's newspaper, the *Daily Telegraph*, and signing them "Colonel Blimp".

In that innings he went on to score 175, and Jim eventually saw the joke. The most repeated joke at his expense was: "Jim isn't a snob: he's perfectly happy to travel in the same car as his chauffeur."

He was a prolific letter writer himself, trying to put the world right, but he was helpful to young cricket journalists, including me.

Everyone was surprised when in 1958, at the age of 50, he married Ann Marion Garbutt, a pianist and golfer, and they lived happily in Delf House in Sandwich which it had a small moat in front of it. She was a daughter of Raymond de Montmorency, a housemaster at Eton College, and had previously been married to a chartered accountant George Carbutt, a close friend of Swanton. In the winter the couple had a property next to Sandy Lane – the most prestigious and expensive hotel of the same name. Everyone agreed that she mellowed him, and together they played golf in foursomes at Sandy Lane and Royal St Georges GC. When Ann died of a sudden stroke in 1998, Jim's iron constitution that had carried him through the jungles of the Far East slowly ebbed away, and he died on January 1, 2000.

A lifelong staunch Anglo-Catholic, his friends of similar faith filled St. Clement's Church in Sandwich for his funeral, with Lord Runcie giving the address. The memorial service was held in Canterbury Cathedral, as he had planned, with Lord William Deedes, one of his closest friends, reading the Address. His estate came to £1,114,531. Sadly, he had no children of his own to leave it to. Nor did anyone think of putting on a Blue Badge on Delf House.

Finsbury Square is a 1.7-acre area surrounded by high rise, commercial properties, and which had a six-rink bowling green of immaculately groomed grass. Previously known as Finsbury Fields, an enterprising developer built terraced houses there, and in the late 19th century the houses were replaced by large scale commercial buildings. In 1784, Vincenzo Lunardi became the first person in England to take a hot balloon into the air from the Square. Around that time it was known as the Street of Sodomites, because it was a notorious gay cruising area.

On August 6, 2005, I was setting out to go and report on the opening day of the football season at the Ipswich v Preston North End game for the *Daily Telegraph,* and tried to park there between a disabled space and a bay marked "Doctor". A white van had strayed two yards into the disabled bay, so I had no alternative but to leave my Honda two yards into the "Doctor" bay. I wrote a note of explanation, blaming the driver of the van for being inconsiderate, and put it on the windscreen. When I returned at 8pm, an unknown warden had replaced my note with a PCN CL79003329.

I wrote to the Department of Technical Services of the Corporation of London, pointing out that some years previously I'd had my Blue Badge supplied by the Corporation so I knew all about parking restrictions in the Square Mile of the City. I added, "Obviously your inspector turned up and the van had departed, leaving me open to criticism. I would be mad to park like that, or be drunk! In the last few years, I am still busy going around the country as a freelance sports writer, and I have been persecuted by various councils, and I've appeared in three recent tribunals, wasting an enormous amount of time, energy, and money.

"Now I face another ordeal. Surely common sense can prevail in this case, because the Square is almost deserted on Saturdays. I could have used a bay further up, but my hip was playing up, which is why I used this one, closest to the station. Also I had to catch a train and was short of time. The "Doctor" spaces are never filled on Saturdays because the offices are closed.

"I can afford to pay the fine of £100 but I object to being harassed unfairly. Any judge would rule in my favour in a higher court if it ever got there. Why should your department be so intent on proceeding with this case?"

A month later, M Guerrati for the Parking Ticket Office wrote rejecting my appeal and asked me to pay the £100 to the "Chamberlain of London".

I posted another letter, addressed to the man at the Ticket Office who had "signed" with a circular squiggle, saying, "Short of crashing into the other vehicle occupying half of my disabled space, and knocking it back into its allotted space, there was nothing to do except park where I did. I explained that to you, and you still insist on wasting more time on this trivial an intensely annoying matter.

"Sadly, I shall have to continue with this charade. I certainly want to appeal, and if it is rejected, I shall be forced to appear before an Arbitrator, and if he is unable to accept my extremely reasonable explanation, I will be willing to go to court. But is this really required for this situation?"

I wrote another letter containing more evidence. "When I arrived, the Finsbury Circus was filled with large vehicles, apparently for making a film. I make this journey a dozen or so times in the winter, and there have been no problems with disabled spaces in the past. But on this occasion, eight spaces were occupied by 'no parking' cones. Two more spaces in the road leading towards Liverpool Street Station were filled – one by a taxi driver whose vehicle showed a Blue Badge and no clock (as if a full-time taxi driver was genuinely 'disabled'!). Realising I would be late, I took a decision to park there."

On November 10, just after the celebration of the 400th anniversary of Guy Fawkes Day, L. Burgess (another squiggle) of the Corporation of London said I had been let off. I felt like burning his letter as my small gesture on behalf of the Gunpowder Plotters who had been summarily executed.

Mr Burgess wrote: "The above notice was issued because the vehicle was incorrectly parked in a designated parking place. A parking bay is defined by white lines on the carriageway, and to be correctly parked a vehicle must be wholly contained within these marks. If this is not possible, alternative facilities must be sought.

"However, after considering the circumstances surrounding your case, it has been decided to cancel the PCN. This decision is not to be taken as a precedent for the future."

Shortly afterwards, I met a friendly lawyer at a cricket dinner at Headley, Surrey, and I told him about this saga. He recommended that I should write to the Department of Technical Service of the Corporation of London and claim damages for being distressed over the PCN 79003329. I followed his advice and, not wanting to break the corporation's budget, I limited my claim to £50. Within a week the cheque arrived. So there: another away win!

READY FOR A PENALTY
SHOOT OUT AT BROMLEY NORTH

In 2005, East Street – adjacent to Bromley North station – was not a place to be seen after 8pm, particularly at weekends. There was a club on one side, which attracted a certain type of person, also a massage parlour, a tattoo shop, and a gym. Halfway down on the right was my favourite Italian restaurant Ferrari's, and with the build-up of worrying incidents in the area, I was toying with the idea of giving it a miss in future. Then the sewer underneath the restaurant flooded and it was temporarily closed down. It never reopened, and another business conveying red meat dishes took over. I took my business elsewhere.

However, there was an art shop in the one-way East Street, and on May 20, 2005, I was trying to park on either side of the road but there were no disabled spaces free – only a "loading" one. I was unloading some of my late wife's etchings to leave with the framer's shop and to collect the framed ones. When I came out, a CEO had put a PCN on the window of my Honda.

Incensed, I wrote a letter of appeal to the Bromley Parking HQ, with copies to the Chief Superintendent at the Bromley Police HQ and also the Chief Executive of the Bromley Council.

In my appeal, I wrote that "the warden claimed the reason for my 'offence' was 'he believed that no loading had taken place'. That is untrue. I am a disabled driver (my file should be at your department; a rather long list!), and I was unloading some of my late wife's etchings to take to the framer's shop and collect the framed ones. With no space available for a meter space and both disabled bays filled, I had to park in the loading area. I am entitled to park there if I was loading up. The sign said 15 minutes were allowed. I was well within that period. As my car was 20 yards from the shop, I didn't leave the boot open. When you read on, you will understand why.

"I know the shop owner well, and he told me a horrific story. The day before (May 19), eight hooded teenagers burst into his shop and threatened to kill him. Within two minutes, three police cars arrived, and all eight youths were taken to the police station and photographed. Three hours later, they were released without charge. This is why decent people like him, and me, wonder whether we are continually harassed by parking wardens on trivial matters, when criminals are free to terrorise the populace whose rates keep these vermin going without impediment.

"I haven't committed an offence on this occasion. I fail to see why I qualify for this £100 demand, and intend to take the matter further if my appeal is rejected. My friend will support me. The week before, his mother died, and his father was still in shock. He said, 'If Dad had been there when these men came in, I am sure it would have finished him off.'

"Across the road, a 'nightclub' has opened, and apparently it will have a 24-hour licence within six weeks. The manager of Ferrari's, the restaurant I visit regularly, tells me that he has to lock the front door at 10pm to keep out potential troublemakers. This council has a lot to answer for, I am afraid."

On June 1, an unnamed person, scrawling a squiggle at the bottom of a letter from the Processing and Representation Parking Team, wrote: "While I appreciate the circumstances you describe in your letter, unfortunately they are not grounds for withdrawing the penalty. The outstanding debt is £50, and if you pay within 14 days, you will only need to pay this amount, otherwise the full charge of £100 will be payable."

I persisted. Among my Christmas cards on December 21, there was a notice from the independent Parking and Traffic

Service saying my appeal would be heard at New Zealand House, 80 Haymarket, SW1 Y 4TE on February 28 at 3.45.

Bromley Council's senior officers had a more enlightened approach to this prolonged, irksome case, and a letter from Miss C Axelson, Head of the Appeal Service, arrived on January 7th, saying, "The London Borough of Bromley has informed me that they will not contest your appeal against the PCN BY24606828. The Adjudicator has therefore allowed your appeal considering your evidence or any details of the case. You are not liable for any further charge(s) and, where appropriate, any amounts already paid will be refunded by the council." Another victory!

Since 2012, when the council was awarded £2m from the Mayor's Outer London Fund, work started on the upgrading of East Street, giving it a continental look with facilities to dine outside of restaurants. The nightclub has gone and there is a prominent sign opposite the railway station saying "BROMLEY NORTH VILLAGE". It may have been a village centuries ago, but not now! The clean-up also happened in Bromley High Street and the Market Square, costing £6.6m. Immense praise goes to Bromley Council!

BIG INCREASE IN STOLEN
BLUE BADGES

L uckily, my Blue Badge hasn't been stolen, but the Local Government Association representing 370 councils across England and Wales said thefts went up from 2,921 in 2017 to 4,246 in 2018, a rise of 45%. This increase marks a rise in thefts for the fifth year running, from 656 recorded in 2013. It meant the 2018 figures were more than six times higher than they had been five years before.

Councillor Martin, LGA Transport spokesman, was quoted as saying, "Illegally using a Blue Badge is not a victimless crime. For disabled people, Blue Badges are a vital lifeline that helps them to get out and about to visit shops or family and friends. Callous thieves and unscrupulous fraudsters using them illegally are robbing people of this independence.

"Despite limited resources, councils continue to work hard to crack down on this growing crime. More fraudsters than ever are being brought to justice by councils who come down hard on drivers illegally using them. It is important to catch these criminals in the act. To help councils in the fight, people must keep tipping us off about people who are illegally using a badge, bearing in mind people's need for a badge might not be obvious."

Blue Badges could fetch £1,000 or more on the black market, costing insurance companies more than £1m a year and millions to councils. According to Metropolitan Police, their officers broke up a North London gang which used young boys to steal badges from cars, being paid £50 for each one. The gang members sold them to other drivers for between £400 to £1,000, depending on when the badges expired. It is estimated a normal use of a Blue Badge saves the owner around £2,500 a year.

In London, Islington, Camden, and Tower Hamlets were hot spots for Blue thefts, and known gangs still operate in Birmingham, Liverpool, Manchester, Sheffield, Leeds, and Glasgow.

Oh, I forgot. My Blue Badge *was* "nicked" when Bromley testers failed me on two occasions, and it took more than a year each time to give it back to me. On another occasion, I went to a copiers' shop to print a copy of my badge to send to the congestion offices, and forgot to pick it up. I was about to drive home when I remembered it was still in the shop. Someone might have realised that it was worth at least £1,000 and made off with it. My car was parked ten minutes' walk away, but there it was on the counter.

EALING COUNCIL LEAD THE WAY

On the day my Freedom Pass arrived, posted from a company in Arbroath on behalf of Bromley Council – many thanks for that! – I noticed an item from *Private Eye*, which was published on February 7, a few days late, under the heading of "Rotten Boroughs".

"Labour Ealing Borough Council has admitted raking in thousands of pounds in fines from residents who had failed to renew their parking permits – because they hadn't been sent reminders. Such fines totalled £2,430 in 2018 but leapt to £147,000 in 2019, reports *Ealing Today*. In common with many authorities, the borough no longer issues paper permits, all records being stored online. The explosion in fines occurred after the council stopped sending people email reminders that their permits were about to expire – leading to more than 3,000 parking fines being issued to unsuspecting residents. The unprecedented happy ending is that it is going to be refunds all round."

In the past, I didn't receive reminders for the renewal for my Blue Badge, and I wrote to Bromley Council and told them they should send reminders. Ditto with the Congestion Charge. Now the badge carries the date of the expiry. On another occasion, I was nicked for having an outdated badge in the Central London Congestion Area. They wrote back, letting me off.

COVER-UP AT TESCO

Tesco have a good reputation for catering for the disabled, and the branch next to a demolished gasworks in Bromley is a good example of it, unlike the posher Waitrose which only has five disabled bays. I've never not been able to park at Tesco. I was coming out of Tesco with my trolley and noticed a middle-aged man trying to park his grubby red Ford next to me a few yards from the entrance, in a space clearly marked "Disabled". He was just about to place his Blue Badge on the dashboard when he saw me limping towards him and hurriedly pulled it off and put it out of sight.

By the time I was about to put my five parcels of goods in the boot, he'd strode off with a footballer's walk – bow-legged – wearing a jersey bearing the insignia of Crystal Palace Football Club. He didn't appear to be disabled. For using a Blue Badge without being a registered disabled person, he could be fined £1,000. It was a shrewd move by the man, because most supermarkets never check on cheats. I've given the registrations of offenders to Customer Service staff, but no action has followed. The offenders should be prosecuted.

SPEED AWARENESS COURSES
SHOULD BE COMPULSORY

Having reached a certain age –- not quite a venerable age needing a stairlift, though – I find that other drivers, particularly impatient young ladies, are continually hooting at me for driving too slowly. This is because I attended a Speed Awareness Workshop at a small house next to Shortlands Station in the borough of Bromley in 2017 and was commended for my slowness. It was overlooked by the railway line from Victoria to the Kent towns, and the noise of trains and the high price of hiring it persuaded the organisers to move to a quieter, cheaper venue soon after.

In the video speed test, I was placed in pole position out of seven markings, classed as "very much slower than average", and my assessor wrote: "Your responses do not reflect a strong tendency to speed. In general this pattern of response is associated with less likelihood of being involved in a speed-related accident. This is an excellent driver profile and one to be maintained."

But tell that to the rest of the nation's drivers. They obviously think I am a pest. I've attracted a few 'V' signs, and when I try to remonstrate with them, I find myself being abused. I don't have a chance to mention Speed Awareness.

I became aware of SAW, short for Speed Awareness Workshop, when the Metropolitan Police wrote to me saying I would be fined £100, plus three points, for being caught driving past Lewisham Hospital, in a totally empty road, just after midnight while travelling at 36mph. But there was a catch: if I underwent the two-hour workshop course and paid £72, the penalties would be waived.

Up until then, I had only had one speeding offence in my 49 years on the road. My only two minor offences were going through a red light on the M6 motorway near Birmingham at 5mph – I didn't know there were red lights on a motorway, but they were flashing above, as three lanes of traffic were going into one lane – and the other one was going through a red light one-tenth of a second too late on a 40mph limit dual carriage coming out of Southend.

I wrote a stiff letter to the Met, pleading mitigation for the Lewisham act of criminality, and asking for my good record to be taken into account.

Another letter from the Met soon arrived, ignoring my plea for leniency, and repeating the offer to attend a workshop or else pay the £100 and be docked three points. I took the easier option and made my mind up that when I turned up, I would give them a severe talking to about the deplorable way this country is treating responsible drivers with a reasonable record.

The letter advised me that I had to arrive before 8.45am, otherwise I wouldn't be let in. I turned up at 8.43, just in time. Nineteen other speedsters were seated at their computers ready for their Driving Risk Profile, and one said, "Another criminal has arrived", and they laughed. There were 11 men and nine women, aged from 25 up to 70, soberly dressed mainly in black, as though they were about to attend a funeral. The lady in charge, a driving tutor, was friendly and jovial, assuring us that we weren't going to take the wheel, only look at real-life situations on film and click on options.

"Were you travelling around 35-36 mph?" she asked, and everyone nodded their heads.

Recently, Jeremy Broughton, formerly the then Government's Transport Research Laboratory, said honest drivers were being penalised. They own up, whereas half of those reported for speeding were let off for various reasons – like being foreigners, displaying false number plates, driving an unregistered vehicle, or not being insured.

"We need to interact and talk," the tutor said.

So I said, "As you can see, I'm older than 25, and I don't see anyone younger than that here, and they are the people who need to be given this course, not us. They commit the majority of offences." There were loud laughs and a few 'hear, hears'.

"Well it's about education," she said.

She asked us, "How many of you know the death figures on the road last year?" Some of the group thought around 5,000, but it was just over 3,000.

"What about casualties?" she asked.

No-one was close. "Almost three hundred thousand," she informed us. "And many of them were serious injuries, like losing a limb. They might be someone you know. It makes you think. Unfortunately for most of us, these statistics mean nothing – until we or someone close to us, becomes one."

We looked at a film of an accident when a young man ran out behind a car, hit his head, and later died. The driver was only travelling at the same speed I had been driving in Lewisham. The clincher came when she said, "When you suffer a serious head injury, the victim's feet suddenly shrink because the blood shoots towards the head. That's why you see shoes lying close to accidents."

A few years ago, just before midnight a fully laden car smashed into a huge tree right across the road from where I live, and one person died. All the proud old trees along that stretch of the road have now been chopped down and replaced by saplings. Two weeks ago, a similar accident happened half a mile away, and a girl of 20 died. There are flowers, usually faded and needing replaced or removed, attached to trees in all parts of the borough – sad memories of more young lives which have been abruptly ended.

Our tutor told us that yellow boxes are usually installed near fatal road accidents for obvious reasons, but 75% of them are not working, which probably explains why so many feckless drivers still speed past my property.

Back at the workshop, I was given high marks for avoiding tailgating. We were shown various examples of driving too close to the vehicle ahead, and I was marked in the second class – "further away than average". My report said: "This is an excellent driver profile, indicating a professional attitude, and needs to be maintained."

The next test was reacting to hazards, like pedestrian crossings, cars coming out of side roads, and old people who looked as though they were about to step into the road. This time I was rated "average", and was told: "One simple method of making many hazards disappear is to slow down."

I look on myself as being a calm individual and not given to road rage, but the Emotion Feedback Test only rated me "slightly lower than average". I would dispute that. I never swear at other drivers; I only make gestures, like pointing a forefinger to the temple.

My report said, "To be safe in today's traffic, you need to treat your driving as a priority and focus your attention on the task. If you let your mind wander, you might find that one day it does not have a body to come back to!"

My marks were dropping fast. In the Distraction Feedback section, I was rated "slightly attentive", and was advised: "There is a clear opportunity for you to change your accident risk by paying more attention to your driving."

Later, the lady in charge asked several people, "How were you caught speeding?" She pointed to me sitting in the last row. "What about you, sir?" she said.

"I saw Lewisham hospital on the right," I said, "and I was thinking that my late wife was treated there a few times, and that might have distracted me. She died on Christmas Day, and my offence for speeding occurred just after Christmas." There was no answer to that, but sadly it was true.

Motorways are the safest roads, with around 6% of the total of deaths, but one in five of accidents on motorways are caused by falling asleep. Drivers are advised to take 15 minutes rest every two hours, but very few do that unless their young children want to stop, continually saying things, like "How far is it?", and other safety-conscience demands.

Some years ago, I was suffering from a severe bout of hay fever and was about to leave Trent Bridge after a Test match to drive back to Bromley, when Ted Dexter, the former England captain and later chairman of selectors, recommended a new tablet to counter my problem. It was around 3pm, and I thought it was safe to take three tablets. They soon worked: the sneezing stopped.

I was driving at almost 80mph when suddenly I woke up with a huge jolt and found myself bouncing into the iron railings on the left side. My Honda Legend swerved back into the middle lane, rocking from one side to the other, luckily missing the other traffic before I regained control. I was able to drive on, and turned into a motorway station to check the vehicle's state. It was severely dented on most of the left side, which cost £1,500 to repair, and amazingly, I have never suffered from hay fever since.

Dexter, known as "Lord Ted", was one of my favourite cricketers, and I've just seen a brief TV clip of him batting in that epic draw at Lord's when he scored 70 in as many minutes against Wes Hall and Charlie Griffith, bowling thunderbolts in shockingly bad light with no sightscreen at the pavilion. Fred Titmus said, "He hit them all over the place. It was electrifying."

Ian Wooldridge and I agreed it was the finest exhibition of courageous batting we had seen. One delivery hit his knee, and he could still feel it at the age of 85; he just had an arthroscopy on it. Shot at while serving in the Malayan Insurrection, he recovered from cancer, and had his leg fractured when his car ran into his leg, so no-one doubts his courage. In the General Election of 1964, he stood as a Conservative candidate in Cardiff against the Shadow Chancellor James Callaghan. Predictably, he lost after he was promoting his latest cricket book he died in 2022.

Nowadays, I always use cruise control, and it is easy to maintain speed limits. I said to our lady tutor, "Why doesn't the Government make it compulsory? It would improve driving standards at a stroke."

She thought it was too expensive. But as demand grows, the price will fall. It should be introduced as soon as possible. By reducing speed, most car drivers save around 10% costs in petrol, and what about the savings of CO_2 emissions and insurance costs? The savings would be enormous.

When I first heard about SAW, I was ready to scoff and complain about the harsh way we were treated – 36mph in the middle of the night, I ask you! But I firmly believe these workshops should be extended to every person who is caught speeding, particularly those who break the limits by greater margins, like the teenage tearaways and the showboating chavs in their 4x4s. We all need to be educated about life and death on the roads.

My printed report concluded, "How you choose to drive is one of the biggest choices you will face in life, as it can directly impact whether you place yourself in a high accident risk category or not. It's about choice."

Thanks to SAW, I choose to observe the speed limits now. If everyone did that, this country would be a happier place and the NHS could concentrate their efforts on the real killers, like cancer which robbed Audrey of a third of her wonderful life – at 58.

The fee for undertaking a SAW went up to £94.40, and in 2020 4,000 drivers attended each day. With more 20mph limits being imposed, that number will rise – thankfully. But I still think it should be part of the application for a driving licence.

Instead of hiring "weirdos" in 10 Downing Street, Dominic McKenzie Cummings – born in 1971, educated at Durham University – and his advisors to Boris Johnson ought to read the letters from perceptive people in the serious newspapers like *The Times*, *Daily Mail*, *Daily Telegraph*, and the *Guardian*.

There are two letters published in the *Telegraph* on February 25, 2020, and I've included them as counter arguments. One is from Roger Lawson, Campaign Director of The Alliance of British Drivers, in Chislehurst (which is part of the Borough of Bromley):

"Sir, Speed-awareness courses do not work; accidents are not reduced. This was made clear by a report published by the Department for Transport in 2018 after research by Ipsos-Mori. The reason why the numbers attending speed-awareness courses have gone up is that police forces like to make money in this way. They are permitted to take a cut of the fees paid."

The other one is from Reg Nuttall of Teignmouth, Devon. Both Chislehurst, with an affluent population of 14,431 and famous for its caves which were used as air raid shelters in WW2, and Teignmouth, population of 15,129 of mainly retired, comfortable people, are full of sensible people:

"During my employment I drove up to 30,000 miles a year and undertook mandatory driver training by the Institute of Advanced Motoring. This formed part of the company's health and safety regime, and as a result the company reported that insurance claims from motoring accidents reduced significantly. Speed-awareness courses target offenders. More effective would be mandatory training and testing before offences are committed. Such a move could save lives and reduce the costs incurred by easily avoidable accidents."

Food for thought for Mr Cummings and his ilk!

APPEARING IN BROMLEY
MAGISTRATES COURT AND LET OFF

In my four years of apprenticeship working as a junior news and sport reporter for the now defunct *Isle of Wight Guardian* at Shanklin, I wrote about many court cases, mainly traffic cases, in Newport Magistrates, and inquests. So I was reasonably knowledgeable about procedure. One incident I remember had a sad ending to a honeymoon at a hotel in Lake. The inquest took place soon afterwards, and the young husband had walked out of the hotel in a dressing gown, gone down the steps to the beach below, walked into the sea and drowned.

He was South African, serving in the Royal Artillery in England. His bride came from the island – the people of the Isle of Wight always call it THE Island. One of my tasks was to ring up the local clergy to ask about prospective weddings, and five days before the groom's suicide, I visited the bride's home and was welcomed by the happy pair.

When I asked her how she met him, she said, "I saw a marriage advert. That's how we met." Her father added, "It all worked out so well. I just can't believe it."

My story appeared in the next edition of the *IOW Guardian,* and her mother rang me at the office in Cross Street in Shanklin and said this wasn't true and she wanted an apology. "It's ruined the marriage," she said, "it will bring shame to the family."

Joan Dodds, daughter of George Gordon Saunders – the owner of the newspaper and printing business – was the editor, and she told me to write it in a discreet way and I did. It appeared in the next week's edition, and no legal action followed.

I gave the story to the Fleet Street national newspapers, and it brought in some cash, which was shared by GG, who contributed nothing except that he was our boss. GG took half, and Joan and I shared the other half.

GG was a frosty character, but years later after he died, I learned that he had endured a terrible time in the Battle of the Somme in WW1 trenches in France. If I'd known that, I would have been more considerate in my dealings with him.

My first and hopefully my last appearance in a Magistrates' Court was on Saturday, February 8, 2002, at Bromley at 2pm, when I was charged with parking on a red line on Tweedy Road not far from home. Two days earlier, I had attended the funeral of my best friend Bryon Butler, the BBC football correspondent, at Guildford Crematorium. The chapel was packed with 250 people, including Ken Bates, the loathed (by many people) former chairman of Chelsea, who had a good relationship with Bryon.

Some years previously, when Chelsea faced going into liquidation, the club's bankers wanted a couple of well-respected football men to sign cheques on behalf of the club, instead of their senior officers. Bates asked Bryon to undertake this task, and Bryon suggested me. Surprisingly, Bates agreed, and each month Bryon and I called in at Stamford Bridge to sign the relevant cheques.

The directors contacted some responsible Chelsea supporters with a view to form another group, called the Chelsea Pitch Owners, to raise money by selling bits of the old Stamford Bridge pitch, which was being replaced, and they took over the responsibility so Bryon and I stood down – thankfully! Stamford Bridge was looked on as one of the most expensive pieces of land in London, and the hard-pressed club directors were vulnerable against overtures from property speculators. But the 13,000 CPO members insisted on a 75% vote to sell the ground to speculators, and Roman Abramovich, an associate of the deranged Putin, respected that during his long reign, until Russia's invasion of Ukraine forced him to sell the club.

Earlier, Bates was forced to sell a proportion of the freehold to David Bulstrode's Marler Estates, who had already bought Fulham and QPR and wanted them to amalgamate. Bates made another deal with Matthew Harding, a fervent Chelsea supporter who made his fortune through insurance and was reckoned to be in the top 100 richest men in Britain. Harding gave £24m to the club, and two-thirds of the money was devoted to building The Matthew Harding Stand, in place of the Shed. His name is still there.

I met Bulstrode and Harding several times, and they were engaging, friendly men who soon fell out with Bates. Bulstrode died prematurely while having sex. A keen cricketer, Harding took me out to lunch a couple times, and I think his intentions about the club he loved were honourable. He was certainly popular with the fans. Bates once told me, "I hear you've joined the Harding gang. Consider yourself an enemy of mine." That was one of his better jokes.

Harding died at the age of 44, when a helicopter flying him and three passengers crashed in Middlewitch, Cheshire, coming back from watching the Bolton v Chelsea game in 1996. The inquest heard evidence that the pilot, who also died, wasn't qualified for flying in those conditions. One of the passengers was a journalist named John Bauldie.

Bates made his money in the British Virgin Islands, with some assistance from the British Government, and paid £1 to take over Chelsea in 1982 when it was destitute. He made it a success on the field, but he didn't make many friends with his coarse comments about others. He was born on December 4, 1931, in West London, and his mother soon died, and his father disappeared, so he was brought up by his grandparents. As a self-made man who wanted to own football clubs, he started out at Oldham, moved on to Wigan, then to Leeds, then Chelsea. He was a long-time member of the FA Council and the other 80 odd councillors were astonished to see him appointed chairman of the committee handling the building of the new Wembley. As a long-serving member of the Football Writers' Association's Facilities Committee, advising the clubs about improving the press facilities, I was invited to one of their meetings, at which his colleagues and I soon realised that Bates did a Maggie Thatcher – he dominated most of the other members. His tenure as chairman soon ended.

He is still hale and hearty, now in his nineties, and spends most of his time with his wife Suzanne, a former journalist, living in Monaco. He told Henry Winter, chief football writer of the *Daily Telegraph*, "I still see Chelsea play."

Enough of the escapades of Bates, and over to Bromley Magistrates to face three magistrates who spent about 20 minutes on my momentous case. They heard evidence from a young girl named Lisa Edge, from the Catford Traffic Warden Unit, saying I'd parked three yards away from a time plate "Red Route – No stopping at any time" on Saturday, May 5, 2001, at 11.49. She had the car reg down as H407 HCR but wrote "Registration should read X407HCR", and added, "I did not see the driver."

Well, I was at my dentist at the time, and I explained that I'd tried to park at the disabled bay but someone had left his or her vehicle there, so I had no alternative but to park on the red line for around 20 minutes. I said there were not enough disabled spaces in the centre of Bromley, and explained that I had been disabled since 1943. "I passed my driving test in 1958, and I've never been guilty of a serious offence," I added.

I mentioned that Audrey had died on Christmas Day, and I told a story about when I was a junior, teenage reporter, working in a newspaper in the Isle of Wight, and interviewed an elderly man about his wife who had just died in Lake. He told me in a halting voice, "We were married 60 years. Do you want to see her?" That was my first experience of seeing someone dead, and before I said anything, he broke down and

BRIAN SCOVELL

cried uncontrollably. Two weeks later, the man died, and the funeral director said he died of a broken heart.

Three days after Audrey died, I suddenly experienced a fit and started shouting out to one of her elder sisters Thelma, who lived in California and had arrived for the funeral. Her husband Stan Schiller, who had a senior rank in the US Navy in WW2 and was a close friend of former President Jimmy Carter, had died some years before so she had also experienced a sad bereavement. Incidentally, Jimmy Carter is still alive at the age of 98.

I shouted, "I could be like that man – dying from a broken heart!" Meaning me. Thelma is a very nice, loving lady, and she calmed me down. Now in her late eighties, though, she tends to forget things. Statistics show that more elderly men die of a broken heart than women. In my case, I keep myself busy writing, giving talks to business and sports clubs, doing my hour-long, daily exercise programmes, walking, travelling, and writing indignant letters to Bromley Council's parking officers.

The kindly chairman of Bromley Magistrates, who appeared to originate from the Caribbean and seemed to be sympathetic, announced after a short adjournment that I would be given a Conditional Discharge – behave or else! A just verdict, and I thanked him - another yellow card.

Eighteen years later, Britain's highest paid footballer at that time – Arsenal's German Mesut Ozil, who was earning an absurd £350,000 a week while not playing in the first team – appeared in the same Magistrates' Court. He was found guilty of driving his Mercedes G-Class Mercedes, costing £160,000, on the M1 at 97mph at 11.50am on July 2, 2020. As a naturalized German national, he apologised, saying he mistook kmph rather than mph. A good effort for getting off! As he lived in Highgate, one wonders how the case was heard in Bromley. He was soon transferred to a Turkish club, so the penalty was a light one.

Under the Hill-Wood stewardship, Arsenal – long-serving chairmen Sir Samuel (1929-1949), Denis John Charles, MC

(1962-1982), and Peter (1982-2013) – rarely wasted money, but his American successors Stan Kroenke and his son Josh have done the opposite. I knew both Denis and Peter – Old Etonians who gave frank replies to questions. How things change! And not for the better.

WE DON'T NEED AN ANNUAL DRIVING TEST!

A ndrew Roberts – no relation of the Churchillian historian – caused a few flutters in early March 2020 when he started a campaign calling for annual driving tests for over 70s. It was very laudable, because his 86-year-old wife Jeanette had been mown down by a car driven by a 75-year-old driver who pressed the accelerator instead of the brake and lost control of his vehicle in the car park of a supermarket in Ruislip. Jeanette died from her injuries, and the driver was arrested and later sentenced for three years in prison. He had only spent three days in jail before he died. It was a tragic sequence of events.

Andrew was shown on BBC television, saying Boris's Government needed to bring in a law insisting on stringent driving tests each year for people over the age of 70. But do we need it? A better solution is to require a doctor's letter confirming that the licence holder is fit to drive. Any signs of the shakes would debar the driver. Now the DVLA in Swansea can insist on someone undertaking a driving test every three years, which is perfectly reasonable.

Statistics about injuries on roads show that the under 25-year-old commit more motoring offences than the over-seventies. Should *they* be made to have an annual driving test? Most drivers of all ages bump into other vehicles when parking. When you are selling your car, the garage salesman first looks at the four corners to see scratches, dent, or discoloration. If there are any, he can knock a few hundred pounds off the sale. Millions of drivers could be careless, including me!

Elderly drivers are slow to react while decisions are called for, but they tend to drive more responsibly and observe the speed limits. With Boris's additional 20,000 police being trained, Chief Constables are warning that drivers who ignore limits will be prosecuted. Up to 80mph on motorways was sometimes permissible, but not now. I try to keep my speed at 70mph, but sometimes it goes over.

Recently, I was edging out of my drive just before Christmas when it was dark. I looked right and left, then right again. Not seeing any vehicles, I moved towards the centre of the road to turn right when a small black car, without lights, shot across my path. I slammed on the brakes and prevented a nasty accident. My road has reduced the power of the street lights after the 2008 austerity imposed on councils to save money, so if there had been an accident, who was the guilty person? I could have had my licence revoked.

Most elderly drivers know when they are no longer fit to drive, but the ones who pass annual eye tests and are assessed by their doctors and given the-all clear should be allowed to continue, especially when they live alone.

The weekly shopping has to be done, and a car is essential. Ordering online or over the telephone has revealed that there is a risk of out of date food being delivered and causing food poisoning.

I have my eyes checked regularly, but my long distance is above average, and I only need glasses for reading.

A YELLOW CARD FOR FRED

Henry Winter of the *Daily Telegraph* is the first person I read about the top football match of the day, and after the Manchester derby which finished United 2, Manchester City 0, on March 9, 2020, he wrote this:

"David James played Fred into the box and Nicolas Otamendi clearly caught him on the right foot. Fred looked up, expecting a penalty, but instead spotted referee Mike Dean marching towards him like an officious traffic warden before showing him a yellow card for simulation. It was harsh on Fred, and the thought immediately took hold of where on earth was VAR?"

In the *Daily Mail,* Mark Clattenburg, who was rated the best referee in England between 2006 and 2017, before he went off to work in Saudi Arabia, wrote: "Fred was booked for diving, but Dean thought the way he went down was not considered with any contact. Otamendi kicked Fred's shin. As a result, a penalty should have been awarded. I wish Dean had been advised to take a look at the monitor at Old Trafford, because I am sure he would have reversed his decision and given the spot kick. Instead VAR made the final decision – and it was a wrong one."

So Fred was badly let down. He emerged as one of United's most reliable players that season. Born in Belo Horizonte, where England lost 1-0 to the USA in the 1950 World Cup (England football's Pearl Harbour), Frederico Rodrigues de Paula Santos earned 11 caps for Brazil before joining Shaktar Donesk FC in the Ukraine in 2013, where he helped to win five trophies. In 2015, he was suspended for almost a year for taking diuretic hydrochlorothiazide – a bannèd substance in the Copa America tournament.

Only 5ft 7, and unable to speak much English, he was signed by United for £52m in 2018 and struggled to hold a place at the start, but his honesty and hard work ethic finally earned him a place. His English has now improved as well.

South American and African players tend to have a more unrefined style of play which features diving in a theatrical way, and they go in for rugged tackling. It makes it harder for referees to control matches. Having seen matches in Argentina, Chile, Uruguay, and Brazil, I know. Home-born players are now copying them, and referees need to punish the offenders. Otherwise the spectacle suffers.

I MANAGED TO EVICT A MERCEDES

After having a meeting in the breezily colourful kitchen in the English Cricket Board offices at Lord's, surrounded by building work to extend the Compton and Edrich Stands at the Nursery End in March 2020, I isolated myself in my car – it was the early days of the Coronavirus panic – and tried to find a suitable place to stop for a snack on the way back to Bromley. It took almost an hour struggling through busy streets before I found one – Dulwich Park. This was before the lockdown.

Remembering that once before I had backed into one of those solid metal bollards at the entrance, which proved to be an expensive mistake, this time I saw two disabled spaces next to a kindergarten on my left. One was filled by a badly parked white Merc, with an elderly man and woman sitting in it, while another Merc filled the other half with an AA vehicle alongside it. The AA attendant had just changed a wheel. The relieved driver – his car had no Disabled Badge – appeared to be ready to drive off, and I started to move forward to take over his space. The driver soon acknowledged the game was up and disappeared down College Road through Dulwich village. I duly took his space outside the deserted school.

Across the road was the Dulwich Picture Gallery, a habitué where Audrey used to exhibit her work. It has been tastefully modernised, and the café was filled with mainly well-off ladies talking in loud voices. The park of 79 acres was created in 1890 and as Queen Mary used to visit it regularly, one entrance is named after her. It is a genteel place ideal for families, and on my many visits I never saw a policeman.

This is not the case at the rival park north of the Thames – Hampstead Heath, which occupies 790 acres and can be traced back to 986 AD. The Heath, now owned by the Corporation of London, has its own squad of 15 or so constables. Murders occur there and male cruising is sometimes prevalent; the singer George Michael used to boast about it. But swimmers love the lakes. Queen Mary also liked the sprawling Heath, but she didn't go into swimming.

Descended from a Duke in Wittenberg, Germany, Mary of Teck was one of the best queens of England. She was born in Kensington Palace and was christened Victoria (after her mother), Mary, Augusta, Louise, Olga, Claudine, and Agnes, in 1867. She married Prince Albert at the age of 24, but within six weeks he died from a pandemic influenza. She then married George V and had six children. She died at the age of 85, just before her granddaughter Elizabeth was crowned Queen in 1953.

MY LONGEST COURT CASE ENDS
EVENTUALLY IN 2006

It kicked off on March 12 and ended, in victory, 24 days later on December 12. The number of words, from both sides, must have exceeded the number of words in Ramsay MacDonald's autobiography – 300,000 in 920 pages. Unreadable!

On Sunday, March 12, 2006, I had to park outside my house for a brief period to let a van park on our drive to transfer my daughter's goods to a flat near Clapham Common. When I emerged, I saw a PCN had been placed on my vehicle, alleging the following contravention: "parked with one or more wheels on any part of an urban road other than a carriageway at 12.14".

The van driver had been sitting in his vehicle when the warden planted the PCN, and the warden should have spoken to him and asked for my car to be moved. I could then have explained the circumstances. As a Blue Badge holder, I could have parked on the yellow line, but a sign high on a post 30 yards from my house on my left indicated that between 7am and 10am it is an offence to enter it at weekends. I could have parked in the bus lane without penalty, but the common-sense approach would be to go on the pavement and not obstruct buses. Even on a Sunday, Widmore Road is busy.

I wrote to Bromley Council's Parking Department and explained this and said I'd appeal if the matter went ahead. The fine was £100.

On June 7, I received a Charge Certificate, saying the amount due was now £150. At the back of the pink form, I was warned: "Filing a false declaration knowingly and wilfully is a criminal offence under Section 5 of the Perjury Act

NICKED!: PARKING FINES AND HOW TO AVOID THEM

191 and you may be imprisoned for up to 2 years, or fined, or both."

Another letter from them said, "On careful consideration, I regret that on this occasion I am unable to withdraw the PCN."

Undaunted, I fired off another missive: "Builders and garden companies park their vehicles on the pavement outside my house regularly, but none of them are prosecuted because the deliveries wouldn't go ahead. The alternative is to park on the road, the worst scenario. Two major constructions of flats are undergoing within a few yards from my house, and I have taken pictures as evidence, including a dent in the pavement outside caused by these weighty vehicles. I am not daft enough to park on the pavement without justification.

"Can I ask you to consider the evidence properly and save unnecessary time and costs? I am prepared to go to an arbiter, but that process, in my view, is superfluous. The Government recently told councils to show more common sense in dishing out PCNs. This is a prime example. Think again!"

I've met Steve Carr, the then Leader of Bromley Council, and I wrote to him when my Blue Badge had been discontinued by Trevor Browne, Chief Officer of Lewis House, Beckenham, and asked him to fast-track my new badge instead of me waiting for eight weeks.

I thanked him and, concerning my latest PCN, I added, "I don't want to appear in front of an arbitrator, but if I have to, I will attend – wasting money and time while so many urgent matters are ignored in Bromley, like excessive noise of sirens through the night by public service vehicles, which is against the law; low flying aircraft ignoring the law; flouting the law about over-development in Widmore Road; and the drunk and disorderly behaviour of many people in this part of Borough, which the police ignore unless someone is raped or physically attacked. On one occasion, on the green at the top of Murray Avenue, my neighbour rang Bromley police, and the offenders were thrown out. This is why me, and 1000s of others in

Bromley are infuriated at what is happening. We are terrorised by over-zealous parking wardens who are not given any discretion, contrary to the latest advice. Someone in your department who is responsible should heed what we are saying. The common-sense approach would be to cancel this PCN!"

On June 9, a squiggle shaped like an 8, without a name, appeared on the bottom of a Letter of Acknowledgement from the Bromley Processing and Representations Team, ending with these memorable words: "If you have previously been issued with a response advising that we are not cancelling the PCN and you wish to take the matter further, you should make use of the formal appeal procedure."

Three days later, I typed out a brief letter filled with overwhelming exasperation, saying, "Your letter addressed to 'Sir/Madam' needs careful reading several times before the recipient is able to find the meaning of it. In three previous letters I have said I want to appeal unless the notice was withdrawn. I set out the reasons, along with photographs, in very clear English. Can I repeat: Yes, I do want to take the matter further; and yes, I am prepared to use the formal appeal procedure. I hope that your threat of adding my name on the council's debtors list, with the attendant further threat of a visit from the bailiffs, has been withdrawn."

On June 13, Mr Carr sent a long, two-page letter explaining why the council turned me down, by one of the parking department's officers Mr Stephens, but some hope was elicited with his final paragraph:

"On a final point, you will be interested to know that I have asked for a review of the parking section to be conducted to look at its working practices, with a view to improving the situation based on the ethos of common sense prevailing. This is the way forward not only for the motorist but the council's parking service as well."

Another two-page letter arrived, from the squiggle signature from Bromley Parking Services, on June 14, rejecting my case.

It said, "Parking in this fashion can cause considerable damage to verges and pavements and a danger to pedestrians."

The photographs of my "offence" showed no damage to the pavement, and there was ample room for prams to pass. Another useful piece of evidence of my appeal to my adjudication at Sutton on August 24 was that the warden wrote "No" to my having a Blue Badge, when it was clearly shown in a photograph. I also produced a letter from Ken Lucas, the man who parked his executive multi-seater van in my drive, confirming that it took a short time to unload my daughter's luggage. In the council's 24-page submission, there was no sign of mitigation which I requested to be brought up.

However, on June 23, there were reports in the daily newspapers about the House of Commons Transport Select Committee calling for a softening of the parking restrictions. The report said: "We condemn councils and their parking operators for poor judgment and lack of professionalism that has brought the system into disrepute. They should concentrate more on helping the 30m car owners to park properly than on raising revenue through draconian and sometimes dubious enforcement." They urged wardens and officials to show more discretion when issuing fines, pointing out that one in five of the 7.1m tickets handed out each year was subsequently cancelled. The 115-page report condemned councils for confusing or out of sight parking signs and lines, and poorly trained wardens.

This confirmed what Steve Carr had written to me, and I thanked him for his help. Mr Michael Burke, of the independent parking adjudication panel, turned down my appeal on August 24, saying, "Having considered all the evidence, I am satisfied that the contravention occurred, and I cannot exercise mitigation."

I persisted, and five days later I wrote saying I was still unhappy about this affair, and thankfully the council decided on a common-sense approach – at last. Miss CA Axelson, Head of Parking and Traffic Appeals Service, with an elegant squiggle, wrote: "Your letter will be referred to the Adjudicator when he/she next attends the hearing centre."

Between 2001-3 Bromley declined to renew my Blue Badge, and eventually I received a fulsome apology. I quoted one of the officers in reply to my latest salvo: "I am sorry that this has taken so long ago and caused you so much distress. I know Mrs Graves has always had a great deal of sympathy with your particular circumstances and has worked hard to find a resolution."

With Steve Carr, Chairman of Bromley Council, Ken Lucas, who gave evidence about how few minutes I had actually parked on the pavement, the Government's committee's censure on "chaotic parking", and Mrs Graves all batting on my side, I felt confident justice would prevail. I'm not superstitious – well, sometimes – but the last two figures in my latest PCN being 13 had brought bad luck, and when the Adjudicator considered my appeal on December 13, I felt twitchy.

The day before, I went to see Lord Mawhinney, the Chairman of the Football League, in Gloucester Place to outline the details of an idea on behalf of the Football Writers' Association, urging managers and chief executives to be more co-operative with journalists. I was still chairman of the FWA Facilities Committee and former chairman of the Association. When Jimmy Hill was chairman of the Professional Football Association, while still playing for Fulham, he used to hold regular press conferences upstairs in a pub in Fleet Street. Half a dozen or so football writers would give the PFA's case maximum publicity and that was a key factor in eliminating the maximum wage, as public opinion swung to Hill's way. The Football Management Committee, headed by the cigar-smoking, blunt Yorkshireman Joe Richards of Barnsley, was always second to any argument. After winning the battle about wages, Hill decided to retire from playing at the age of 33. He joined Coventry City, whose chairman Derrick Robins was an enlightened cricket lover, and he gave Hill licence to launch the Sky Blue Revolution, as he called it.

Hill rang me on a Friday early in his first season and said, "Do you want to report on what I am doing? We can come up with a good story every day." Sol Chandler, the sports editor of the *Daily Sketch*, wasn't an expert on football, but he knew a good news story. Every day we had a whole page to expand on Jim's new ideas.

Coventry shot up the Third Division, and when the club reached the First Division in 1967, he suddenly quit as manager and became a TV presenter. Sky Blues, as they still call them, introduced their own song, the first all-seated stadium, a train devoted to their fans, and Hill was the man who suggested three points for a win. He was a true footballing pioneer and legend.

They put up a statue of him at Highfield Road, and he deserved it. As a free-thinking person, he was often criticised by lesser people, but his television career was eminently successful for many years. In his latter years, he sadly succumbed to Alzheimer's. As I played in one of his charity matches, I could vouch that he hardly headed the ball. He preferred it on the ground. He married three times and fathered five children with Gloria and Heather, and when he was diagnosed as suffering from dementia in 2008, his third wife Bryony lovingly cared for him and wrote a book about his cruel descent into insensibility. He died on December 19, 2013, at the age of 87.

Mawhinney (1940-2019), born in Belfast, was a former Conservative MP who spent seven years as a President of the Football League. At my first meeting with him, he didn't think my idea was workable. "Most managers look on the Press as a menace," he said.

At a second meeting, he was more receptive, and when we were about to approach the League Managers' Association to take it further, some strident managers and chairmen pooh-poohed my suggestions which Hill pioneered at Coventry, and hardly any club followed his example. The gulf between the Press and professional football still remains, but the pandemic has forced the errant owners to burst the boil of greed and think about the poor spectators who were terribly exploited. Now Marcus Rashford, MBE, and Raheem Sterling have given a lesson to the owners.

My parking case, BY08650013, had been rejected by one Adjudicator, but common sense at last took over. Hugh Cooper, of the Independent Tribunal for Parking and Traffic penalties in London, based in Sutton, ruled in favour for the case to be thrown out.

On December 13, 2006, Mr Cooper accepted my case, and a five-page document, full of mumbo-jumbo jargon, concluded that I was not guilty. So endeth the longest saga. And it saved £100.

IS BROMLEY ONE OF
THE BUS LANE BANDITS?

Under this heading, my favourite newspaper, the *Daily Mail*, carried a revealing story about how many drivers get off for driving in bus lanes. It went on: "Up to 86% of fines overturned on appeal after councils turn their roads into money-making traps. "

The AA, RAC, and the other motoring organisations, called it "staggering" and urged councils to send letters to offenders to warn them that if he or she did it they would be fined £130. Top of the Bus Lane Bandits League was Sandwell – a densely populated borough of around 354,000 inhabitants south of Birmingham, which houses

The Hawthorns, home of the yo-yo West Bromwich Albion Football Club. Apparently, Sandwell has a notorious road where drivers cruise along, with prostitutes waving a hand to them to stop. In July 2017, 173 out of 201 appeals were successful – 86%. The Borough is twinned with the Indian city of Amritsar, famous for General Dyer ordering a massacre in 1919 when British and Gurkhas soldiers killed 376 and wounded more than 1,000.

Second was Doncaster in South Yorkshire, with 310,00 souls, most of whom voted for the former Labour leader Ed Miliband. They voted 67% in favour to leave the EU. Having been to Donny, as they call it, it hasn't any noticeable features, but I later discovered there was a long list of famous people living there, including Tony Christie (of *Amarillo* fame), Jeremy Clarkson, Thomas Crapper who invented the flush toilet and who is buried in Elmers End Cemetery in the Borough of Bromley (next to W.G. Grace), as well as Kevin

Keegan, Diana Rigg, Bruce Woodcock, Lesley Garrett, Graham Rix, and many more.

A large number of 658 motorists there were excused in 2018 – 80%.

Bottom of the league was Coventry with just 12% successful, and close to the bottom – on 15% wins – was Bromley, nearby Bexley, and Nottinghamshire. English councils made a record £92.5m from bus lanes in 2018/19, up from £39m in the previous year, earning them £59.2 after costs.

THE DAY THAT OVER-70s WERE ORDERED TO GO INTO ISOLATION

It was the day that Boris read out the latest restrictions on Operation Coronavirus at 10 Downing Street, flanked by Professor Chris Whitty, Chief Medical Officer, and Sir Patrick Vallance, the Chief Scientific Officer. Professor Whitty soon had to retire because he contracted the virus, as did Boris.

They "strongly urged the over-70s with a prior condition"– like my pacemaker, which had just been boosted – "to agree to isolate oneself for 12 weeks". Balderdash! I already avoided crowds, restaurants, the Underground, empty buses, crowded shops with people overloaded with loo paper and kitchen rolls, and studiously washed my hands for more than 20 seconds.

I was looking was for a free parking space near the Post Office in Chatterton Road, Bromley, to renew my £145 road fund licence, now known as Vehicle Tax. Actually, Bromley haven't had a proper Post Office for some years. The main one is now on the first floor of WH Smiths in the High Street, and parking is prohibited. So I go to the more friendly, much smaller one in Chatterton Road, which is at the rear of a chemist's shop.

Conveniently, it has a disabled space right outside. As I approached it, I saw it was occupied by a medium-sized car with no Blue Badge displayed. Normally I would have shown mine to the driver – an oldish man wearing a cap – and told him he was risking a £1,000 fine. I heeded the advice from HM Government that elderly people should be helped by others, but it might have caused a row, so I turned round my car and parked at a nearby bay.

There were a dozen people in the Post Office, all spaced out two metres from each other, as required. The young man in front looked as though he came from the Caribbean and was carrying a large parcel marked "FROM CHINA". Donald Trump had been saying on many occasions that the virus originated from China, so I took a step backwards when I saw China, almost knocking over a middle-aged woman wearing an Indian sari and coughing into a hanky. I had to grin and bear it. A cheery lady without a mask dealt with my application efficiently with a smile.

Back home with my daughter and grandson, I checked with the latest figures of death and suspected cases, and compared them to the biggest pandemics in history:

Proportion of global population killed:

Athens 430 BC, 33%

Antonine AD165-180 (Roman Empire), 40%

Justinian 541-750 (Byzantine Empire), 13-26% of world's population

Black Death 1347-5 (Europe), 30-60% of world's population

Columbian Exchange 1492 onwards, 90% of Native Americans

Great Plague of London 1625, 25%

3rd Plague Pandemic (China & worldwide) 1855-1859, undisclosed

Russian Flu 1889-90 (spread to Northern Hemisphere), undisclosed

Spanish Flu 1918-9 (worldwide), 50m plus

Asian Flu 1957-8 (China and on to Europe/Americas), 1.2m

Hong Kong Flu 1968-70, undisclosed

H5N1 1997-2000s 1st bird flu from Hong Kong, undisclosed

Sars 2002-3 (worldwide), 10% mortality

Swine Flu 2009-10 (Mexico, spread worldwide), 0.08 mortality

MERS 2012-8 (Middle East & outward), 38% mortality

Ebola 2014-6 (Western Africa), 11,325 deaths

The worst plague, Spanish Flu, had the highest number of victims with an estimated 50m or more around the world: far more than the total deaths in WW1.

When I was growing up in the Isle of Wight, a man used to deliver Corona bottles of lemonade, and we collected a penny from every empty bottle we returned. The word "corona" comes from the Ancient Greek, meaning wreath or garland around the moon and the stars.

The word "coronavirus" apparently originated in Wuhan, Hubei in China, when the first person caught it late in 2019 and died. The droppings of bats were picked up by pangolins – a large, scaly animal weighing about 70lbs and four feet in length, which is trafficked by Chinese who remove the scale, which is similar to human fingernails, and eat their skin. As bats live in dark, murky places, they pick up all sorts of viruses. This one, known as severe acute respiratory syndrome (SARS – COV 2) has now spread to most countries around the world, and panic ensued. I decided to avoid any kind of travel – train, Underground, bus, motorcycles, bikes, and electrified scooters – and drive alone, isolated, with windows firmly shut.

IT'S NOT AGE THAT MATTERS, IT'S HOW HEALTHY YOU ARE

Professor Karol Sikora, a leading cancer specialist at the University of Buckinghamshire Medical School, wrote this under the headline in the *Daily Telegraph* on March 18, 2020, and I second his resolution:

"Many over-70s are fitter than those with poor lifestyles. Shutting them away is not the answer. On Sunday morning I woke up with a jolt. The plan (proposed by the Government) had shifted to cocoon over-70s in their homes for four months. At the same time, special powers would be introduced to allow the arrest of those who broke the quarantine rules. Had the world gone crazy?

"I declare a conflict here – I am 71. I work full time and am reasonably fit. The thought of being locked up fills me with absolute horror. Until now our Government's response on coronavirus has been laudable, and I've been very supportive. Not the hysteria we've seen in the US and other countries, but measured, scientifically based, and sensible. This new bombshell was simply not thought through.

"The death rate is higher in infected older people. That's clear from China, Korea, and Italy. On their way to heaven, they use up NHS resources: ventilators, ITU beds, and nursing time, all in short supply.

"Locking people up for their own protection seems a logical policy to save resources. "But it's not age that really matters – it's the state of health prior to infection. Many 50-year-olds are burdened with serious comorbidities – diabetes, chronic lung disease, heart failure. Lifestyle issues – obesity, lack of exercise, smoking and alcohol abuse, also threatens longevity.

"I've been a consultant oncologist in the NHS for 40 years. When I started, we had all sorts of cut-offs at certain ages. Gradually we came to realise it wasn't the absolute biological age that mattered but health and lifestyle status. The ageist policies were all discarded 20 years ago. Most healthy septuagenarians are fine to stay in society."

A few days later, a suntanned Karol made a good impression when he was interviewed on BBC1's Breakfast programme. Soon he became a TV star.

"I am an optimist," he said. And after the second month of lockdown, he urged a gradual return to work, "Otherwise the economy will suffer."

He followed up with another damning article in the *Daily Mail*. He wrote: "Our healthcare system is abandoning its most basic responsibilities. As thousands of Britons are discovering – anyone who is struck down by a serious acute illness or has developed worrying symptoms of disease – the new reality is a dangerous one. Reports today say that some stroke and heart patients are routinely waiting for an ambulance, while 2,300 cancer diagnoses are being missed each week because they are not going to see their GP, or because they are not referred for urgent tests and scans in hospital. Indeed, the diagnosis system has all but seized up. Abandoning Britain's non-coronavirus patients, as we are doing, is unacceptable – and a strain on us all.

"It is absurd that London's vast new Nightingale hospital is virtually unused nearly three weeks after opening. By Monday, it had treated only 41 patients. And more of these hospitals are opening around the country."

ANOTHER OF BORIS'S IDEAS
GO THROUGH THE WINDOW

Before Boris succumbed to Covid-19, as it then became, he spoke about advising elderly people to turn up at 7-8am at supermarkets and be helped by their staff. Meaning that fit people would wait until 8am to be let in. So I rose early and drove off to Tesco at 7.50am and joined a long queue of vehicles – almost gridlocked – and when I eventually saw Tesco's car park was full, and all their roads were jammed, I proceeded on to the Co-Op in Chatterton Road. The road was busy, and in the rush I failed to notice an empty disabled space right outside the store. After a possible joust with another man driving a Mercedes, I managed to slide into another nearby space.

Lots of people were going to the store – hardly any pensioners. There were half a dozen small trolleys outside which needed a pound to release them. I put my hand into my trouser pocket and discovered eight coins but no pounds. I asked one of the staff if he could help, as suggested by 10 Downing Street, but he said, "Sorry, I don't have any pounds," and carried on counting the bare shelves.

A young lady in her late twenties swept in and I asked her.

"Sorry, I don't have any money," she said.

She wore a black jacket with "Tottenham Hotspur" on it, and I said, "You're a Spurs fan then! I wrote Bill Nicholson's book!" and she roared with laughter.

Suddenly a male over-70 was going out the door, and I tackled him. He held up his hand and said, in a rather surly manner, "No," and rushed off.

I was about to drive off when a middle-aged blonde woman came in. I offered my coins, totalling a pound, and she smiled and said, "Here is a pound." She refused the coins and wished me well. What a gesture!

Armed with the only trolley, I walked around trying to find fruit and green veg but there was none, though there were plenty of packets of crisps and other unhealthy items. I rummaged around and paid £13 on three ready meals, two soups, and one Swiss roll, by swiping my Visa card then made off. I tried to find the kind lady with the pound, but I couldn't see her.

Two days later, I arrived at the Sainbury's store in oddly named Locksbottom (the PC activists ought to change that name by now!) at 7.02am – supposedly reserved for essential NHS staff and carers, elderly people, and the disabled between 7am and 9am – and discovered a plentiful supply of fruit and veg, which is my stable diet. Soon the place was filled with trolleys with people of all ages, with most of them ignoring the broadcast appeals to restrict themselves to only two of any items.

One grim looking, able-bodied woman in her fifties was coming towards me with her trolley, and when hers brushed mine she shouted, "It hurt me and you didn't say sorry." I observed she was wearing black gloves which would lessen any impact, if any.

Over the years I notice that more disabled people would make way for me, or give up their seat to me. I toyed with the idea of saying, "Sorry, but I am disabled," but merely said, "Sorry," as she disappeared into the mass of shoppers and their overladen trolleys.

My daughter warned me that the Sainsbury's spacious car park was also used by the patients and staff of the nearby Princess Royal Hospital, where I've spent spells for various ailments, and she thought that I might catch the virus. So I decided that I would stop using it until the crisis was over.

The following Saturday, I was the only Disabled Badge holder using one of the five out of a total of 206 – parking spaces reserved for the disabled in Bromley South's Waitrose superstore between 8am and 9. It is now overshadowed by an immensely high tower block of flats with no visible car park.

A massive queue of huddled customers with trolleys stretched back to another car park, positioned two or more metres away from each other, not speaking much, and mostly wearing fur-lined Eskimo hats. The scene was like an airport where passengers trudge up and down in lines separated by barriers – in this case, connected, unclean trolleys tied together. And with no attendants, I hobbled off to find the start of the queue. Suddenly, a young lady attendant appeared and ignored the Government's advice to help the disabled and told me to go right to the end of the queue.

Half an hour later – having taken my medication in the cold wind – a male attendant from Sierra Leone said, "Follow me." I proceeded up the slope, but when I was close to the entrance, a woman who bore resemblance to the one I had bumped into the previous week shouted, "That's the end of the queue," and agitatedly pointed to where I first set off.

Luckily, the attendant waved me on, and the senior manager was standing by the entrance and apologised. "The first attendant was new," he explained.

These unthinking, rude people should be shown a yellow card, and if they do it again they should be ordered to go to the end of the queue or pay a fine of £60 to the relief fund. I should have gone up to the woman and said politely, "Madam, I can show my scar to prove that I've been a victim of a German bombing raid in 1943." But I decided not to – the wind was howling, and I might have contracted a germ or two.

Two weeks later, I turned up at Waitrose on a Friday at 8am, parked in the number one disabled space, stumbled out of my now dirty Honda, and made my way towards the entrance. Thereupon a nasty incident ensued, with a gaggle of middle-aged women shouting, "Go to the back of the queue!"

I turned to try to point to the sign "Disabled and Vulnerable People Take Precedence" which was half hidden out of sight from the protestors. I tried to placate the women and said in a loud voice, "I've been disabled since 1943." I spared them the gory details, but on reflection I should have told them about my Herman Goering tip and run bombing raids in the Isle of Wight.

Two Waitrose under-managers came out. One didn't respond, but the other one did. I told them they should move the sign further along so that people in the queue could see it and not lead to unpleasant cricket-style sledging. One said they would move it. As I drove off – waving out to them – the sign was still obstructed.

Another development of the time was that the Government cancelled speed awareness courses.

Cyclists and joggers were taking over the almost deserted roads, and my friend Paul, who lives nearby, said, "There is no etiquette shown to walkers. We have to get out of the way." A lifelong supporter of Ipswich FC, he has now cancelled his renewal of his season ticket costing £500. "Football will never be the same," he said. "I'm not missing it. And the longer it goes on, more and more clubs will go out of existence." A month later, he changed his mind and paid up.

COMMON SENSE FINALLY EMERGES

As spring burst out in the landlocked kingdom, councils all over the country eased off on enforcement of the laws about parking. Instead, they were using common sense. Havering Council was one of the first to allow people to park in residents' spaces. Newham Council confirmed it would penalise drivers if they parked in an obstructive or dangerous way. Kensington and Chelsea jumped in and told people they wouldn't be penalised if their parking permits had expired. And Cornwall decided not to charge for parking in March and April.

It must have cost a lot of money, and with buses outnumbering cars, there were no problems about finding a space. NHS staff and carers had the priority and weren't charged.

A PLEA FROM THE SHIRES

Letter to the *Daily Telegraph*:

"Sir, Despite the pandemic, Essex County Council still requires my 86-year-old, frail, and recently widowed mother to attend a Blue Badge medical assessment in a public library in a town 23 miles from the hamlet in which she has lived for 46 years, and where she wishes to stay and remain independent. Because the computer says Yes.

Pamela Voice, Pett Level, East Sussex."

ONE FOOT OVER IN BLACKBURN

"Picking up medicine for my 91-year-old mother, I was fined £100 because one wheel of my car was one foot over the line in the parking space.

Steve Catterall, Blackburn, Lancs."

I know the feeling!

WAR ON OBESITY

"We know that obese people are susceptible to coronavirus, so aren't they being told to stay at home?

Steve Catterall, Blackburn."

You're right, Steve! Boris is now staying most of the time in Downing Street and has lost several pounds, or possibly stones. Steve is obviously a keen writer to the newspapers, but he has no chance of beating Lord Lexden, the historian of the Conservatives and Deputy Speaker of the House of Lords. He was christened Alistair Basil Cooke in 1945, and he isn't the one who delivered those marvellous letters from America to the BBC. Almost every month, a Lexden letter from the small Essex hamlet of Lexden appears in the heavy, serious newspapers, usually correcting historical facts.

OVER-70s SAY THEY AREN'T DECREPIT

After two months of Government lockdown and Boris had been saved by some dedicated doctors and nurses at St. Thomas' Hospital – where I was taken a year previously and discharged myself because I had recovered – I saw two more indignant letters printed in *The Times* and the *Telegraph* which hit out against ageism.

The first one was written by a retired doctor, saying he intended to shop every day defying the order of shopping "infrequently". He said, "There is little risk to catch the virus in a supermarket."

Unless everyone was sneezing or coughing! In my experience, I can't remember ever seeing a full belter of a sneeze in my two Waitroses in the Borough of Bromley. Trains and buses attract sneezers, not disinfected Waitroses.

The other letter came from the Mayor of Buckingham, named Mark Cole:

"Sir, You report on the 750,000-strong force of volunteers (April 11), but what was not mentioned is there is an army of us who are not being permitted to help. We are the 70 and overs."

LET OFF BECAUSE
A QUESTION OF SIGNAGE

The high-rise houses and flats cost around £200,000 in Edson Street, off the High Street of Bromley, in 2004 when I was presented by a PCN by a parking attendant at 12.28 on April 2. In 2020, the price has more than doubled to almost £500,000. It's a short walk to the shopping centre and Bromley South station, but this is extortion of the worst type. In 2019, the average cost of properties went up by 8.3%, and in 2020 even higher.

I was forced to park in a residents' space, and Bromley is in the minority among the councils who insist that the disabled ought to pay if they don't have a residents' permit. So I wrote one of my longer than usual letters, urging the Parking Department to change this procedure because there aren't enough disabled spaces for the Blue Badgers.

On that day I had to go to a dinner at Three Bridges Cricket Club, and one of the players collapsed at the wheel on his way and crashed. Luckily, he survived.

More than a year later – when I almost forgot about the Edson Road case – it was adjudicated by Gerald Styles under Section 73 of the Road Traffic Act 1991, on September 19, 2005. I attended the hearing and pleaded mitigation. After half an hour, Mr Styles intimated that he was on my side and ruled that the case turned on a longitudinal bay by the gutter and the council used the wrong surface markings – shot down by false signage.

The letter of reprieve came as a surprise. Mr Styles – no relation to Nobby Stiles of Manchester United and

England – sent a 900-word "Adjudicator's Reasons", and it must have arrived at Bromley's Parking Department like one of Nobby's crushing tackles from behind. I was at Wembley in 1966 when Nobby snared Portugal's Player of the Tournament, Eusebio da Silva Ferreira, in the semi final of the World Cup. I met Eusebio several times in the tournament, and he was one of the most sporting, nicest young footballers I've ever met. He called me "Mister". I think he dyed his hair. When he died, he was given a State Funeral.

Norbert Patrick Peter Stiles – his proper name – was born during a bombing raid in Collyhurst, Manchester, in 1942, and he was delivered by two female neighbours. His father Charlie was an undertaker. Nobby wasn't your usual footballer – balding, small, wearing dentures from losing front teeth in his teenage years, short-sighted and having to wear glasses. He wore thick-rimmed glasses normally but used his contact lenses when he was playing. The fans loved him, particularly Alf Ramsey, the England manager.

During the World Cup, Alf shielded Nobby after he scythed down the French player Jacques Simon in an early match, putting the Frenchman out of the tournament. FIFA warned the FA that Stiles could have been banned for violent conduct, but Alf told the FA that if that happened he would resign as manager. I interviewed the likes of Bobby Moore, George Cohen, Geoff Hurst, Martin Peters, Gordon Banks, and Jimmy Armfield – all very amenable and friendly, but I never got past a "Hi" when Nobby was around.

His 28 caps over five years were curtailed by the emergence of Alan Mullery – a nice, adjusted, now 81-year-old, who ironically was the first England player to be sent off in 1968. After Nobby managed Vancouver Whitecaps and Preston, he finished his footballing career as a youth team coach at Manchester United. When he retired his businesses, he had a stroke, and he was forced to sell his World Cup winning medals and European Cup medals for £200,000. The buyer was Manchester United, and the medals are displayed in the club's museum. Nobby died of dementia on October 30, 2020.

That weekend, it was confirmed that the revered Bobby Charlton was suffering from dementia. His brother Jack had died from it three months earlier, aged 85. A campaign was growing about footballers heading the ball and causing the illness.

But John Charlton, son of Jack, put another perspective when he said in *The Times*: "I do have a problem with people trying to tie it to playing football. I'm not saying there definitely is no link, but just that I don't believe it has been proved. It's an old people's disease, and lots of old people get it – Sean Connery wasn't a footballer, Barbara Windsor wasn't. I'm just concerned people are using the 1966 team to gain more publicity and more funding to do all these studies. My Uncle Bobby rarely headed the ball, and there are lots of other players of that generation who would also have headed the ball a lot and they haven't developed dementia."

Almost half of the 1966 World Cup winning side had dementia – Jack Charlton, Ray Wilson, Martin Peters, Nobby Stiles, and Bobby Charlton. Only Jack headed the ball frequently; Wilson used his head infrequently; Martin headed mainly in attack; and Nobby only occasionally headed, because he was only five feet six inches tall. Bobby Moore left Jack Charlton to deal with the high balls, and Geoff Hurst and the late Roger Hunt headed mainly to try to score. Geoff is in good health after having a pacemaker fitted. Alan Ball, who was a similar height to Nobby, died of a heart attack after tackling a fire in his garden.

A *Daily Mail* reader, Norman Brill of London N20, made an excellent point about the subject: "Unfortunately many of my friends have been stricken with various forms of dementia. Not one of the ladies has ever headed a ball."

My football playing days started in goal because I felt my stiff leg would be a handicap running around out in the field, but after our almost nightly six-a-side football sessions in the

Croydon YMCA gym, where I lodged for almost a year before the secretary threw me out, I decided to be a striker.

One day, the secretary Leslie Wheelhouse answered the communal phone in the hall, and someone said, "We need to speak to Brian Scovell of the *Daily Sketch*."

Wheelhouse said to me, "Do you work for a national newspaper?" And I owned up. "This place is for hard-up students," he told me, "not well-paid reporters in Fleet Street."

Running the *Sketch* football team, and after the *Daily Mail* side, I invited some ex-pros to guest for us, like the mischievous Thomas Henderson Docherty, the humorous Tommy Harmer, the loquacious Danny Blanchflower, the England cricketer Graham Roope who taught me how to dive and not get injured, the combative Geoff Arnold, the placid Arnold Long, and the great all-rounder Micky Stewart. The Doc was manager of Chelsea at the time, and in a match against Brian Glanville's Chelsea Casuals, he launched a fierce sliding tackle on Hugh McIlvanney OBE of *The Sunday Times* and dumped him in the mud.

Hugh looked up to the Doc and said, "Tommy, this is a friendly game."

But the Doc snarled like old-time Hollywood actor James Cagney (1899-1986), "There's nae such thing as a friendly." Cagney was similar in height to the Doc, at 5ft 5.

Not everyone appreciated the Doc's occasional waspish cracks, which ended with a sting, and Hugh didn't see the joke. I knew Tommy's first wife Agnes, and they had four children, but in 1977 when he steered Manchester United to victory in the FA Cup Final, he was summarily sacked because he'd had an affair with Mary, wife of the club's physiotherapist Laurie Brown. I knew Laurie, because he'd previously worked for Lancashire CCC, and he was a very nice man.

The Doc joked, "I was sacked for falling in love."

The Doc and Mary married, and it was one of the happiest footballing marriages, lasting 43 years, and they had two more children. When Tommy died at the age of 92, in December 2020, Mary was sitting with him.

If I had known that he had the second posh Christian name of Henderson, I could have teased him about it. Not many Hendersons come from the Gorbals, and he said in his autobiography, which was published when he was 78, "Illness and malnutrition were a constant threat to family life. No human being should have to live in the conditions that we endured during my early childhood."

His father departed, leaving his mother to struggle with bringing up a big family, and young Tom was allowed to leave school early. He joined the Highland Light Infantry and saw the King David Hotel blown up by Irgun terrorists in Tel Aviv in 1948, when 91 people died.

Danny Blanchflower played in one of our matches at Woolwich Garrison, and he was instrumental in laying on most of our six goals by half time. Back in the dressing room, he started to get changed. I said, "There's another 45 minutes to go."

"I know," he said, "it's all over."

He then went home, and we played the rest of the match with ten men. We just held on to record a 6-4 win.

At another game, at the National Football Centre on an artificial pitch at Crystal Palace, I managed to head three goals in 15 minutes. The then Palace manager Bert Head was watching, and he said, "If you hadn't had your stiff leg, I could have signed you." I think he was joking.

I was never good at heading, but my hat trick was made easier by the pinpoint crosses from my good friend Rod "Rocket" Gilchrist, who became assistant editor of the *Mail on Sunday*.

In my sixty-odd years I've never worn a cricket helmet, but I was hit by cricket balls on the head on seven occasions, and so far, dementia hasn't afflicted me. In 1976 the English Press team toured Barbados, managed by Trevor Bailey, and I edged a full toss in the nets and needed seven stitches in my left eyebrow.

When I arrived at the hospital, a hundred or so patients were queuing to see the English doctor. Told I was an England cricketer, he invited me to jump the queue. He was a Sussex supporter, and when I said I was reading John Snow's book *Cricket Rebel*, he said, "He's my hero." Next day, I presented him with the book.

I doubt whether any doctor bettered his immaculate stitching, and the following day I opened with John Jameson of England and Warwickshire, and he scored most of the runs in a stand of 90. I scraped 15, all singles.

The worst injury came two years later while playing for the Woodpeckers wandering side at the beautiful ground at Withyham, owned by the 10th Earl De La Warr. An 18-year-old quick bowler, Steve Deathridge, bowled a bouncer when I was 80 not out, close to the tea break, and I failed to get my feet in the proper manner to try and hook it. The ball came off the edge and snapped off three of my front teeth. Slightly concussed, I felt my body slowly crashing into the ground like a victim in a road accident. I spat out a mouthful of blood and said to the home umpire, "Good thing I'd completed my shot and I can resume."

"Oh no," he said. "You fell on the wicket, and you are out hit wicket."

Audrey drove me to a hospital near Tunbridge Wells, where an Indian doctor said, "I can't do anything for that, you'll have to see your dentist."

I did – next day. It cost me £500.

Several years later, I was sitting outside in the Withyham pavilion and, not having met the Earl, I noticed an elderly man sitting there. I asked, "Who owns the ground?"

He said, "I do."

He also owns the popular Dorset Arms – a high-class pub and restaurant – and his father, the 9th Earl, was responsible for building the striking De La Warr art deco modernist building overlooking the sea in Bexhill. It was opened by the Duke and Duchess of York in 1936, at a cost of £80,000 from private loans. He was the first Labour Mayor of Bexhill, and although many of the inhabitants disliked the building at first, now it is a major attraction. The council wanted to give him the freedom of the town, but he turned it down. In 2015, £8m was spent on renovations at the pavilion.

A few years later, another tearaway teenager hit me on the left side of my jaw at Beddington CC's ground, and I had to go off for an ice pack to reduce the swelling. Wickets were falling, and I decided to go out again. The bowler had been rested, but the skipper Brian Swain brought him back on, and another bouncer – which I tried to avoid and failed miserably – landed on the other side of my face. Except for not being able to eat solids for a few days, I didn't need treatment.

The skipper said, "This one has knocked your face back into place."

A young tearaway bowled a beamer at me at Knowle Park on a hill in Sevenoaks in 1992, and it hit me on the back of the head, causing a noise like church bells ringing out. Jeanette Pheathan, one of the wives, swathed my head with copious bandaging, and Audrey drove me to the nearest hospital. Not knowing the way, she stopped to ask a middle-aged couple for directions. They took one look at my bandaged, blood-covered head, and they walked off, obviously thinking I was a football hooligan.

The doctor decided a plaster was sufficient, and when we returned, nine wickets were down, and I resumed batting. The bowler was still bowling, and his first delivery was a bouncer which I ducked under. The umpire signalled "no ball".

I said to the bowler, "Are you putting me back in hospital?"

Our number 11 was bowled in the next over, and I was saved from more bouncers.

An injury to my head occurred in the luxurious pavilion of the Western Province CC in Cape Town in 2017, when I tripped over and crashed into a wall. As I lay on the floor, I noticed a portrait of my cricketing hero Sir Garfield Sobers was hanging on a wall above me. I used to write his articles and wrote his first autobiography.

One of the nurses who treated me turned out to be a daughter of the great South African batsman Barry Richards. I wrote Barry's articles for syndication to worldwide newspapers after he started playing for Hampshire in 1968, and for several years later. He only played in four Tests before South Africa was banned by the ICC because of apartheid.

The treatment by a young lady doctor at a nearby private hospital – 17 staples in the back of my head – was unequalled, and it only cost £128.

Before he died in 1997 at the age of 78, I interviewed Denis Compton about the wearing of helmets, never having worn one. "Today's batsmen are cowards," he said. "No-one in my day wore one because we knew how to avoid being hit. Keep your eyes on the ball and move out of the line. That's the way to hook the ball."

I said, "You needed one when Ray Lindwall hit your head in the Old Trafford Test in 1956, when you went off to have treatment."

He made a wonderful riposte: "Yes, but I came back and scored 145."

Compo had several stitches inserted in his forehead, and he returned with the score of 119-5.

My last football game took place in 1985 at the old Highbury ground, on my 50th birthday, and by then I was back in goal. Don Howe, a long-time friend from my days at the *Wolverhampton Express and Star* cricket team, arranged the match. And Liam Brady, Wally Downes, and some young pros turned out for the opposition, while Trevor Brooking and Tommy Harmer played for us. I let in six goals and Don presented me with the ball and an Arsenal jersey as man of the match because I was the busiest player. We lost 6-2.

I attended Danny Blanchflower's funeral in December 1993, after he died at the young age of 67. He wasn't one of the footballers who went in for heading, but he died of dementia – a sad ending for one of the brightest intellectuals of the game. Rain was pouring down as we trudged several hundred yards to see the coffin lowered into the grave. Suddenly, the sun appeared, and a shaft of sunlight landed on it.

Tommy Harmer said, "Typical of Danny; he was blessed."

Danny's greatest summing up of football, which is immortal, is now displayed at the new Spurs ground:

"The great fallacy is that the game is first and last about winning. It is nothing of the kind. The game is about glory, it is about doing things in style and with a flourish, about going out and beating the lot, not waiting for them to die of boredom."

Following the other Mr Styles's reprieve, I wrote to the Bromley Parking GHQ: "Apologies for the trouble over this! I have never been prosecuted for a motoring offence, and I haven't been penalised for entering a bus lane for 50 years. (Actually my memory let me down; I have been done for straying into a bus lane in the same road some years ago.)

"I live in a very busy road and hardly use my car in the rush hours, because it is almost impossible to get into the proper lane because of unhelpful drivers who fail to let me out of my drive. Normally I check with the first sign on my left, but it was hidden by a tree. I enclose a picture of the evidence. Had I seen the sign clearly, I would have changed lanes.

"On another matter, I was gestured by one of your parking attendants who told me not to park in Cork Street, the street leading to the Fire Brigade headquarters. I explained I have used that road in the past after being told by the Parking Department that it was permissible for Blue Badgers to park on double or single lines. I asked the attendant, 'Has that been changed?' She said the road was now a 'no loading' area and except for a tiny sign saying 'no loading'", there were no other more distinct, bigger signs.

"A week later a driver was being booked, and I asked a female attendant when the change was brought in. She said gruffly, 'Dunno, speak to the council.' With people being cautioned there ad lib – two more victims were also booked while I was there – your attendants need more training. It doesn't cost anything to be polite! You want to pass this to the chairman of the Parking Committee.

"They should copy the example of the young lady I spoke to at your department to ask for a picture of my 'offence'. She was extremely polite and had a good sense of humour."

My appeal was rejected, and I had to pay up.

WE WOULDN'T RECOMMEND
GOING TO SWEDEN

As Boris returned to duty at 10 Downing Street. the man who advised the Swedish Government not to go for a lockout but to carry on regardless – the State epidemiologist named Anders Tegnell – explained his reasoning. Apparently, Sweden has a high mortality rate for over-70s, and the Government adopted his suggestion that they were the only section of the populace to be kept in their homes.

Whereas around 800-1,000 died each day in the UK during lockdown before it went past the curve, Sweden's population of 10,183,100 lost a daily average of 75 at the same time. The conclusion is that Britain is too crowded.

These are a sample of quotes from dissatisfied "wrinkies" – over-70s who have a habit of touring colonial countries to watch the England cricket team.

John McEwen, of SW1: "There is a widespread 'elderly' contempt for the woke-driven pandemic policy, the craven subservience to discredited scientists, insulting war comparisons, deification of the heroic but ill-managed NHS, totalitarian clapping, arrogant directives, officious policing, closure of houses of worship, the brute ignorance of Christianity. If the lockdown is not speedily lifted, we 8.8 million 'elderly' voters will take revenge at the general election."

Margaret Armstrong, of Newmarket: "Please do not treat us oldies as if we are irresponsible children."

D. Goldsmith, of North Wales: "Please don't patronise people who have reached my age – 86 – by referring to us as vulnerable. We experienced WW11, the Cold War, and an array of crises."

NICKED!: PARKING FINES AND HOW TO AVOID THEM

A. Gray, Surrey: "Then there are reports that people of over 70 are immediately given Do Not Resuscitate forms on admission to hospital. What is going on? (I have had one and put down 'please put me down for a second innings'.) This has to stop. It is about time everyone is treated with respect and dignity, despite their age."

Most "old stagers" still drive, and after a certain age they have to be tested for their eyesight and physical condition. Many are being stripped of their licence. How many tearaway teenagers lose their licences? Not many!

SAD END FOR MICHAEL ROBINSON

As April 2020 set a new UK record for sunshine, the news came through that Michael Robinson – the former Preston, Manchester City, Brighton, and Liverpool centre forward – had died in Madrid of skin cancer at the age of 61. He was famous as being the first English footballer to settle in Spain, and he became one of that country's most popular football commentators and analysts. This is what his family said:

"With enormous sadness, we inform you of the death of Michael. It leaves us with a great emptiness, but also innumerable memories, full of the same love you have shown him. We will remain eternally grateful to you for having made this man so happy, he never walked alone, thank you."

I met him on several occasions, and he loved chatting away to everyone about his favourite subject – the world game of football. He was more of an honest bustler, like Tottenham's Bobby Smith, and lacked the grace of Ian Rush or a Kenny Dalglish, whom he played with at Liverpool. He always recognized a face.

The previous week, the BBC showed the fascinating film *Diego,* one of the previews of which I attended at the Bromley Odeon. The producer, Asif Kapadia, answered questions after the showing, and I asked him why he used so much of Diego hurtling along on his way to matches in his Ferrari without being caught for speeding?

"They didn't dare to upset the Naples fans," he said.

Maradona had close links to the Mafia, and that was another reason.

The truth came out much later, when one of Britain's most respected football agents Jon Smith said, "The police gave him dispensation to go through red lights, to stop people jumping on his car when it stopped. I worked with him after the Mexico World Cup for a while, and he was an absolute delight, a wonderful human being."

I reported on Argentina's 2-1 victory over England in the 1986 World Cup, in the Estadio Azteca in Mexico City on June 22, and Maradona and his colleagues were fired up to take on Bobby Robson's team to avenge the retaking of the Falkland Islands, the sinking of the battleship Belgrano, and also the sending off of the Argentinian captain Antonio Rattin, which probably cost them the game in the World Cup in 1966.

After a tepid first half, Maradona seized on a defensive mistake by Steve Hodge, and he chased the bouncing ball into England's penalty area. Six feet tall Peter Shilton advanced and should have punched the ball clear from 5ft 5 inch Maradona, but he admitted, "I punched fresh air, and he beat me to it."

From my seat in the press box – filled to its capacity of 1,500 – it looked as though Maradona's fist sent the ball forward and over the line. But I couldn't be sure. Maradona screamed, "Goal!" and his players joined in. He called his act of skullduggery "The Hand of God" but should have said "The Hand of a Cheat".

Shilton and his colleagues protested to the referee and linesman on that side in vain, but the incensed Robson declined to rush onto the field and try to change the decision. Robson, who was a good cricketer, had been taught throughout his youth about sportsmanship and not to cheat. Today, VAR cameras would have ruled out "God's goal".

Four minutes later, in the 55th minute, Maradona waltzed round Peter Beardsley, Peter Reid, Terry Butcher, Terry Fenwick, and then Butcher a second time, and slotted the ball past Shilton. All four could have hacked down the most kicked footballer ever in the game, but the British stiff upper lip prevailed. It still rates as the greatest solo goal in the history of World Cups.

Years later, Shilton gave a damning verdict on the 'Hand of God', saying, "He didn't show any remorse or say sorry."

The polite Robson described Maradona as "a rascal". No, Bobby; he was a scoundrel.

When Maradona died on November 25, 2020, aged just 60, it was the same date as George Best died fifteen years before from a heart attack, and the eulogies were fulsome. Maradona came from the slums of Villa Fiorito, and the critics praised his generous spirit and excused his excesses – cocaine taking, associating with the Mafia and prostitutes, kicking opponents in riots, and his blatant cheating, which should have soiled his hero status. But it didn't. One factor in his favour was his bravery. When he was felled, invariably he would get up.

In four World Cups, he was fouled on 152 occasions, at the rate of seven per game or one every 12 minutes. And there were many occasions when the offenders weren't punished. One glaring one was when he was elbowed in the face in the England v Argentina match in 1986 by Terry Fenwick.

Maradona was recuperating at home on November 3, 2020, after a blood clot had been removed from his brain, and six days later he was pictured smiling with his 39-year-old doctor Leopoldo Luque. He had a live-in nurse and a cook, with several relatives close by, but on the 24th November he had a heart seizure, and nine ambulances turned up – too late. The first ambulance took half an hour to arrive.

On the 28th, the police were granted a search warrant from a judge, and they raided Maradona's villa to investigate any "irregularities" about his treatment. Dr Luque said, "They were trying to find a scapegoat."

In Maradona's medical history there was no mention of him being bipolar. In Gary Lineker's fascinating BBC programme, which was reissued after the Argentinian's death, there was a scene where Lineker was sitting next to Maradona in his box in the La Bombonera Stadium – the home of Boca Juniors FC – during a tempestuous derby game. Maradona suddenly jumped to his feet shouting and screaming after seeing one of his players had muffed a shot. His face was contorted, and he pointed to the offender and swore. A minute later, his demeanour changed abruptly, and he was applauding and smiling. It might be an explanation of his unusual behaviour throughout his life.

Like Best, he destroyed himself.

Controversy had followed him through his short life, and it was still there after he died. Three days later, his funeral took place in Buenos Aires, as the nation came to a halt to honour its greatest footballer – and everyone went into a frenzy.

With the Brexit talks reaching a climax, French President Emmanuel Macron was accused of stirring up unnecessary trouble between Britain and France. In a 600-word tribute to Maradona, Macron said, "It fell to Maradona to write the history of a country scarred by dictatorship and a military defeat. This resurrection took place in 1986, in the most geopolitical match in the history of football – a World Cup quarter final with the England of Margaret Thatcher. On June 22 in Mexico City, he scored the first goal with God as his team mate. The miracle was disputed, but the referee saw nothing: Maradona's bluff won the point. What followed was 'the goal of the century'. In the same match, both God and Devil, he scored the two most famous goals in football history. There was a King Pele, now there is a God Diego."

One wonders whether Macron is bonkers!

Gary Lineker scored his sixth goal near the end, and he won the Golden Boot for being top scorer in the 1986 tournament. Argentina beat West Germany 2-1 in the drab final, and Maradona temporarily displaced Eva Peron as the country's number one hero. After he died, he drew hundreds of thousands of people to the streets, probably more than Eva.

Nottingham Forest's left winger Steve Hodge, whose sliced pass fell to Maradona for the disputed goal, went to him at the end of the game to ask if he could swap shirts, and Maradona willingly agreed. Hodge sold it for a reputed £7.6m Maradona's family has claimed the shirt wasn't the one he wore in the final – obviously.

On a subsequent visit to Buenos Aires, I went to the deserted Boca FC ground and wanted to inspect the press facilities. A friendly, English-speaking official led me to the 250-seat press box, which was over a corner of the pitch.

I said, "It's difficult to see the far side."

And he replied, "That's the idea of putting it there!"

We had been discussing the frequent riots which sometimes close the ground.

THESE BOOTS WERE WALKING
ALL OVER SPAIN

The person who was responsible for Gary Lineker suddenly becoming a millionaire was his agent, Jon Holmes. Jon doesn't like the word agent, because many of them are dodgy people who almost ruin football clubs and make fortunes for themselves. He prefers the description of financial advisor and PR expert. And he makes a pile as well for being straight, hard-hitting and honest, helping the likes of Michael Atherton, David Gower, rugby's Brian Moore, and Anna Soubry, who is a barrister and a former MP.

After Mexico, he arranged a transfer taking Lineker to Barcelona, which earned him £1m. He also did a deal with the Quaser company, who manufactured a more comfortable type of football boot allegedly made from kangaroo leather to take on the German Adidas. Spain loved Lineker, mainly because he took Spanish lessons and he scored goals profusely, including a hat trick at Real Madrid's Santiago Bernabeu stadium. Eighteen days later he scored all four goals for England against a shocked Spain's two less imposing goals at Barcelona's Nou Camp.

I reported on that match, too, and the sheen of Lineker's achievement of netting four times in 33 minutes was somewhat tainted by headlines afterwards about the terrifying scenes outside the ground before the kick off, involving drunken English hooligans and vengeful Catalans. Torrential rain fell and that helped the Spanish police, who arrested 18 people. More seriously, three people were stabbed.

We didn't see the incidents, as we were sitting high in the press box. But a Fleet Street reporter from the *Daily Star,* sitting near me, was phoning a detailed report on the incidents to his newspaper.

I said, "You are doing a Des Hackett." Desmond was the *Daily Express* football correspondent who often embellished his stories. He was famous for wearing a brown bowler and using his imagination. Everyone loved him.

The bogus reporter laughed. But two hours later, he had the last laugh. "I took a chance," he said. "A scoop!"

Four years earlier, I was at the Bilbao San Mames Stadium for the England game against France. The temperature was 100F and the players were soaked with sweat, wearing the wrong type of material used in their shirts. In these World Cups, I made sure I was sitting in my seat for an hour before the kick off. Those who weren't settled down missed the opening of the match: the unmarked England captain Bryan Robson headed the first goal in 27 seconds – a record in World Cup tournaments.

A CLASSIC HEADER FROM ROBBO

A fussy referee might have disallowed it, because his stocking on his right leg was exposed, and the law doesn't permit that. He later scored a second goal in England's 3-1 victory.

Today, the popular Robson is a well-paid ambassador for his old club Manchester United and counselled the elderly and vulnerable, especially during the pandemic. He is now recovering from cancer. He is a battler, and his prospects are good.

DAY FOR LIBERATION
FOR THE OLDIES

In the week of the 75th anniversary of Victory Europe, May 7, 2020, the over-70s and Blue Badgers were finally liberated. All but the infirm and vulnerable with health problems were let out, and most of the credit went to the combative social activist, 54-year-old Jewish Orthodox Baroness Rosalind (she prefers Ros) Miriam Altmann, CBE. In a series of sparky speeches delivered with a smile, she said that social unrest would break unless the rules were relaxed.

"They risked going to prison rather than being forced to isolate at home."

Britain has almost 9m mentally sound, extremely fit over-70s and the number is growing fast, and 1.5m were classed as vulnerable.

The Baroness was briefly Secretary of State for Pensions and Child Maintenance in the Theresa May Government in 2015-6 before she resigned because the lack of measures to help the poor. She played key parts in introducing the winter allowance, free eye tests to allow drivers to continue at the wheel at an advanced age, and bus passes to get the populace out of their houses and spend more to boost the economy. Her political career started in the Labour Party, then she flitted over to the Conservatives, then became an independent.

An equally combative Sir Graham Brady, Chairman of the trouble-shooting 1922 Committee and MP for Altrincham and Sale (where the highest paid Manchester United players hang out), launched a broadside, saying, "We have today the healthiest, most active elderly generation of all time, and it would be tragic if the government threatened this by trying to extend the so-called lockdown for those judged to be most of risk based on age. Why don't we just give them the best information and advice and let them risk themselves?"

Born in Salford – walking distance from both Old Traffords – in 1967, Sir Graham went to Altrincham Grammar School. And when he first became a Secretary of State, he resigned in protest against David Cameron's policy to change the status of grammar schools. He was soon back in the Cabinet, though, and he is one of the most active MPs, serving on loads of committees. He also voted against the Marriage (Same Sex Couples) Act in 2013. His wife works with him, for which she is well paid.

People like Boris – whether they are for or against him – Ros Altmann, and Graham Brady, had the verve to convince the public that they are right. Sadly, the former Minister of Health Matt Hancock, who is a useful cricketer, Dominic Raab, and their cohorts Sir Patrick Vallance, Professor Stephen Powis, and Professor Chris Whitty, all lack the same appeal.

Did 10 Downing Street's War Cabinet soften their approach to the Oldies after reading these letters in the *Daily Telegraph*?

"Sir, My husband is in his eighties and I am in my seventies, and we run a commercial bee farm. Our sales of honey are booming, and fellow bee farmers – most of them past normal retirement – report the same. If this group of people is incarcerated, simply on age, who will look after the nation's bees?

S, Reed, Oakhanger, Hampshire."

"Sir, Evidently researchers at Warwick University have a clear understanding of the kinds of discrimination tolerated in modern Britain. Hence their willingness to advise compulsory incarnation of old people but not of fat people.

Dr Julian Critchlow, Tregaron, Cardiganshire."

"Sir, I no longer watch the gloom of the BBC 6pm Coronavirus bulletin. For weeks it has been a catalogue of intermittent bad news. No wonder the country is in the grip of hysteria.

David Palfreyman, Poynton, Cheshire."

"Sir, We know that 90% of deaths from Coronavirus are in those with pre-existing health problems, but little has been said about tackling these problems before the next wave of Covid-19 infections. For instance, obesity – with its complications of diabetes, high blood pressure, and cardiovascular disease – is one of the commonest co-factors. Obese patients admitted to hospital with Covid-19 are 40% more likely to die than other patients. Excess alcohol consumption and high blood pressure makes the obesity worse. These are important issues for the Government.

Professor Roger Williams, Institute of Hepatology, King's College Hospital, London SE5."

Roger was the consultant who treated my late wife Audrey in her last years before she died on Christmas Day, 2000, in room 147 in Cromwell Hospital, after I'd retired from the *Daily Mail* after 40 years. He was a wonderful, kind man, and was still working at several hospitals in London – aged 88 – when he died on July 26, 2020. He pioneered many medical innovations in the field of hepatology, including the first liver transplant in the UK.

The last time I saw him, I asked about Audrey's chances of surviving him, and asked, "Is it fatal?"

He didn't want to be unkind, so he said, "Well, there are cases where the patient survives." He left us with a smidgeon of hope.

I was extremely proud to know this remarkable man, who was one of the greatest men of medicine not just in Britain, but the world. He hardly drank, campaigned against needless consumption of alcohol and obesity, played tennis, and his slimline build was exceptional – not a pound overweight.

He was a keen yachtsman with his own yachts, and he once said, "I don't want to linger; I prefer just keeling over." He did. He was playing tennis when he had a fatal heart attack.

A month before Audrey died, I was walking from Piccadilly Circus Underground station round the corner to speak at the Middlesex Wanderers' annual dinner at the nearby Café Royal. The chief guest was Dave Mackay.

The pavement was packed, and progress was slow. Suddenly a coarse looking man in his forties shouted, "Get moving, you fxxxxxx cripple, get moving." You don't expect to be threatened in the centre of one of the most civilized capitals in the world. I was unable to oblige, so stopped and stood aside to let him pass.

Dave Mackay was a true Braveheart who recovered from two broken legs and never pulled out from tackles. I learned a lot from him on trips, or in the pub next to the old White Hart Lane after matches. I asked him if he had a story to relate for his speech.

"Once," he said, "we were on a trip to Portugal, and we were having difficulty in finding taxis in the early hours."

I spoke first. Noticing a banner across the far wall said 'Middle Sex Wanderers', which had come from the Wanderers' recent tour to Japan. So I started my speech and pointed to the banner and said, "You didn't tell me you were poofs."

Some laughed – Dave did – but others remained poo-faced. At a male dominated function it might have been appreciated, but not now.

Dave came out with his long-winded story about a taxi on a tour to Portugal, which turned out to be non starter. But the rest of his speech held the attention of 350 men and a dozen or so women.

Audrey went back into Cromwell Hospital after refusing to take more chemotherapy. She said, "It's worse than the pain from my liver."

On December 23, I had a premonition that she was going to die. Saint Audrey's birthday was on June 23 in the Seventh Century, and that was the reason why my wife's parents had named her Audrey.

Another doctor recommended sleeping tablets, and that caused her to go into a coma. She didn't come out of it. By this time she was making awful noises – the start of a death rattle. On Christmas Eve, just before midnight, a young Australian doctor Luke Bennett from Brisbane – a cricketer – asked us if we would like more morphine to end her life. Without hesitation, we agreed.

I was dozing at 8.30am in the next room when John Motson shouted, "Ipswich have scored!" on "Match of the Day". I went to Audrey's room and soon realised she was in her final death throes. Hearing is the last function to go, and she heard my eulogy about her, how she helped so many people. I ended by saying, "You will be carried to heaven by a tide of love." A single tear rolled down her cheek, and her heart stopped forever.

Half an hour later, a nurse came in and asked us about Christmas lunch.

"Can you come back?" I said. My son Gavin and daughter Louise weren't thinking about lunch.

A few minutes later, the phone rang. It was Professor John Shepherd, a consultant at Bart's Hospital and a long-time cricketing friend. He commiserated then said, "We are getting the lunch ready in my house. Why don't you all join us?" We were relieved. That lifted our spirits, and we enjoyed a day which we will never forget.

John and his wife Alison now live in Cowes, Isle of Wight, overlooking the yachts in a 17th century house which was owned by one of Nelson's Admirals. In 1982, they invited us to stay at their then house in Tampa, Florida, and we accepted their kind offer. When we came home, Audrey had problems with her health, and another consultant at Middlesex Hospital diagnosed chronic active hepatitis.

She had frequent stays in hospital, and John reckoned she caught it while eating seafood in Tampa. For him to ring us and entertain us for lunch was one of many psychic experiences I've had ever since.

Audrey's in-house nickname was "Dollies", short for "Dolly Wallies" – and her spirit is still pulling strings!

Roger wrote a handwritten letter to me, dated December 29, 2000, and said, "Dear Brian, I was very sorry to hear from Dr Akeel Alisa of your wife's death on Christmas Day. I do so hope the ending was peaceful for her. It was such a big tumour to try to treat and there was a little chance, but sadly it was not to be. My greatest sympathy to you and your family.

Yours, Roger Williams, CBE, MC, FRCP, FRCS, FRACP, FRCPath."

Almost 20 years later, when Covid-19 arrived, the quality newspapers picked up his theme about obesity, and several put it on their front pages. Donald Trump should have acted long before the outbreak began, because one in every three Americans is overweight through gorging on cheap fast food and takeaways. In Britain 13m are officially considered obese.

Luckily, I can just about get into my wedding suit – we were married at Brompton Oratory in 1965 – and my weight of just under 78 kgs then has never changed, except during my recent illness when I lost nearly two stone, but I soon regained it. I gave up red meat and Coca Cola many years ago, but have big helpings of extravagant desserts and ice cream.

Three months before Audrey died, Roger had suggested a liver transplant for her, but we were told that it was a risky enterprise, so she turned it down. His most famous patient was the mercurial footballer George Best, who had a transplant in 2002, and Roger waived his fee for the surgery. Best's liver was in tatters, and he died on November 25 in 2005, aged 59, from major organ failure.

Like his mother Anne (1922-1978), George was an alcoholic. His father Dickie, a member of the Belfast Orange

Order, drank rather less and lasted 87 years. One hundred thousand people took to the streets to watch the cortege pass by in Belfast, and the City Airport was later renamed after him.

George always boasted that he loved boozing, women, and fast cars, and in a television interview he said his desirable occupation was "screwing". Manchester United manager Matt Busby used every dodge to curb his excesses but finally gave up. Best was twice convicted for dangerous driving and served two prison sentences. One wonders how many parking offences he committed, and acquittals!

He was blessed to have extraordinary natural, uncoachable talent, based on the gift of superb balance, only rivalling Messi and Maradona. Admirers, particularly journalists, kept telling him he was a genius who was the world's best footballer. He believed it, and that was part of his downfall. Even geniuses need to meet certain standards of fitness, and also behaviour. I met Stanley Matthews and Tom Finney on several occasions, and one of them should have been a mentor for Best. Both men were peerless in every respect.

I interviewed Best several times, and though he left school at 15, he passed his 11 plus and was very bright, good enough to complete *The Times* crosswords most days in his final years. You couldn't dislike him, only his wayward life – he was kicked out of many of the 18 clubs he signed for. In his comparatively short, first-class career, he scored 207 goals in 586 matches, most of which were stunners.

I was at Wembley Stadium in the European Cup Final in 1968, when he virtually beat Benfica in extra time on his own. But he was less successful in international football, scoring only nine goals for Northern Ireland in 39 matches. Finishers like Cristiano Ronaldo, Lionel Messi, Jimmy Greaves, and Pele were better than him at putting the ball in the net, whereas Diego Maradona and Johann Hendrik Cruyff – the Dutch master whose sporting name was simplified to Johan Cruyff – probably matched Best's one v one skills.

I managed to get a spare ticket for the European Final, and Audrey wanted to see it. She enjoyed the occasion, but only went to two football matches in her life – that one and the World Cup Final two years earlier. She should have got a medal!

Leading up to the England v Holland friendly match at Wembley on February 9, 1977, I was sent to interview Cruyff, and a Dutch colleague Lex Muller warned me he might be a bit moody. When the interview started, he spoke to a number of journalists from other countries, as well as Holland, and he spoke in their languages with great fluency. He switched to English, and then became gruff and unhelpful. I thought he was rude, and the interview was curtailed.

The match kicked off in front of 90,260 spectators, who were excited to see Cruyff's artistic Total Football, and he didn't let them down. He totally dominated the match and covered almost every square yard of the pitch. England's young prodigy Kevin Beattie said, "He ripped us to pieces."

Cruyff had 61 touches – an exceptionally high figure – while Trevor Francis, who was making his way into international football and was half Cruyff's age, mustered just 21. Cruyff laid on the first goal for Jan Peters and played a key part in the build-up to the second goal, also for Peters. And Cruyff and his players were given a rousing standing ovation at the end.

After the match, Lex tipped me off that the Dutch players had refused to play the day before until the FA paid them extra money. Cruyff had conducted the negotiations and the FA relented, otherwise the game would have been called off. Cruyff made many more contributions to his sport than Best, and his international record was vastly superior – 33 goals in 48 matches. His first-class tally was 297 in 511 appearances. He was pioneering as a coach and manager, at Barcelona in his prime, with new ideas which were copied. But he blotted his behaviour record by being a chain smoker, which caught up with him when he died from lung cancer at the age of 68. So, like Best, he helped to destroy himself.

IS THERE IS A PLOT TO TAKE THE DRIVING LICENCES OF THE OLDIES?

As a drawn-faced Boris addressed the nation on Step One of Operation Lockdown early in May, evidence came from some oldies that their driving licences were being unduly held up at the DVLA in Swansea. At the time, 141 people died of the virus in Wales, a much lower figure than in England (32,692 deaths from 2,007,146 tests), and there must have been an army of statisticians all round Britain dishing out the facts on a daily basis. Maybe some of them could have been drafted to the short-handed DVLA.

One vital fact was missing: how many driving licences of over-70s were still waiting to be issued? Roger Brain, of Devon wrote, "On March 1, just days after being reminded I needed to re-apply for my licence, I returned the necessary forms, and on March 16 I re-sat my DVLA eye test. I am still waiting to hear from the agency, and my current licence expires on May 1. I suggest that a delay of more than two months is not significant but displays yet more discrimination towards the older generation."

Kate, of Weymouth: "I returned my application on April 2 by hand-signed delivery. Having heard nothing by April 17, I checked the DVLA's online progress facility, which said (and still says) "awaiting application return form". My email chaser of April 17 was automatically acknowledged, but I have received no further contact. Fortunately, Ian Squires (Letters, May 8), I can take comfort from DVLA information document ING188/6 which says if the proper application has been returned, I may continue driving under Section 88 of the Road Traffic Act."

YORKSHIREMAN LOSES HIS RAG

Not many people are calm and orderly when they discover he or she been booked by a Civic Enforcement Officer, as they are now known. But 40-year-old Alex Owers from Willerby – a small town in the East Yorkshire Riding – took it too far; much too far. He illegally parked outside a café in Kingston upon Hull and seized the PCN, crumpled it, and started to shove it into the officer's mouth.

Sue Evans, prosecuting in the case at Hull Crown Court, said, "He held the officer's head in a headlock and said, 'Eat it now, you can have it.' The poor man's gums started bleeding, and he tried unsuccessfully to press his panic alarm. Owers then stamped on his mobile and kicked him. Several people tried to help, and some took pictures of the incident. He pushed another man into his car in front of his terrified child."

Owers wasn't arrested at the incident but was later charged after being identified from pictures. On March 29, when the lockdown started, he tried to buy petrol at a petrol station and abused the man in charge. After being refused, he spat into the protective shield of a police officer. He was found to be three times over the limit, and he was sentenced to undertake 100 hours of community work. He had completed 85 hours. His defending lawyer said he had drinking and betting problems and, with three children, he was now remorseful.

Judge Nadim said, "The message needs to be loud and clear that that sort of conduct won't be tolerated." And he sentenced him to 23 months.

RISKING ANOTHER PCN

We have been warned that we will soon live in a cashless society, but I still like to see these new, shiny plastic fivers, tenners, and best of all the £20 notes, which not long ago were worth £5.

I needed to withdraw £500 from my current account at the High Street branch in Bromley and, having been sent a new Visa credit card instead of my debit card, which had been hacked, I made a personal appearance to join the well-spaced, masked queue outside Barclays Bank in the Market Square.

My right leg – the one that doesn't bend more than five degrees – was playing up, and I needed to park close by. Told by several people that Bromley were suspending parking fines, I tried it out. The nearest road to the bank has been a minefield for me: I've had three cases lost there for parking when I was not "loading", so I left my Honda right next to the bank, in one of the three spaces designated for taxis.

I spent a convivial 30 minutes in the bank trying to convince a young lady member of staff to allow me to take the money without having a debit card, and being asked tough security questions like my mother's maiden name and to name the details of one standing order. The absence of a debit card was explained by Barclays whose HQ sent a second credit card, not a debit one. The second one was the same colour.

After another wait, eventually the bright new twenties emerged, and the teller put the gleaming 25 notes into a small white envelope and handed it over. She didn't need to count them. It's done by automation.

As I was about to get into my car, I looked up and saw a CCTV camera staring at me. Not another £65 fine!

Another piece of Trumpism – fake news – was that the parking wardens were being stood down during the lockdown. I drove up the upper High Street, past the newly opened but now shut up Picture House, and saw a male one and, round the corner, a female one.

I was dreading to see yet another PCN. So far, one hasn't appeared.

CASH CRASH

"Sir, Our cleaner has now returned. She gave us her bank details for payment. When restaurants and hotels open up, even for the porter it will be digital. All large shops that I have been to recently, including those frequented by builders, have a card-only rule. Cash is now finished in this country and may never return.

Dr Michael Pegg, Esher, Surrey."

TONY KAY'S UNLUCKIEST
PARKING OFFENCE

While isolated during May of the pandemic year of 2020, I started to re-read my cherished football and cricket books in my library in our house in Bromley, and the first one was Arthur Hopcraft's *The Football Man – People and Passions in Soccer*. It is unequalled in giving piercingly accurate insights into players and officials who shaped the post-war years of professional football, before he went on to become one of the country's best scriptwriters.

A self-confessed loner who refused to travel on the London Underground, he was born in Shoeburyness, and at 16 began as a trainee journalist in Stafford before joining the *Guardian* and the *Observer*. The book starts off with interviews with George Best, Bobby Charlton, Duncan Edwards, and then on to Tony Kay. Most of today's generation wouldn't know of the red-haired, fiery, temperamental, wing half with a bite, who played for Sheffield Wednesday alongside the England centre half Peter Swan and centre forward David Layne.

The trio was talked into fixing a game at Ipswich in December 1962 by Jimmy Gauld, a Scot who played for Swindon Town. All three put £50 at odds of 2-1 on Ipswich, and Ray Crawford scored both goals in a 2-0 victory for Ipswich. The FA had a rule to punish players who bet against their own side, and they were sentenced to prison for four months and banned from football for life. Gauld sold his story to *The People* newspaper and was paid £7,420 – equivalent to around £143,000 today – and he incriminated no less than 33 footballers, some of whom also went to jail.

Hopcraft wrote, "Of the three Wednesday players Kay was the most of colourful and notably articulate. He was 27 and played once for England under Alf Ramsey, scoring a goal in the 8-1 victory over Switzerland. He was an extremely tough, quick, enterprising half back of the combative, all-action kind: very much like Nobby Stiles.

"I went to see him in 1967, and he looked haggard, but not in the debilitated sense of a man gone to seed. He looked like a hard-driven athlete. He had red, scrubbing brush hair, and he wore thick-rimmed glasses. He exuded an exaggerated ruefulness, a bitter and aggressive self-mockery. There was a distinct TV-age, showbiz edge to his back-street wit.

"'The cops have it in for me; must have,' he said. 'Have you ever heard of anyone being booked for parking by a copper on a horse? That's Anthony's luck.'

"The resentment poured out of him, as he built up a picture of a victimized upbringing. 'I've always hated referees,' he said. 'Who are they? All the week in their offices, scribbling away, and on Saturdays they're saying, "Right, now you do what I tell you or you're going to be in my little book."' He did a wickedly observed impersonation of a hunchbacked, myopic referee writing in a notebook, his hands up his nose.

"He told a story about Jimmy Hill at Fulham. 'He was towering above me. Every time I went up for the ball, there he was, just leaning over the top of me. I thought, *Right, I'm not having this all the game. Next time I'll have his shorts off him.* Well, up we went, and I shoved me hand out and I missed 'em. Instead, I caught him right between the legs. He screamed the place down.'"

For a while Kay was the costliest player in the League when he was sold to Everton for £60,000 in 1962, and when he came out of prison, he wrote to the FA regularly to appeal against his life ban. Each time he was rejected. All the others were allowed to continue playing professionally.

Hopcraft said, "Professional sport made him, tested him, and broke him. He was one of football's tragic casualties because he was so strongly equipped in nearly all aspects. His counsel said in court, after his conviction, 'He has given up for £150 what has in fact been one of the greatest careers of any footballer. He was tempted once, and fell.'"

The former sports editor of the *East Anglia Press*, Tony Garnett, remembers that game at Portman Road, which was fixed, and said, "There was no sign of the players making deliberate mistakes to ensure Ipswich finishing on the winning side."

Last word from Anthony Herbert Kay, born on 13 May, 1937, and still going strong: "Ipswich always beat us anyway."

Many football experts thought he should have been picked in Alf Ramsey's 22 for the World Cup instead of Nobby Stiles, who was a Catholic. They thought he was a better all-round player. Both excelled at "stopping" the other team's star, often by brutal means, but Nobby was more popular, with a better sense of humour. He wore contact lenses when he played, his front teeth were false, and he took them out when he played, too. His hair was receding quicker than Bobby Charlton's, and both had the comb-over style to try and hide their baldness. His popularity was shown when he sold his World Cup medal for £160,000 and his European Cup winning medal for £69,000.

Kay was slightly taller than him, with a full head of hair, and when he was excommunicated for life, he found it difficult. The FA refused to allow him to restart his professional career, and they used his example to deter others from fixing matches. The punishment was too severe. No wonder he came over as a moaner.

Nobby was one of Manchester United's ambassadors, but at 73 he contracted prostate cancer, and he died from cancer and dementia in October 2020. He hardly headed the ball, because he was only five feet six inches.

Someone who headed the ball constantly was Swan, as a dominating centre half, and he, too, descended slowly into a state of dementia before he died in January 2021. In 2016, a ghost writer helped him to write a wonderful expose of the illness. He said, "I was brought up to cry, but now I'm crying all the time with this Alzheimer's."

I met him a few times, and he had a gentlemanly way of conducting himself. But on the field, when he donned his very short shorts, his bulky, muscled legs were rather intimidating. Bobby Moore wore short shorts as well.

Swan was picked in the England squad for the 1962 World Cup tournament but dropped out with severe dysentery. After coming out of jail, his chances of being Moore's partner in the 1966 tournament had been dashed. Jack Charlton took over. The FA cancelled his life ban in 1972, and he managed Bury and Matlock Town before he ran several pubs.

He came from a mining family, and he had six brothers. When he married, he and his wife had five sons. The odds against that must have been a million to one – worth a bet!

CAROLINE NOKES MP RIGHTS
A PCN INJUSTICE

On Stage Two of restoring normal life on June 2, 2020, the chamber of the House of Commons was occupied by no more than a dozen MPs, along with the Speaker and his assistants, including the lady who has to lift the weighty golden mace and march off when time is called. Simon Clarke, the eager beaver Conservative MP of Middlesbrough South and East Cleveland – known as one of the most deprived areas in Britain – had the floor for more than half an hour. He was the Minister of State for Housing, Communities, and Local Government, and his subject was private car parks and how to remove the abuses perpetrated by the greedy owners.

Fielding at wide fine leg some 30 feet away was Mrs Caroline Nokes, nee Perry, who is recognised as one of the good-lookers in the House. Mr Clarke, a gentleman, soon made way for the MP of Romsey and North and South of Southampton, to recount her story of a constituent Guy Hindle. He was booked for a trivial parking "offence" and refused to pay the whole amount. As a determined North East Yorkie, he spent another 20 months firing off angry letters with the help of Mrs Nokes, and in that time the £15 fine rose to £247.62. It was subsequently cancelled.

Mrs Nokes asked the Minister when the report on parking generally was to be published. The Hon. Member of Middlesbrough said it would be later in the year and that it would make life easier for England's harassed car owners. The Government had provided for free parking for NHS staff, carers, and other essential workers. Welcome news about showing common sense and compassion, instead of strong-arm bullying.

A BRUSH WITH A SEAGULL AND A CLOSE-UP OF A SLAVE TRADER

Bristol, with its half a million cosmopolitan population, holds great fascination for our family. Once I drove to an art exhibition there with some of Audrey's work, and while they were unloaded, several crashed onto a concrete floor and the glass broke into hundreds of pieces, causing havoc.

The West Country has been kind to me for many years, seeing not a single instance of the motoring virus PCN. On another occasion, I was invited to speak to a cricket club in the pavilion of Somerset County Cricket in Taunton – famous for Harold Gimblett and the two Sirs, Viv Richards and Ian Botham. I was given a seat a long way from the top table, and when I rose to pick up the hand mic, someone made off with it. The speech was barely heard, and having run up 300 miles and an overnight in a hotel, I was rather surprised to see the organiser asking me for the £32 for my dinner. I had to pay up.

In 2018, I arranged to report on a cricket match at a school in Bristol against a team of veterans from the Forty Club. To avoid running up a big bill for travel, I went by train. While I was waiting for a taxi, I sat on a wall and opened my M&S plastic box and took out a prawn sandwich. I was just about to take a big bite when a large, white seagull sitting nearby swooped and whipped away the sandwich then speedily fluttered off. I had to admire its dexterity; I didn't feel any pain or discomfort. It could have knocked out one of my 11 implants or two crowns!

Twenty minutes later, I was relating that story to the cricket master, when he said, "Do you know Sir Gary Sobers is here?"

I wrote Gary's first autobiography in 1988, and I first met him when he captained the West Indies in 1963 and virtually beat England on his own. It was a huge honour to work with the greatest all round cricketer of the lot. One of his dearest friends, the late Tony Cozier from Barbados, who was also reporting the series, was too busy to ghost write books so he put forward my name to the publisher. Sadly, Winston Anthony Lloyd Cozier, to give his full name, died aged 76 on May 11, 2016, and his wife Jillian died four years later on May 12, aged 75 – a huge loss to the cricketing world.

I sat down with Gary at Colston's, and he told me, "I organise some tours for English schools to take part in the Barbadian Youth tournament."

Gary represents the Barbados Tourist Board. Having had six operations on one knee, he now has difficulty walking. He still plays a few rounds of golf, but he doesn't drive any longer, so the Board lay on a chauffeur-driven car for him.

At the time, students from the local university were campaigning to have a statue removed of Sir Edward Colston – the slave trader who transported around 84,000 slaves from West Africa, now Sierra Leone, to the Caribbean between 1680 and 1692 to work in the fields under a blazing hot sun and cut down the sugar cane which had just started becoming popular in England. A quarter of them died on the way, and their bodies were thrown overboard.

A Portuguese explorer, Pedro de Sintra, discovered West Africa in the 15th century, and local African kings sold slaves to him. English explorers followed on, and that was the reason for the creation of exporting slavery. So, blame the tribal kings in West Africa!

David Olusoga, a British-Nigerian historian, broadcaster, and BAFTA award-winning presenter and filmmaker, published his definitive book *Black and British – A Forgotten History* in 2016, and mentioned that fact. And his three-part television programme was shown on BBC in 2020.

Today's students in Bristol ought to be told that fact. They wanted to have the school renamed, and we were told a decision had been made to retain it. But a primary school named Colston was to be changed.

Besides being one of 15 children of a rich merchant, Sir Edward was also Bristol's biggest benefactor. He financed two schools, a concert hall, and much-needed infrastructure, with two roads named after him. In 1895, the town council built an 18ft high Grade II listed statue of him on Colston Avenue, close to Colston Hall, and it has now been shamefully renamed. Colston School is one of the finest rugby schools in England with a reputation for producing international stars.

Grade II listing by the organisers of the National List of Historic England to preserve old buildings and statues means it is an offence if a property or statue is altered without permission. I know this because my art deco house was built in 1933, and if I want to make changes, I have to contact Bromley Council for clearance. We moved there in 1978 and we have kept it in good condition with no changes. People often stop to take pictures of it.

Was anyone prosecuted over Sir Edward's statue which was radically altered and is now lying in a museum? Some weeks later, some were leniently treated in court. In October, six men and a woman were charged for bringing down the Colston statue, and the men were fined £100 each and given two weeks social work. In December, three more men and a woman were charged with the offence. The cost of restoring the damaged statue came to £13,000, but so far those guilty have yet to contribute.

Thomas Guy, the slave owner whose money built the original Guy's Hospital in London, would be unhappy about his statue being removed.

Obviously, Gary Sobers knew about Sir Edward, but he didn't give an opinion on him nor about the statue being thrown into Bristol Harbour. He has a great sense of humour, and if he had he might have turned into a joke.

Sitting in my lounge on Sunday June 7, 2020, I saw the live pictures of thousands of people demonstrating in Bristol calling for that to be done. It was carefully planned, and masked, hooded young men and women used ropes to attach the statue then, with a succession of yanks, it toppled over like Saddam Hussein's was felled by US and Iraqi soldiers in Baghdad in 2003. There were no police to prevent these happenings, which was understandable, because if they arrested all of the demonstrators it would have needed a whole battalion of officers.

American activists were pulling down the statues of generals, Christopher Columbus, and others who affront today's students, and now all five statues of General Robert E. Lee, the legendary general of the Confederation, have gone. You might as well remove the large number of memorials for our best-read author Charles Dickens, because A.N. Wilson called him a sexual predator when his wife was put in a mental home after having ten children.

Will Churchill, Nelson, Wellington, Montgomery, or even Queen Victoria's 77, have their statues destroyed?

The first Afro-Caribbean Mayor of the Bristol Council, Marvin Rees, said he had been campaigning for four years to discard the statue of Sir Edward, but a US professor I heard on a BBC programme had a different view. "They should let it remain, to remind the next generations what had happened."

I agree with her. That is good sense.

On the same day, a fired-up section of demonstrators rioted in Parliament Square, and one crossed out the name of "Churchill" and scrawled "was a racist". I read most of Churchill's volumes and I saw little sign of him being racist. Quite the reverse. On TV. a young girl said. "He was a racist because he didn't like Gandhi."

Over that weekend, the film *Gandhi* was screened, and I watched the 191 minutes and was totally enthralled. It had a budget of 22 million dollars, earned £127m, and won eight Oscars. The cast included many stars, and Ben Kingsley shone the brightest. Mohandas Karamchand Gandhi, a lawyer, was assassinated in 1948 aged 76. Why are the good guys assassinated, not the tyrants?

I didn't hear anyone on the BBC saying we need a Gandhi today, someone leading a non-violent resistance movement and going on fasts, instead of what Boris described as "thuggery". The answer is to banish hate and replace it with love: Joe Biden preaches that as President of the USA.

These are the words I wrote on Audrey's gravestone in Chislehurst Cemetery: "She brought beauty, laughter and love to the world." It is beautifully positioned under trees next to a field used for exercising thoroughbred horses. When we visited – because her parents were buried in the same grave – she would feed sugar cubes to the horses.

On April 24 in 1965, we started queuing at 9pm on the South Bank to see Churchill lying in state in Westminster Hall, and it took four hours before we reached the Hall. He'd reached the age of 90, escaping death so many times. We all owed a debt to him for giving us our freedom. He was the greatest Englishman of his time.

George Floyd, who died in Minnesota when a policeman kept his knee on his neck and caused his fatal cardiac arrest, was lying in state in a church in his native Houston on June 9. The crowds were impressive, but nothing like Winny's turnout.

There was a surprise development a month later, when Sir Edward Colston's statue was pulled out of the River Avon, renovated, and locked away in a museum. Another sculpture of black bronze – called "A Surge of Power" – of 31-year-old dancer and black activist Jen Reid was craned up and stuck on Sir Edward's vacant plinth. She had her right fist held high and was dressed in a short skirt. Miss Reid turned out to be a former lover of Marc Quinn, the sculptor who made a bronze statue of the model Kate Moss. And he also made the "Alison Pregnant" sculpture which stood on Trafalgar Square's Fourth Plinth between 2005-7.

Mayor Rees said on BBC Radio Five: "It is increasingly delicate for me, because every time I talk about race as a black politician, I'm boxed in – all I do is talk about race. The irony is nearly 300 years after Colston died, aged 84, he's coming back to get this first black politician. This is not about taking down a statue of Jen, who is a very impressive woman. This is about taking down a statue of a London-based artist who came and put it up without permission."

The council wanted to charge Mr Quinn for putting up Miss Jen's sculpture, but they favoured putting up a memorial to honour a local man named Paul Stephenson, who helped end the 60-day strike in 1963 when Roy Harper, a Jamaican driver, was harshly sacked by the Bristol Omnibus Company. To qualify for putting up a statue, it is a necessity that 80,000 people sign a petition. At the time of writing, the figure fell 5,000 short.

My friend Sir Learie Constantine, when he was the first High Commissioner for Trinidad and Tobago, played a leading part in finding the solution to the bus strike, and he was also a key figure in creating the Race Relations Acts in the 1960s. Had the strike happened in London, there would have been justification for going ahead with erecting a statue of him, because he was the man who broke the colour bar by winning a High Court action in 1944 after being ejected from a hotel because he was black.

On another visit to Pocklington School, near York, to report on a cricket match (which was rained off), I saw the statue of William Wilberforce, the hero of slavery. A converted Christian, he joined up with a number of like-minded philanthropists to form The Anti Slavery Society in 1787. As a friend of William Pitt the Younger, who followed his father as Prime Minister, Wilberforce became one of the finest and most persuasive public speakers in Parliament, and in 1807 the vote was 283-16 in favour of ending slavery. With so much money to be made from slavery, it took 26 years to bring about its end. He died three days later, aged 74. Today's generation should read about him, celebrate his life, and follow his peaceful preachings.

Early in 2021, Exeter's Labour council voted in favour of relocating a statue of General Redvers Henry Buller – Commander-in-Chief of the British Forces in the Zulu War in 1879, who was awarded the VC – near Exeter College, at a cost of £25,000. When the country was in the direst economic crisis since WW2, this seemed to be an extravagance of the worst kind. The excuse was "because of his links to colonial campaigns". Buller served in both Boer Wars 1899-1902, fighting the white Afrikaners, and made his name by relieving Ladysmith on his fourth attempt. The MP Leo Amery criticized him in *The Times*, and opponents branded the General "Reverse Buller". As a result, Lord Roberts took over.

The grossly outnumbered Afrikaners eventually surrendered, and throughout England relieved local councillors named hundreds of roads and buildings after Buller, Roberts, and the likes of Ladysmith and Mafeking. Are these names to be changed? Redvers was the son of a respected long-serving MP in Exeter, and he married Audrey Jane Charlotte Townshend, daughter of the 4th Marquess Townshend. He also had a good reputation for handling his troops. Now the woke brigade has branded him as a villain. His statue was paid for by the public who thought he'd done a good job. Perhaps the woke brigade might pay the £25,000 to move it to an obscure place where no-one can see it. Early in 2021, Exeter Council changed their minds. The statue stayed.

The only Redvers I knew was Redvers Dundonald, known as King Dyal. In his bright coloured suits and incessantly smoking a pipe, he attended every Test match in Barbados for four decades and gave his opinions in a singsong voice. He sometimes went to Lords as well and was very entertaining. He is no longer with us, and he was buried at sea. He ought to have a statue at the Kensington Oval in Bridgetown!

There are around 12,500 statues in England, 3,400 of which are protected, but the Government has now brought in legislation to extend to all 12,5000. Communities Minister Robert Jenrick said, "We don't want to see the errors of previous generations. Proper processes are now required. It was wrong that statues are being removed at the hands of the flash mob or the decrees of a cultural committee of town hall militants and woke worthies. Proper process will now be required. It will need planning permission after consulting the local community. We live in a country that believes in the law, but when it becomes to protecting our heritage, due process has been overridden. That can't be right." Hear, hear. Afterwards, the statues of Sir Francis Drake and Baden-Powell were reprieved, and others were safe from demolition.

On January 5, 2022, the educated populace of the shires were startled to read and hear about the Colston Four being not guilty of any of the charges for damaging Sir Edward Colston's statue. A jury voted 11-1, like the England football team last year when they outplayed San Marino by a similar score last year in a World Cup qualifying match. The Four – Rhian Graham, 30, an event manager from Bristol, reared in Norfolk; Sage Willoughby, 22, a carpenter; Jake Skuse, 37, locally born; and Milo Ponsford, 26, also a carpenter from Hampshire (no relation to the great Australian cricketer Bill) came out with these mortal words: "We didn't change history, we rectified it."

The *Daily Mail*'s highly paid columnist Richard Littlejohn countered with, "They must be stark, raving mad."

They were lucky to be living in a sane, democracy at the same time as the bulk of the protesters in the 19m population of the former Soviet satellite Kazakhstan, which boasted a lot of natural sources. A statue of ex-dictator Nursultan Nazarbayev was torn down there, and a number of renegades were shot and killed by police and Russian soldiers.

Sir Tony Blair picked up a pile of cash when he acted as his PR, and Prince Andrew had dealings there as well. Not a good place to live! Nothing to compare to Bristol, where Sir Edward Colston did so much, paying for schools, roads, and concert halls.

WERE GAS MASKS REALLY
NEEDED IN WW2?

Hard on the news about Stage Four in the fight against Codiv-19, a gigantic U-turn happened on July 24, 2020. Suddenly we were back on the leash and told if we didn't wear masks in supermarkets and shops, we would be fined £100. The shop owners had forked out to pay for the safety-first precautions, like plastic in front of tellers, sanitisation stands for customers entering and leaving, and ensuring no-one was within two metres of someone else.

I think Boris and his Cabinet were thinking about pubs flouting the regulations, rather than orderly restaurants. Musical, drunken, drugged raves were almost ignored, with the police totally outnumbered and unable to make mass arrests.

The subject of wearing masks brought memories of Churchill's edict in 1940, when the nation was ordered to wear gas masks because he feared the Luftwaffe would drop gas bombs on Britain. Thirty-eight million of these ghastly, huge, heavy Mickey Mouse-like contraptions were provided, and they cost just two shillings. Not one person was fined for not wearing one. (In wartime, people observed the regulations, or else.)

I remember the one I had in a cardboard box, made in a factory in Blackburn. Directly the siren went off, we would huddle in an area below the stairs – we didn't have the luxury of a John Anderson shelter. We were asked to have a rattle and use it to attract attention if we were bombed.

In WW1, gas was used extensively by the Germans and by us, but though it caused deaths and sickness in the trenches, often the wind changed, so the gas drifted back to our own soldiers. In 1939, Hitler gave the order to build up large stocks of noxious gases, much more than the British Army had available from Porton Down, but he didn't use it and nor did Churchill.

As it turned out, gas masks weren't needed. We were lucky in the Isle of Wight, having two radar stations, both of which were walking distance from our houses. The first one was hidden half a mile from where I was born in St Lawrence, and the other one on 800ft St. Boniface Down. They tracked early onto incoming raiders, so we had plenty of time to take proper precautions.

A number of countries claimed they invented radar – Radio Detective And Ranging – and a German scientist, Heinrich Hertz, first experimented with it in the 1890s, while another German, Christian Hulsmeyer, first applied for a patent for it in 1904. An Italian nobleman inventor and engineer, Guglielmo Marconi (1874-1937) from Bologna, had connections with Queen Victoria and came to live in England. His first meaningful telegraph message was transmitted from Freshwater on the west tip of the Isle of Wight from the Queen to her son Prince Edward on the Royal Yacht. In 1909, Marconi won a Nobel Prize. Back in Italy in his latter years, he became a fervent supporter of Benito Mussolini.

In 1935, a Scots physicist named Robert Watson-Watt discovered the secret of identifying aircraft from long distances, and the Germans followed suit. Then our Government ordered a string of radar stations to be built along the south coast of England. The Nazis underestimated the importance of radar, and my father worked on the St. Boniface Down one, which was bombed several times. There was only one occasion when it was out of action – and just for one day.

Hermann Goering ordered pairs of FW190s – the equivalent to the Spitfire – to take over, and they flew a few hundred feet above the sea to avoid detection. They were called "tip and run" raiders.

The Germans developed and built a host of radar systems, but Hitler made a catastrophic mistake when he told Goering to switch from attacking English radar stations and airfields to concentrate on bombing London and other cities. These terror tactics failed, and the British Army, which had been routed in France, was reconstructed after the escape from Dunkirk.

A SURPRISING, SUCCESSFUL APPEAL

I have strayed from PCNs and contesting them, but one of the nicest parts of London, the Royal Borough of Greenwich, did the decent thing once and let me off. It occurred in Burney Street, close to the Royal Observatory and the Cutty Sark, on October 10, 2001. I was taking some of Audrey's etchings to the Greenwich Printmakers shop in the market to allow another member, Theresa Pateman, to colour them to sell for prospective buyers.

Greenwich is blighted by having a polluted one-way system around the centuries old market, and it is almost impossible to park. The Burney car park was full, and I saw a gap outside the Health Centre which was marked by what I thought was "Disabled". I was late, so backed into it, got out, and headed off on the short walk with the artwork. When I returned later, there was a PCN on my windscreen. I ripped it open and it said: "Your vehicle was parked in a Doctors' Only bay." Drat it!

Next day, I didn't have time to reply. My close friend Bryon Butler's memorial was being held in St Bride's Church – the journalists' church off Fleet Street. And the former England football manager Sir Bobby Robson – a much-loved man – and I were the main speakers. Bryon died after surviving five bouts of cancer, and Bobby did the same before he died in 2009, at the same age of 76.

The church was crammed, the choir was magnificent, and it was a fitting tribute for someone who wrote beautiful prose and spoke in the burr of a man of Somerset. Bryon was a footballing equivalent of cricket's distinctive John Arlott, whose burr came from Hampshire.

When it was Bobby's turn to give the address, he turned to me and said, "What do I say?" I was taken aback. Too late; it was time for him to go up to the pulpit. Without notes, he spoke movingly with humour and great respect for 20 minutes or so.

When it was my turn, I said, "Bryon braved five bouts of cancer before he was bowled out by a fifth, and he was the bravest person I've ever met." He loved cricket and was an off spin bowler when he was available, which was seldom.

Eight days later, I received a brief letter from David McCollum, Greenwich's Director of Strategic Planning, which stated the bare facts without any jargon, and I wrote a letter explaining that my wife had died on the previous Christmas Day at the age of 58 from cancer of the liver. It was my first visit to the Printmakers' shop since she'd died, and that brought tears tumbling down my cheeks.

He wrote back, "However, in view of the circumstances, I am prepared on this occasion to cancel the notice." That was class from a classy Royal Borough where Liz Truss lived.

There are almost as many statues in Greenwich than in Parliament, and the one of General James Wolfe of Quebec dominates the town of 32,000 from a hill close to the Royal Observatory. Two kings, William IV and George II, each have a statue, but there was nothing for Henry VIII, despite being born in the Palace of Placentia in Greenwich. Others are of Admiral Nelson, Emma Hamilton, Captain James Cook, Sir Walter Raleigh, and Yuri Gagarin. So far none have been toppled, although Sir Walter was a well-known slave owner.

I hadn't been hit by a PCN for almost two years – chiefly because my travelling had diminished, for which councils' parking departments would doubtless be relieved. But I continue to be active to support keen, mentally alert oldies who still drive and keep to the speed limits. As for diversity and equality, I am renewing my campaign about Learie Constantine. He should have a statue erected in Parliament Square, because no-one did more for diversity in Britain – BAME (Black, Asian, and Minority Ethnic), as it is now known – than him.

Too many young people fail to read enough history to help mould their attitude to life. Recently I was speaking to a PRO employed by a county cricket club, and he said, "I've never heard of Learie." Worse happened some years ago, when I addressed 80 media students at Portsmouth University and asked them, "How many of you have heard of Hermann Goering?" Two put their hands up, and one thought he was a Bundesliga football manager.

Instead of pulling down statues, the activists should organise a fund to cover the cost of the fourth black statue in Parliament Square for Learie – £150,000 – along with the ones of Mahatma Gandhi, Nelson Mandela, and the black suffragette Millicent Fawcett, and it should be placed near Churchill's. However, there are 77 of Queen Victoria, all untouched! In Belgium, there were 60 of King Leopold II, but one has been beheaded in Gent. His great, great grandson King Philippe apologised for the wrongs of his ancestor in the Congo in the 1860s, and doubtless others will follow.

Churchill's statue has been defaced several times and, on occasions, boarded up. It was unveiled by his wife Clementine in 1973 and was one of 12 statues in Parliament Square, mainly of British Prime Ministers. Abraham Lincoln's statue was daubed there in 2020. There is also one of Field Marshal Jan Smuts, the white South African Prime Minister between 1919-1924 and 1939-48, who supported segregation but later changed his mind. He was the only person who signed the two peace agreements for the First and Second Wars.

Despite having the support of former Prime Minister Theresa May, Lord Norman Fowler, the Speaker of the House of Lords, and Sadiq Khan, the Mayor of London, my efforts for funding a Learie statue were drowned by a flood of intelligible jargon from a succession of civil servants. However, I discovered that a bust of Learie was stored in the National Gallery.

Baroness Maddock, the Chairperson of the House of Lords Work and Art Committee, applied to borrow it, and it was unveiled at the Queen's Robing Room in the House of Lords on May 1, 2019, by Baroness Floella Benjamin – a Trinidadian who lived in Beckenham, near us. When she first arrived from Trinidad, she was greeted by a number of a jeering white neighbours, and police were called. There were no arrests. She is now chairperson of the £1m Windrush Museum project, which will probably contain some of Learie's memorabilia. The National Museum of Port of Spain has just over 19,000 items in his name.

Thirteen months later, Baroness Maddock, the highly regarded Liberal peer, died at the age of 75. She was said to be kind and patient, with a touch of the Jamie Lee Curtis about her. In the by-election at Christchurch in 1993, she turned a Conservative majority of 23,015 to a Liberal majority of 16,427 from a field of 14 candidates. One put up for the Sack Graham Taylor Party, who attracted very few votes. I knew him well; he was a God-like figure around Watford.

With public opinion rapidly growing towards diversity and equality, it is now time to put up a statue to give a heartening message to the next generation and telling Learie's story as one of our nation's real genuine heroes. It began when his grandfather Lebrun was one of the last slaves to be transported to the Caribbean. When he landed in Venezuela, he wanted to go to Trinidad. He found a canoe and, with a young lady, set out to row the seven miles to Port of Spain. A mile short, the canoe sank, and they had to swim the rest of the journey – exhausted but triumphant.

SHANE WARNE'S STATUE

Australians honour their sporting heroes, sticking up 70-plus statues – mainly cricketers – long before they die. But the lovable larrikin Warney departed shockingly early at the age of 52 in March 2022, after a suspected heart attack. His life-size statue, made in bronze in 2011, was surrounded by flowers outside the Melbourne CC Ground, and three weeks later 50,000 went to his two-hour memorial service there – a record in the Southern Hemisphere.

A host of Test players, politicians (including the then Premier Scott Morrison, who was booed), singers, actors, personalities, and people who met him, all reminisced about this remarkable man. His father, Frank, and his three grown-up children spoke from the heart. Greta Bradman, granddaughter of Sir Don, started off by singing the National Anthem. An estimated one billion people watched the proceedings around the world.

The Southern Stand, boringly named, was renamed The Shane Warne Stand. It seats 45,000.

I was sitting in the old press box in Old Trafford on June 4, 1993, when he bamboozled Mike Gatting by a fizzing leg break, pitched an almost two feet outside the leg stump, and flicked the off stump. Had Gatting stretched his left leg well forward, he could have used his pad outside of the leg stump and no umpire would have given him out. It was called the greatest wicket of the century, even of all time.

The name of Shane, a rarity, originates from the Irish and means "God is Gracious, Destiny and Luck". He certainly had luck in taking his first ball of an Ashes series.

At the age of 17, he joined a Bristol club called Imperial CC as a batsman who could toss up a few leggers. He was very popular, with a big appetite and liked a pint or two. He occupied a bedsitter upstairs in the pavilion, and the club laid on ample amounts of refreshment and gave him £6 each week providing he rolled the pitches, but he rarely helped out. He was too busy playing for other clubs who were short.

In 1991, he was signed as the 21-year-old overseas player for Accrington, David Lloyd's club, in the Lancashire League. And his figures with both bat and ball were mediocre – hardly a superstar ready to terrorise the world's leading batsmen. But they loved his antics – wine, women, and an odd diet for an athlete. They called him Mr Vegemite who rarely washed up in his chaotic, rented house. They didn't sign him up for a second year.

Back home in Australia, he got down to serious work under Terry Jenner, who played nine Tests and became a renowned coach. He was also an inveterate gambler and was convicted for six years for stealing, with his sentence commuted to 18 months. He taught Warne to trick batsmen into being dismissed by all sorts of deliveries, mainly imaginary. And his mastery of leg spin and conmanship helped Warne to pass 700 wickets – second behind the equally tricky Sri Lankan Muttiah Muralitharan.

In the World Cup in England in 1999, people were writing Warne off, and most of the critics wrote that it was the end of his career. However, a good contact told me that Warne was angling for a new contract and definitely wouldn't retire. My story was splashed in the *Mail* after he took 4-33 and was voted The Player of the Final. He was exhilarated when I shook his hand after the interviews.

Later it came out that some of the Pakistan squad had enjoyed a late night, accounting for their slapdash 132 in 39 overs, with the top score of 25 from extras. Australia won by eight wickets in 20 overs – an embarrassing rout.

Last time I saw Shane at Lords he had retired and was concentrating on his TV and radio commentaries, as well as advertising, especially his transplant hair business, from which he made a pile. I shook his hand firmly and he yelled, saying, "It's bruised!"

When he died on his bed in the afternoon in an expensive villa in Thailand, one friend in their group tried to revive him but failed. The verdict was natural causes from a heart attack. But it was odd, according to the *Sunday Times*, that two female masseuses and a pedicurist had visited his room. The police were satisfied there weren't any drugs and "special" massages.

The weakest handshake I experienced was one from Gordon Brown, who succeeded Tony Blair as Prime Minister. As he supported Raith Rovers, it was an unusual place to meet in the boardroom at Wimbledon FC. Former chairman Sam Hamman had invited us.

FREED AT LAST!

My hundredth day hibernation in the second quarter of 2020 fell on June 23, and Boris heralded it with rousing Churchillian phrases in Parliament. The date coincided with Audrey's birthday; she would have been 78.

My three-year-old Honda HR-V saloon was creaking through lack of exercise, so I booked a 10,000-mile service in the Honda service centre in Orpington on that day. Going up a hill, I noticed two vehicles with PCNs displayed. If I'd stopped and knocked on the door of the owners, I could have volunteered to organise an appeal for them.

Instead, I was too busy later in the day writing to Oliver Dowden, the former Culture, Media, and Sports Minister, asking him to support my campaign for a Learie statue. While in my 40 years working for the *Daily Mail*, I interviewed nearly all the 14 sports ministers, and in my letter I said the best one was the former referee Denis Howell (1923-1998), a Labour MP for two Birmingham constituencies, famous for ending the drought in the summer of 1976. His appointment coincided with heavy rain, and he was renamed Minister of Drought. He did a lot for charity and was actually at a charitable function when he died from a heart attack. He was looked on as a hero to Brummies, understandably.

Oliver sent one of those automatic replies, and I never heard from him.

THE CASE OF DRIVERS
HAD BEEN NICKED BY CRANES

The funniest parking story of the year, or maybe ever, in Great Britain, took place in late November 2021 when the 47,501 inhabitants of the austere Berkshire town of Wokingham learned that cars had been taken illegally by cranes overnight. Poppie Platt started her article in the *Daily Telegraph*: "Drivers were given parking tickets after council workers lifted their cars with cranes to paint double yellow lines underneath.

"Volker Highways, a contractor, carried out the work at night, and drivers whose cars were parked along the lines were issued with tickets the following day. (Up to then, the road wasn't restricted.)

"A Labour councillor, Shirley Boyd, said, 'I think residents were incredulous. Some were laughing because it was bizarre. They couldn't believe it. When I discovered, I was furious because we'd been treated appallingly."

The PENS of £70 were withdrawn.

MY FINAL PCN KNOCKED OUT

My daughter Louise was driving my old Honda Accord GF56VWY on December 29, 2021, through prestigious Dulwich Village before my grandson Sebastian and I had blood tests and checks in Kings College Hospital. The average price of houses in the Village was topping £1,650,000, and one of our best friends, Barbara Owen-Browne, lived there in Aysgarth Road before she died from cancer.

I had given Louise the vehicle some years before, but it was still registered in my name for economic reasons. We were alleged to have been going northward, past Pickwick Road on the left. Our longstanding friends Professor John Shepherd and his wife Alison, of Barts Hospital, lived nearby in centuries old Pickwick Cottage before they moved to a centuries old mansion owned by one of Nelson's admirals in Cowes, Isle of Wight.

The two lengthy, error-filled letters from London Tribunals Environment and Traffic Adjudicators and Southwark Council arrived, and one had a cardinal mistake – namely using Souzer as my second Christian name, not Souter.

I once interviewed Brian Souter, the owner of buses and transport who was one of the richest men in Britain. There's a revealing story about Souter, a sept of the Scottish McDonald clan. I was originally christened Brian David Scovell, and my grandfather Andrew Souter was a cabinet maker who helped build ships in Halifax, Nova Scotia, in WW1, where my mother Maude (who hated the name and preferred Kitty or Poppy) was educated. Andrew was like a volcano – ready to explode any moment. His beautiful wife couldn't handle the rows, and walked out and never saw her daughter again. My mother contracted polio at the age of four when this happened, leaving her with a permanent limp, and she was the most stoic person I ever encountered. She had strong principles and passed them to us.

Andrew's brother, a bachelor, had been provost of the fishing town of Lossiemouth, Morayshire, where former Prime Minster Ramsay MacDonald (first Labour Premier 1866-1937) was born out of wedlock, and was a close friend. They played golf together on the windswept course... very poorly.

Andrew's brother owned a smart gentlemen's shop, and he also owned several seine net fishing boats. When he died in 1947, the bulk of his fortune went to Andrew. My grandfather hated going out in a fishing boat, because two Andrews in their family had been swept off boats in gales and drowned in the previous century. He didn't want to make it a hat trick.

Our family was still living in Ventnor, Isle of Wight – roughly the most southern part of the country – and Andrew and his solicitor pleaded with us to move to Lossiemouth, 640 miles away, to care for the provost in his final days and clear up his affairs afterwards. They offered to pay all expenses and give a lump sum of £6,000 to my mother to buy a house nearer the sea.

Ventnor was named after the vents, and our second house situated in the danger area had walls and floors cracking up, so our mother saw a chance to move to a safer part of lower Ventnor. We moved house just in time, as it was demolished shortly afterwards.

We packed our essentials and went off on the Flying Scotsman to Aberdeen then on to windy, gaunt Lossiemouth, population 7,450. It has for many years been the home of the RAF, with hardly a single fishing boat remaining. The deafening noise of jet planes needed earplugs.

In 2004, I went back to Lossiemouth and saw the tiny cottage where MacDonald was born and lived with his typical Scots hard-driven mother – the father disappeared. A small plaque signified that he had been the first Labour Premier, but there was no statue or bust. He was the first Premier to fly to a

Cabinet meeting from Lossiemouth to Hendon, and in a taxi to Westminster. He died aged 71, in 1937.

Late in December 1947, a Big Freeze set in for several weeks. The harbour froze over, denying the fishermen and their families of "fries" -- the word in that part of the country to pick up a dozen or so fish, tie them together with string threaded through their jaws, and take them home. We qualified for "fries", as Andrew inherited three vessels. Often, we couldn't get out from our flat, and I was unable to attend Elgin Academy six miles away for much of the time. Pipes were frozen and roads were treacherous. It was an experience not to miss.

Andrew told my brother Allan Bertram and me that he would give us £500 each on condition that we change our second Christian name to Souter. I did, but Allan stuck to Bertram and kept the money. I put the money in my bank for ten years, and when I learned to drive I used it to buy a good condition Morris Minor, which served me well for a few years.

Bertolt Brecht, the German (1898-1956), was one of the outstanding writers of the era when MacDonald was preparing to be on a comeback in 10 Downing Street. Brecht was an orderly in WW1, and the horror he experienced influenced his writings, particularly *Life of Galileo* in 1947. That could be used today.

Heroes like Alexander the Great, Queen Boadicea, William Shakespeare, Napoleon Bonaparte, the Duke of Wellington, Horatio Nelson, George Washington, Abraham Lincoln, Simon Bolivar, Mother Teresa, Florence Nightingale, Otto von Bismarck, Mahatma Gandhi, Nelson Mandela, Sir Jack Hobbs, W.G. Grace, Charles Dickens, and Queen Elizabeth II, have inspired the young through the ages. Some were at fault by modern standards, but they nonetheless need to be remembered.

In the 1930s, the *Daily Herald* offered people a free set of the works of Dickens, and my mother changed from the *Daily Express* to the *Herald*, and I still have them. There are countless reminders about Dickens around the world. He was born in Portsea Island in Portsmouth in 1812, and moved to London, then to Sheerness, Chatham, Camden Town, Southwark, Charing Cross, Covent Garden, Broadstairs, Boston, New York, Washington, Switzerland, then Paris, and he died in Higham, Kent, in 1870. He was interred in the Poets' Corner in Westminster Abbey. Five years previously, he was in the only first-class carriage where no-one died when a train crashed in Staplehurst. Many lives were lost.

In the 1830s, he spent several months working on one of his most successful books, *David Copperfield*, and with literary friends in Bonchurch he would climb the 800ft St. Boniface Down in Ventnor. When I was a Boy Scout, as a patrol leader, we would do the Dickens' climb. For Dickens to do it regularly, plus having several mistresses with eight children, perhaps that might have been the reason he died prematurely from a stroke, aged 58, in 1870.

I've been to Dickens House, now a museum in Broadstairs. And in June 2020, a former Green Party councillor, Ian Driver, was charged for scrawling "Dickens Racist" on the Victorian cottage. He said Dickens had insulted Jews, and in particular pointed to that devious character Fagin. He is now branded as a racist by a minority.

BE MERCIFUL, YOU BAMEISTAS!

On March 16, 2022, a letter arrived from Michael Burke, an Adjudicator, delivering the verdict for my 20/12/2021 Dulwich case: guilty. He ignored nearly all the points I had made in my weighty defence. I had to pay up – £130: a pound for each foot Louise went in a bus lane before she was allowed to go into the crowded lane on the right.

Mr Burke ruled that I was guilty on another PCN case outside of my house in March 2006, but after 284 days I had reversed it on that occasions with a lot of sweat and toil. In my weakened state in March, however, I couldn't repeat it, so I grumpily paid up with a plea asking them to reconsider.

A month later, Kirsty Moore at Southwark Parking Services sent a curt letter, saying, "Thank you for correspondence received in connection with the PCN JKO5763754. We can confirm that your case is paid and closed, therefore no further correspondence is required."

A FOOTBALLING HERO FROM GUERNSEY, A SMALL ISLAND WITH A POPULATION OF 63,000, COMPARED TO THE ISLE OF WIGHT'S 142,000 WHICH HASN'T PRODUCED AN ENGLAND INTERNATIONAL

One of my footballing heroes was Matthew Le Tissier who played all of his 17-year career with Southampton FC. He was the first Sky football analyst to object about the alarming aims of the BAME who suddenly dominated British sport. He said, "I support BAME, but don't believe in defunding the police and destroying capitalism." He was sacked by Sky soon afterwards.

He was born in St Peter Port in Guernsey, and hardly any player in the history of the game has matched his success rate in penalty taking – 48 out of 49. His tally of 164 goals from 461 first team matches as a midfield winger is almost unequalled. He looked lumbering on the field, but his fast thinking and great skill with the ball made up for that. He only played in eight internationals until the then England manager Glenn Hoddle, who was similar in style but more of an athlete, left him out. Matt played with a smile and brought his humour to Sky programmes.

In Easter 2022, he had to resign as one of the club's ambassadors, after being caught out on Twitter. He made the mistake of questioning reports that Ukrainian people had been wantonly shot dead and thrown into trenches by Russians soldiers. Was it a life ban? The directors should give a time limit.

As a boy listening to commentaries of Test matches and football internationals while lying in hospitals, Denis Compton was my cricket hero and Stanley Matthews my first footballing hero. In later life, I met both of them on numerous occasions. Once I interviewed Stan in a hotel in Edinburgh, on his 67th birthday – he was still playing charity matches – and asked him what he wanted to drink. He said, "I only drink water." He was a lovely man.

Another footballing hero of mine was the left winger born in Cardiff, now aged 44, named Gareth Bale. He is quicker than Le Tissier, and his hair is drawn back to a bun at the rear of his head. The bun habit is growing, and the brutal Spanish Atletico Madrid player Felipe, who crashed into the back of the head of Manchester City's Phil Foden and left him bandaged, wore a bun in a European Cup tie. He was sent off for another foul on Foden near the end. Realising that he had ended up off the pitch, Foden rolled over and over to stop the game by getting back on the pitch. That incensed the Spanish players, and it led to a fracas. To stop these rollers, referees should book them for ungentlemanly conduct. Diego Simone, the frenzied coach, was also booked.

Real Madrid paid £86m for Bale and he hardly played for them after he fell out with the coach, but his statistics of 106 goals and 67 assists in 256 appearances was most impressive. His annual salary was astronomical, engineered by Jonathan Barnett – the 72-year-old super agent boss of ICM The Stellar Sports. I first met him early in 1995 when the *Daily Mail* wanted to sign Brian Lara, after he broke the Test batting record of Sir Gary Sobers of 365 by ten runs.

Lara preferred a younger ghost writer. But when I told my agent Jane Bradish-Ellames that I had written the books of Sobers and Sir Clyde Walcott, President of ICC, she told Lara, and he soon changed his mind: I was the man. It was the most exciting summer of my life, catching up with the engaging but elusive superstar.

In his final seasons with Real Madrid, Bale improved his handicap, playing golf more than appearing in the Santiago Bernabeu Stadium with its capacity of 81,044. But he was intent on playing for Wales to qualify for the 2022 World Cup. Against a dedicated Austrian side in a qualifying tie, he won the game single-handedly with two stunning, long-range shots. Messi, Suarez, di Stefano, and Gento wouldn't have done that.

When Gareth won the Football Writers' Association Footballer of the Year trophy in 2012-3 – I've attended nearly all the awards since 1960 – I was in the VIP room when I noticed a middle-aged couple standing self-consciously. I asked them, "Are you with a club?" The wife, Debbie, said, "We are the parents of the winner – Gareth." Clang! They were delightful, and when Gareth came in, his father Frank introduced me to him. I told them an amusing story about David Beckham when he was the winner. He had come in and started shaking hands with almost everyone, including me. An hour later, he was still shaking hands. He approached me and said, "I'm David Beckham." I said, "I know. You told me. Have you got dementia?"

A two-part documentary on the errant Paul Gascoigne was shown on BBC2 recently, but with him not fully co-operating, it was a mess and relied too much on the *Sun* former editor Neil Wallis. I first met Gazza at a drinks party in Sardinia at the start of the 1990 World Cup, and the purpose was to encourage the journalists to be more responsible and not file inaccurate stories. Rupert Murdoch's *Sun* and Robert Maxwell's *Mirror* were in a bruising circulation battle, and the sports editors ignored the FA's appeal. Bobby Robson battled on and showed how he was a wonderful sportsman, treating the *Sun*'s football writer and the *Mirror*'s to a lunch after the tournament ended.

I introduced myself to Gazza and I said, "With your talent, you could go into telly after you retire and make a fortune. Look over there – copy Gary Lineker."

He said, "I certainly will." But he did the opposite. I covered the start of his short spell in Lazio, and the players joked about him and the exasperated coach Nereo Rocco, which probably helped to drive him to an early death at the age of 66.

With my last lap hovering in the distance, my final ambition is to honour my friend Learie with a worthy statue with these words "Lord Learie Nicholas Constantine of Maraval in Trinidad and Tobago and the Palantine of Nelson in Lancashire (1901-1971): Dynamic Cricketer, Barrister who broke the colour bar in Britain in 1944, the first Afro-Caribbean Lord in the House of Lords in 1969, and no-one did more to bring about diversity than this much loved man."

BORIS STUMPED ON
RECREATIONAL CRICKET

B oris Johnson who plays tennis – badly – doesn't really
know how to pick up a cricket bat properly. That probably
was the reason towards the end of the first Covid-19 lockdown
when he used the word "vector" to say recreational cricket
had to be banned. I thought the word might be derived from
Ventnor, where I grew up, but the meaning is "carrier of
disease or infection". He had the impression that the virus
would attach itself to the cricket ball, and the players risked
being rushed off to hospital. Only a Boris would use a word
like vectoring! Now the MCC, who are responsible for the
laws, have banned spitting on the ball.

Another cricketing friend is Dilip Jajodia, whose company
makes the Dukes ball. Boris described it "inexplicable" and
explained how the ball was treated with a substance that
protects it. In his column in the *Daily Telegraph*, Michael
Vaughan, the former England captain, led the campaign calling
for the Government's ban to be rescinded, and was supported
by the then captain Joe Root and acting captain Ben Stokes.
Later, Vaughan was banned by the BBC and Sky for talking
about a group of Pakistani cricketers as "you lot". What a
farce! He went on a diversity course and was later reinstated.

Boris was interviewed by Nick Ferrari on LBC and stuck to
his story about the threat of vectoring, but in his 5pm press
conference at 10 Downing Street, he was asked about amateur
cricket. "Well, I was stumped this morning, but after talking
to our science experts, we've now changed our view." Boris c
Vallance b Whitty 0.

In his book, *Life in the Fast Lane – The Johnson Guide To
Cars*, published in 2007, Boris confessed that while studying

at Oxford he let parking tickets pile up on the windscreen of his old Fiat 128. He boasted, "I parked all over the place, my favourite spot was the yellow lines in Jowett Walk. Sometimes, it is true that I got a ticket, but what did I care? I had Belgian number plates. I let them pile in drifts against the windscreen until – in the days before they were sheathed in plastic – the fines (PCNs) disintegrated in the rain."

Did he apologise to Oxford City Council, and what did the dreaded triumphant trio of Rachel Reeve, Sir Kieron Starmer, and Angela Rayner say?

ANOTHER PRIME MINISTER
IS BOOTED OUT

He was one of the world's all-time all-rounders – Imran Khan, who I interviewed him occasionally when he played for Worcestershire in 1973-6, Sussex in 1983-1988, and as an inspiring captain of Pakistan.

His father must have been a rich man to send an 18-year-old to Oxford University to graduate, and Imran spoke in a posh manner and was a good-looking young man who attracted young ladies. When he joined Sussex, his flat off Kings Road was visited by a large number of rich, beautiful women, including the heiress Jemima Goldsmith, who was one of his three wives. An anti-Imran demonstration took place outside her house, and police broke it up.

With strong opposition in the Sussex ranks, he speeded up, his action improved, and he matured into one of the fastest bowlers in the world. His rousing speech in the 1992 World Cup in Australia – "You have to play like cornered tigers!" – inspired his Pakistan team to win their first World Final. His mother, Shaukat Khanum, died in 1985 from cancer, aged 63, and he launched an appeal to build a cancer hospital in her name with his World Cup winnings donated to the fund. It was duly built, and it was the first free hospital in Pakistan.

Realising that many of the political leaders were corrupt, he joined the PTI party and soon played key roles, setting out his desire to do away with corruption and help the poor. With his charisma, he was elected the 22nd Prime Minister in 2018. None of them has lasted the five-year term. Nawaz Sharif, who had three spells, was sentenced for ten years for corruption and now lives in London.

With the economy going haywire, Imran blamed the USA for interfering in his country's affairs. He supported the Taliban takeover in Afghanistan and made a cardinal mistake by visiting Vladimir Putin to agree trade arrangements at the same time as Russia invaded Ukraine. The rival party, the Pakistan Muslim League, called a motion to remove him, and they secured enough votes to get rid of him. They replaced him with the younger brother of Nawaz, Shehbaz Sharif, who is 70 and also faced charges for corruption.

The military is all-powerful in the fifth biggest country of the world, which has a population of 220m and has nuclear missiles. About 28 years ago, I sat next to a cricket lover General Pervez Musharraf at an ICC lunch in London. A very impressive man, in 1999 he took over as President of Pakistan to restore order. He insisted that fiddling was out, but in 2008 he was deposed in a coup.

Following his removal, Imran – now approaching 70 – called for protests demonstrations in the streets, but he hasn't been reinstated. Huge crowds blocked the cities and towns for his return, with social media joining in with support. They campaigned for the removal of General Qamar Javed Bajwa, the head of the Army, who denied that the military ordered Imran's sacking.

WHEN THE RIGHT TIME TO RETIRE

In my case, as a cricketer 50 years ago – and on my 50th birthday, as a footballer. One of the greatest English women pace bowlers, Anya Shrubsole, gave up international cricket when she was 30 – a perfect time. In the ICC Women's Trophy in New Zealand in 2022, she was puffing in her second spell in the final against the best side, Australia. She said, "At the top level you have to be 100%, and I just felt I didn't have in it me any more."

After she took 6-46 to win the 2017 Final, watched by one billion around the world, I met her at the Cowdrey Lecture at Lords. Nicknamed "Hoof", she has proved to be a wonderful ambassador for the game. Born in Bath, her father was a keen cricketer, and she made her debut for Somerset at the age of 12.

Joe Root has the record of 64 Tests from 2017 to 2022 and 10th of the England captains with 42.2 in the percentage best wins, ahead of Alastair Cook, Ray Illingworth who died in 2021, and Nasser Hussain who was bottom with 37.8. However, Nasser is one of the best all round cricket commentators.

Too many captains are selected as the best player of the team, and the popular Joe was chosen for that, but he wasn't tactically aware and took too much notice of the coaches. He was too nice. Top of the percentage wins were WG Grace and Douglas Jardine, both with over 60%.

After winning only one Test in the last 17, Joe should have quit, because the criticism affected his family. He made the mistake of following the party line, excusing the 1-0 defeat by a mediocre West Indies side. Ben Stokes took over, but he has a history of a damaged left knee and a seriously broken finger.

HENRY KISSINGER IS STILL WORKING AT 98!

In the World Cup in Spain in 1982, a small group of my journalist colleagues and I had reported on a game in Madrid then went out to relax in a nightclub. A bespectacled, tubby man in his late fifties approached with his glamorous wife, and said, "Did you enjoy the game?"

He introduced himself and his wife Nancy, who was wearing a brace on her teeth. "I'm very keen on soccer. I was President in the US League and played when I was in my teens," he said.

We spent a couple of pleasant hours with the former US Secretary of State. He was renowned as a negotiator for peace around the hotspots of the world, including Vietnam, when he was awarded a Nobel Prize. He handed it back because a majority of Americans opposed the war, and 58,220 US servicemen lost their lives. Richard Nixon was President, and he sanctioned the US involvement and also the withdrawal, before the Watergate investigations forced him to resign.

Henry was born in Germany, and his Jewish family migrated in 1938 to New York. He told us, "I played with a club in Germany for a while, and my love for the game remains." He appeared to be very informed about current players and trends, and if he were here now, he would be the right man to find a solution to stop the moneyed clubs from forming a European League. He is now busy writing books.

PCNs SET A RECORD IN DORSET

The sprawling genteel town of Bournemouth, which includes Christchurch, was the first in the country to use CCTV cameras in 1985. And on June 25th, 2020 they needed every camera working at full pelt. Lockdown had just been marginally lifted, and the population of 465,000 suddenly found themselves outnumbered by half a million intruders. The ten large car parks soon filled up with people ignoring the Government advice about social distancing, and parked all over the place without thinking they would be booked. They were mistaken.

Surprisingly, only 558 were issued PCNs, but that's a record in the town. If they all paid up, the income would have been a substantial amount, though not enough to pay the bill for picking up the massive amount of litter, including steel small phials containing laughing gas which couldn't be recycled. Dorset Constabulary – one of the smallest in England – was overwhelmed. Even the Hong Kong Chinese special forces wouldn't have coped.

Council leader Vikki Slade said angrily, "We are absolutely appalled at the scenes witnessed on our beaches, particularly at Bournemouth and Sandbanks, in the last 24-48 hours. The irresponsible behaviour and actions of so many people is just shocking, and our services were stretched to the absolute hilt trying to keep everyone safe."

I've visited Sandbanks several times, and normally the owners of the overpriced mansions are fed up to seeing motorists slowing down to gaze at their houses, but on this occasion it must have been execrable and gridlocked. Harry

Redknapp and his delectable wife Sandra lived there. Now they have moved, as Harry is a TV star.

In an earlier public opinion poll, 88.3% of the population of Bournemouth said they were happy and contented living there. But had the poll been conducted on that day, I'm sure the percentage would have been reversed. Tolkien the author, Shelley the poet, and a Hancock – not Matt, but the comedian Tony – all lived in Bournemouth. And Freemen of the town included Winston Churchill, Geoff Hurst, Bob Geldof, and Eddie Howe – the manager of the local football team. When they were relegated, genial Eddie resigned, and he has since uprooted from the peace of Dorset to face the fanatics at St. James Park, Newcastle, where he has won them over.

There are many statues or memorials in Bournemouth and district, and Lord Baden-Powell's is now boarded up after being classed as "vulnerable". We are vulnerable against the threat of the organising activists who want the police defunded, capitalism destroyed, prisons closed down, and all statues dumped and replaced by ones of the like of Lenin, Putin, Marx, Che Guevara, Fidel Castro, and Hugo Chavez, the late President of Venezuela who died from cancer in 2013. Che, the guerrilla leader and revolutionary, was executed by a firing squad, aged 39, in 1967, and Fidel, who was reckoned to survive 600 aborted assassinations, died of natural causes at the age of 90.

When decisions are made for future statues, there will be nothing for the champion parking orderly who invented the Parking Charge Notices!

My final words are about "going on one knee" as a reminder of recognising what we need to do: observe the Golden Rule to "treat others as you want to be treated". I wouldn't be able to do it, because if I tried it I wouldn't be able to get up due to a left knee which has been half replaced by titanium, a stiff right leg, and two right hip replacements in

1997 and 2013. A German security officer with a sense of humour at Nuremburg Airport some years ago said to me, "You British are made of titanium."

BATTLING THROUGH
THE BOLLARDS

As the days slipped by much faster than the gridlocked roads of London in the final week of Codiv-19, I have added a few words of cheer. On August 19, just before the schools opened, I was about to back into a disused "Disabled" space at the Widmore Road M&S garage when a white van darted into it. I had to move forward ready to back closer to the building, as a woman driver in a black limousine nearly collided with my dark blue Honda. I stopped, and the van driver – a greyish haired, middle-aged man – strode up to me, and I expected a volley of abuse. His exact words were, "I'm terribly sorry. I didn't realise you were going into the space, and I apologise."

My next port of call was to leave my tax returns with my accountant, whose office is in Chislehurst High Street. It was raining, and as I approached, I thought it might save my bulky package from getting wet if I parked right outside on a bus stop. Disabled drivers can park on single yellow lines, but we are prosecuted for parking at bus stops. I decided to be cautious and left my car on a yellow line, not on the bus stop.

Suddenly, a white-helmeted, Deliveroo-type motor cyclist dismounted and left his machine right behind my car. On his yellow bib it said, "Civil Enforcement Officer". He glanced at my Blue Badge but didn't speak to me, then he proceeded to cross the road to photograph two 4x4s with the view of issuing PCNs. It was a lucky escape!

There was more good news. When Gill and I parked right outside my son Gavin's new property in Fulham, we learned that the road is one of the quietest in London and without yellow lines.

But the return journey to Chislehurst was horrendous. Fulham to Chislehurst, where Gill lives, is 16.2 miles. We departed at 4pm, hoping to turn off the Fulham Road towards Battersea Bridge; a vain hope. In a stretch of 400 metres, we were becalmed for almost 25 minutes, with lots of impatient drivers trying to force their way onto Fulham Road from side roads. One nosed almost up to my right bumper, daring me to give way, which I prudently did. Had I not done so – with his expensive car used as a battering ram – there might have been a crash, and as an oldie I would have been guilty. There were hundreds of red bollards, leaving only a single, narrow lane, and when we reached an 'S bend' the road opened to two lanes. Several cars turned into the inside lane, and I followed. Too late I realised it was a bus lane.

If charged, I will refuse to pay up! Though I wasn't charged on that occasion.

By dodging down to unexplored side roads, I managed to join the Embankment, going east at a snail's pace, and I had my first experience of Boris's cycle lanes. For several miles from Battersea Bridge up to Lambeth Bridge, there was only one lane for vehicles. The other lane was coloured blue for cyclists. Motor cyclists were using the bus lanes. Are they fined? I doubt it.

Just approaching the Royal Chelsea Hospital for old soldiers, two cars had stopped, and the male driver was taking pictures of his car, indicating the woman driver in the other vehicle had bumped into his. Neither Gill nor I saw any sign of damage, and it reminded me of when a woman in Westerham claimed that I had backed into her car. Her 4x4 had a thin, three-inch long scratch, and I had to pay £330.

The woman in this case was still sitting in her car, and a dog was leaning over her shoulder, ready to bite the other driver. We departed, leaving the two drivers at odds.

The next obstacle was Lambeth Bridge, and it resembled the Tour de France with dozens of cyclists weaving through bumper-to-bumper cars gingerly inching ahead. I managed to avoid any crashes.

Half an hour later, we were slowly heading down the A2 and reached New Cross. I nominate it as the worst snarl-up in London. It gave us the chance to look up to see the four statues at the top of Deptford Town Hall, built in 1905. Some activists slapped red paint on the first one – Sir Francis Drake (1540-1596), who was branded now as a cruel slave owner. The second one was Robert Blake (1598-1657), who was an authentic slave owner. The third one was our greatest maritime hero, Lord Horatio Nelson, who allegedly supported slavery. The fourth statue was an Admiral with no name.

Activists who toppled Edward Colston's statue in Bristol would need an Exocet missile to blow up Nelson's Column, which was built in 1884 at a cost of £47,000. It is 51.6 metres in height, including the 5 metres of the statue of Nelson. Over the years, a number of fearless people have scaled it but hardly any defaced it. Evidence has now emerged that a letter Nelson wrote, agreeing with slavery, has proved to be a forgery, and only 1% of the today's population would want to blow it up.

Our hazardous journey took three hours and 35 minutes at an average speed of 4mph. The worst place for gridlocks in the 92 countries I've visited is Bangkok in Thailand, where we managed to get round a roundabout once in 15 minutes.

Is there a solution to overcrowding in Britain? Too many people, too many elongated lorries, vans carrying ready-to-eat-in meals, too many cycles, too many red cones, and too many statues which are defaced and defrocked? But we don't want too many statues being toppled, though some military leaders that no-one has heard of need to be pruned. We have an excess of diesel cars, and particularly those hotted-up electrified scooters, which now cost from £149 up to £799. I, and some others, walk on pavements, and we stop when scooter owners whizz past without warning. They remind me of "Whispering Death", the nickname of the great West Indian

Michael Holding, who has now retired as a cricket commentator.

Fortunately, the Minister of Transport Grant Shapps intervened as the autumn lockdown began in October. Earlier in the year he had sanctioned the first payment of £250m of a £1billion investment to allow councils to close down roads, widen pavements, and introduce more cycle lanes. Most of the councils overacted, and the Minister warned them they would have their quotas cut unless they showed common sense, talk to residents, and adopted practical solutions to avoid unnecessary traffic hold-ups.

The Police and the Ambulances Service raised objections about excessive delays in dealing with life and death issues. So far, I have been rushed to hospitals on 13 occasions – with my accident caused by septic arthritis in 1943 (Ryde Hospital); twice with heart attacks – Bromley Hospital (now defunct), St John and St Elizabeth and Wellington in St John's Wood, Orpington; and five with collapses – Kingston, Princess Royal, Royal Free (Camden), Lewisham, and St. Thomas'. Another was in Cape Town, and I've had five falls with head injuries, and been taken to our local Princess Royal University – Pru for short.

Once the winter gales swept in, lots of cyclists reverted to public transport or driving cars. The answer was to work from home until Covid is killed off. And now councils were changing their minds about bicycle lanes. Some were ripping them up.

I SIT IN THE RECLUSIVE, SANCTIONED ROMAN'S CROCODILE SEAT

When Putin ordered 160,000 soldiers to invade Ukraine, I recalled that some years ago I had sat in Roman Abramovich's seat, made in crocodile skin, in his private box at Stamford Bridge. He wasn't there at the time, but a member of staff showed me around. He said it cost £30,000 to see a match in Roman's elegant seat, as the man himself rarely visited London.

His influential director of Chelsea, 47-year-old Marina Granovskaia, whose parents were Russian and Canadian, worked for him since 1997 and supervised the transfer of the club to another company.

NICKED IN A YELLOW BOX

As I was about to finish my manuscript to send it to 40 publishers, a letter dropped on my doormat. On the back it said "Wandsworth Borough Council", so I knew what it was: a Penalty Charge Notice. One of Wandsworth's most profitable money earners is the yellow box, and on August 9, 2020, I strayed a yard or two in one of their hideous, huge yellow boxes at the junction of Putney High Street, SW15. Nicked without a single excuse!

I wrote a cheque out for £65 and posted it with a second-class stamp.

This was my third PCN for being caught by the yellow peril. I was delighted to contribute to the cause – paying for repairing potholes and for putting up notices in Wandsworth's parks saying, "This is not a bin, take your litter with you."

GOVERNMENT LAUNCHES
A PARKING COWBOY BLITZ

On the last day of Rishi Sunak's restaurant discount on August 31, the Government came out with stringent new laws curbing the activities of the rogue private firms who specialise in handing motorists rip-off parking tickets. Communities Minister Robert Jenrick, the 39-year-old MP for Newark, said, "These new measures are a victory for millions of motorists. They will stop these rogue parking firms using aggressive tactics and giving out unfair parking tickets with no right of appeal, while boosting our high streets by making it easier for people to park near their local shops. Our proposals will restore common sense to the way parking fines are issued, by cracking down on the worst offenders who put other people in danger and hinder our emergency services from carrying out their duties.

"At last, common sense will prevail, and I hope these laws apply to local councils who run their parking policies. Hospital car parks should be free, and relatives should produce a letter to prove that patients are being seen by relatives. That would stop people parking randomly."

Fines are being raised to stop people parking on pavements, and the penalty is a mere £70. However, many roads are so narrow that parking on half a pavement is now permissible. News came from the Ministry of Transport that they were planning to make a concession about bus lanes. A first offence would be excused, but a second was mandatory. One small step for mankind!

Before the semi-lockdown in October, I was astonished to see my car being the only vehicle parked in the Beckenham Spa when I went for my 2pm appointment for exercising my legs, arms, and back. The other nine spaces for the disabled were empty, and also the pay spaces were unfilled.

Suddenly an expensive black 4x4 sped in and parked next to me, in a space marked "Motor Cyclists". The driver was a tall, blonde woman, and as I got out, I looked at the windscreen of the vehicle, but there was no Blue Badge displayed. Having been fined for parking in the "Motor Cyclists" in the past, I was about to warn her that she might be prosecuted.

There was a delay at the counter, and I waited to see the outcome. (Yes, they don't take cash now. Luckily, I had my debit card with me.) As I walked off to the pool, I heard the lady – early thirties, I guessed – tell the attendant, "I'm on Universal Credit!"

Made me wonder how many people cheat.

A DRUNK IS NICKED!

At around 3am on Monday, September 27, a car driven by an intoxicated driver crashed into a tree on the wrong side of our road, Widmore Road, 30 metres from the white wall in front of our art deco house. He was arrested, and several police vehicles arrived to remove the damaged vehicle. Some years ago a similar thing occurred, when several people were injured on the other side of the road. And in WW2, a stray bomb destroyed two houses nearby and they had to be rebuilt.

However, our beautifully constructed house escaped damage. Not a green tile roof was displaced nor a wall. It won a national design award in 1933, was copied at the Ideal Home Exhibition, and was given a Grade II rating. The architect was Lt Col Albert Leigh Abbott, MC, TD, FRIBA (1890-1952), who was an Ulsterman born in Hendon. In the First World War, he was awarded the Military Cross as a Major, for valour.

Our house was built in partnership with Lovell and Tanner, but the company was dissolved, and a new one took over in partnership with Beswick and Shires. That was dissolved in 1952, shortly before Abbott died. He was living at 15 College Road, West Dulwich, when his car caught fire in his garage, and he burned to death. A coroner delivered an open verdict.

His finest design was the Ulster Memorial at Thiepval in North France in 1921. The 36th Ulster Division lost more than 5,000 Orangemen, and five were awarded VCs. Other designs were the German Embassy in London, the Australian Pavilion Empire Exhibition in Glasgow in 1938, and more than 1,000 houses.

We are now trying to classify our property as a Grade I to qualify for a Blue Plaque to commemorate Lt-Col Abbott as the designer.

WHAT CAN WE DO ABOUT
MENTAL HEALTH?

Prince William is campaigning for this to be taken up, as though half the country is suffering from it. Yes, there are many people who are worried about their future and are on depression medication, but is the state of Great Britain in 2020-2022 more debilitating than in 1940 when hundreds of thousands of bombs dropped from Luftwaffe bombers, killing many more than the current death rate from Codiv-19? If Hermann Goering had put out of action all the 14 radar stations along the South Coast, the Battle of Britain might well have been won by Germany's Nazis. Fortunately, he failed.

As someone who experienced both WW2 and Codiv-19, I was invited by the Football Writers' Association and the FA to speak at a conference, via Zoom, late in the summer of 2020. Carrie Brown, the FWA chair, conducted the discussion admirably and an hour whizzed past, so it was too late for me to deliver my little speech. The event concentrated on the stories of young journalists and footballers, who spoke at length about their problems. There was not much forthcoming about the solutions to overcome them. A brisk walk around the block is more beneficial than taking tablets, most doctors tell us!

In 1940, we weren't eating blueberries flown in from Peru, or avocados from Kenya and French beans from Morocco. We grew our own vegetables and fruit in allotments, or in gardens, for those who were lucky enough to have them. British Airways now say that Britain's biggest "port" is Heathrow. Eighty years ago the busiest ports were London, Liverpool, Cardiff, Bristol, Southampton, Hull, and Belfast, and all were heavily bombed.

The community spirit, which dominated our lives during the war has slowly returned. In those days, the ones suffering were helped by others. Bikes predominated; few could afford cars. Humour eased the strain of wondering when the sirens were about to blare out warnings that the Luftwaffe were on their way. Hundreds of thousands of small children were evacuated to towns and villages out of range of the German bombers, and lived with strangers for years.

My mum was my number one hero, and she had a tough life. She was born in 1908, and her mother – a beauty descended from the Spanish – abandoned her as a young child, and my mum never saw her again. That meant she had to be brought up by aunts in Lossiemouth. She contracted polio at that time, and she was lucky to survive. For the rest of her life she had a pronounced limp, but she carried on without complaint.

Her father Andrew's nickname was "Gee Whizz", and he was descended from two generations of the same name – Andrew Souter – who had drowned. My mum went to a school in Amhurst, Nova Scotia, and had good grades in the high school, but when they returned to Lossiemouth she left school at 14 and worked as a junior cook in a mansion owned by Ramsay MacDonald. Ramsay's parents, John, a farm labourer, and Anne, a housemaid, never married, and he was classed as illegitimate.

In 1924, MacDonald formed a National Government as prime minister for nine months. In the Depression he took over as premier in 1929-31, before he was voted out. His story from poverty to riches, through hard work and persistence, hasn't really been matched in British political history. It was a good lesson for my mum to adopt, and she had the same attributes.

When MacDonald accepted an invitation from a millionaire to stay at his opulent mansion in the Undercliff in the Isle of Wight, he took my mum with him in his party. That led to her meeting my dad, Percy Henry John Scovell – formerly a farm labourer, who became a carpenter – living in nearby Niton.

After a whirlwind courtship, they married, and their first of many houses was the historic Toll House in St. Lawrence, built in the early 1800s. When Percy finished a job, he was sacked but didn't lounge around waiting to be hired by another builder. He did odd gardening. There was no proper dole at that time.

When the war started, my mum took a menial job as a waitress in The Black Cat in Ventnor's High Street. She was too intelligent for that, but she had no alternative. When Percy found another lengthy job, working on the radar station at St. Boniface Down, she ceased being a waitress. Eighteen months later, another part of the High Street – 50 metres away – was bombed, and seven people were killed. The area now is a car park, with a memorial mentioning the incident.

Living on his own in a small flat with a perpetual wind off the harbour, "Gee Whizz" asked my mother whether he could live in the top floor of our large house close to the sea. We were taking visitors to augment our measly income, so she said no. Undaunted, he sold his property and bought a flat overlooking Ventnor's Town Hall, 400 metres from our house. He used to sit at the top of the beautiful Cascade, looking out on the remains of the pier, which had been partly destroyed to frustrate any Nazi landings.

I was taking out our terrier Winston for runs at the time, and I usually popped into his flat to listen to his diatribes about the Socialist government, particularly the Health Minister Aneurin Bevan (1897-1960). The son of a Tredegar coal miner, he was a firebrand of a speaker, and I reported on one of his fiery speeches in the *Isle of Wight Guardian*.

When I left home to work for the *Wolverhampton Express and Star*, my grandfather scrawled a weekly letter to me, even more vicious in tone about Clement Attlee's Government. He died at the age of 87, and only my parents went to the cremation. My father died at the same age several years later.

When I spent my two years in hospital, I thought it was the best period of my life – reading lots of classical books in bed. I was convinced it gave me a writing style of sorts, and I wonder why today's youth can't write good English, only abbreviated phrases on social media.

Rather oddly, on several occasions I wrote to my mother from the hospital, saying I wanted her to send me reels of cotton. She asked me why, and I said, "We tie cotton on the legs of the Daddy Long Legs." It was a game we played from our beds, aerial battles bringing down others' flying insects.

Penicillin was in its infancy, and a boy named David Prior from Freshwater and I were the first patients to be given it in the Isle of Wight.

We had a young lady teaching English, Literature, and Maths in our block in the Lord Treloar Cripples (Sic) Hospital in Alton, and I had access to a portable radio and a copy of the *Daily Herald* to learn about my sporting heroes like Denis Compton and Stanley Matthews. At the age of seven, I wanted to be a Fleet Street sportswriter.

Most of the time I was in plaster casts and extensions on my right leg, but when at last I was allowed to try to walk, it proved to be very difficult. Once I became more mobile, the teacher brought a bat, some stumps, and some bouncy balls to play cricket. It was the start of my 70-odd years' love affair with the most cerebral, enjoyable sport. I still needed crutches, and when I batted, I put them down to try to hit the ball. Once I connected, I'd pick them up again and start running. I never ran a two, only singles.

My friend and colleague Lawrence Booth, the editor of *Wisden Almanac*, wrote a remarkable review filling a page in the *Daily Mail* on Armistice Day in 2020. It contained 600 pictures taken in India by former Australian captain Steve Waugh, entitled "The Spirit of Cricket". One picture stood out: it was captioned, "Inspiring: a disabled bowler on crutches." Using one crutch, the bowler released the ball four feet high; his left leg had been amputated above the knee.

I went on three cricket tours of India where everyone loves the game, and regrettably many desperately poor people cut off an arm or a leg to gain sympathy while begging in the streets.

Waugh was one of the outstanding Australian captains who played it hard. He used the phrase "mental disintegration" about sledging opponents. I ghosted some of his articles after he retired, and I was impressed by his thoroughness. He reminded me of Bobby Simpson, who was similar. On another tour of England, Bobby – then retired from playing – was writing for an Australian newspaper. Sometimes I would ask him if he could phone my copy to the *Daily Mail*. He always did.

In the winter at Alton, we weren't able to see our relatives for three months, for fear of catching flu. There was no talk of mental health. Anyone who behaved oddly in the Isle of Wight was stuck in the workhouse at the Whitecroft Hospital.

The hospital at Alton was named after the Lord Mayor of London, Sir William Purdie Treloar, and was built in 1908 by public subscription. The *Daily Mail*'s owner, Lord Northcliffe, was a subscriber who helped our soldiers to recovery from their wounds in the Boer War in 1903-5. No-one was discharged within a week; more like months or a year. In 2000, the hospital was demolished, and a housing estate took its place.

I was eventually discharged and resumed my education at Lowtherville Infants School. My mum told me to ignore the taunts from other boys – she told me "sticks and stones might harm you but not words", and I always bear that in my mind. But as a precaution, she took a part-time job as a waitress again to pay for me to go to a private school, Ventnor College. The Headmaster Charles Green had been a sprinter in his youth, and he claimed he ran the qualifying heats for the 100 metres in the 1908 Olympics in London.

I heeded my mum's advice to ignore taunts; it was called mental strength. The Head introduced boxing in the school's sports, and after a three-round contest was declared a draw with a boy named Donald Badman, I announced my retirement.

In my teens I loved seeing Neil Tarleton, Bruce Woodcock, Randy Turpin, and the Yanks champions Rocky Marciano and Sugar Ray Robinson on Pathe newsreels. But when I was given a press ticket working for the *Daily Sketch* at the Earls Court Arena to see professionals in action, Turpin was sitting behind me and was coming out with gibberish. I realised that boxing was barbaric, fights were often "fixed", and I came to the conclusion it should be banned. Turpin was punch drunk. Today the word is dementia.

Not long afterwards, he committed suicide, shooting himself at the age of 38, leaving behind four young daughters. His father came from British Guyana and was the first black person to live in Leamington. Randy's nickname was the Leamington Licker, and he became a hero when he beat Sugar Ray Robinson in July 1951 in the Earls Court Arena. Sugar Ray may have been disconcerted when a seven-year-old girl was abducted in Windsor where he was training, and was raped and murdered. No-one was arrested. Two months later, Sugar Ray won back the world middleweight championship in the Polo Grounds, New York, by a tenth-round TKO.

One of our teachers at the College was Charles Salisbury, who was luckily my mentor. He was a very successful cartoonist who made a reasonable living out of magazines like "Punch", "Answers", and "Tit Bits", but following a long strike by NUJ members and with no income, he had to take a teaching job. He was married with a son and daughter, and lived close to our latest house in East Street, near the Fire Station. Round the corner was the Seely Library, paid for by the West Wight Seely family. A later relative is the current IOW Conservative MP Bob Seely, MBE. Each Saturday, Charles would take me to the library to choose books to read for my English Literature A-Level exam – mainly classics. I read two or three a week, and I recommend any potential sportswriter or author to do the same. Books and libraries are still around, thankfully.

My mother gave up her waitress job because the condition of her hip deteriorated, and she couldn't find the money to pay the fees for Mr and Mrs Green's College, so I had a short spell at the Ventnor Secondary School. The Labour Government brought in O- and A-Level Certificates, and I passed my seven Os and started studying for four A-Levels.

Just before Winston Churchill took over as Prime Minister late in 1951, aged 77, I had passed my seven subjects at O-Level – most easily, although I scraped through maths. I wasn't given pocket money, but I was earning seven shillings and sixpence whenever I had a football report published in the *Isle of Wight Mercury*. My mum had found one of my reports and taken it to Roy Wearing, the editor, and said, "My son's report is better than your correspondent's." The then writer was a compositor, not a budding writer, so I was hired.

I also took two dogs out twice a day for an old lady who was unable to walk. One, which was completely mad, once bit my left hand and wouldn't let go. It took several minutes before he released my blood-covered hand, and I still have the scar. As the lady raised my stipend to ten shillings, I carried on as a professional dog walker. On top of my match fee, it enabled me to see most of the films shown at the nearby Rex Cinema, which has now been turned into luxury flats with the best view of the Esplanade and beach.

My dad was in and out of jobs, so money was tight, and I had to leave school at 15. I spent several months unemployed, frantically trying to find a suitable job. I wrote to the five Isle of Wight newspapers – the *County Press*, the *Guardian*, the *Sandown Chronicle*, *Ryde Times*, and the *Mercury* – and was told there were no vacancies. Only the *County Press* has survived. I was trying to court the daughter of the chairman when I joined the all-girl class where shorthand and typewriting was taught. I think my efforts were in vain.

I received a curt reply from the editor and the girl was warned off, but I did pass my 120 words a minute in Pitman's.

The only job available was as a junior clerk in the Road Fund Licences Department in the Isle of Wight County Hall in Newport, with a salary of two pounds fifty a week. By that time I had signed up with an Oxford University postal course to be guided to pass my four A-Levels– English, English Literature, Economics, and British Constitution. A fifth of my weekly income was spent on a six-day Southern Vectis Bus Company ticket for the 45-minute journey to Newport and back – no free tickets for teenagers, unlike now! The hour and a half on buses each day was worthwhile – reading and studying, and looking at two glamorous young ladies who got on the next stop and worked at Barclays Bank where I took the bag with money and cheques every weekday. By the time I plucked up the courage to speak to them, both had regular boyfriends.

I was quite shy around this time, but that soon changed when the January rush of customers seeking to have their road fund licences renewed. The queue stretched out onto the steps to the County Hall, and I had to shout the names of the lucky ones. Those with queries had to be sorted out by me, and my diffidence soon disappeared.

I never spoke to the Oxford teachers: it was all done by correcting my work with helpful suggestions. There was no Zoom then, nor any technological aids! Today's Royal Mail wouldn't cope with the massive amount of material being sent to and from Oxford.

In 1953, I contacted the National Council of Journalists to ask how I could go in for their Certificate of Journalism and Diploma of Journalism – the equivalent of gaining a First at a university. I hadn't heard of anyone in Ventnor going to the 40 or so major universities in England. Nowadays, half of the island's 18-year-olds and older now go to universities. Too many, I fear.

I've given lectures on sports writing to nine universities in the South of England, and I advise the students to get to know influential people, and to start writing their stories, blogs, podcasts, etc, and try to persuade employers to take them on – not to waste four years enjoying themselves in university, and to avoid excessive drinking. Not surprisingly, only one university invited me back, and they failed to arrange a date.

My Certificate of Journalism was speedily granted by passing the necessary examination, and my four A-Levels were taken into account. The Diploma was more difficult, though. I needed to write a thesis of 10,000 words – or more – on an original theme. Again, luck came my way.

I wrote my final application to join a daily newspaper and it was successful – after 150 knock-backs – and I joined the staff of *The Express and Star* at Wolverhampton. The editor, Clem Jones, was a friend of Enoch Powell and he used to vet Enoch's speeches. Around that time, Enoch was looked on as a possible prime minister, and Clem told him that his speech about blood flowing like rivers caused by immigration would finish his career. He was right.

Enoch lived in Tettenhall Road, and Clem fixed up a room for me as a lodger there with an elderly lady who was a fan of Enoch. I once spent two hours with him, and he was certainly a highly principled intellectual.

On the train journey from Ventnor to Wolverhampton, I was shocked on the final stretch from Birmingham to Wolverhampton. From the Garden Isle to the Black Country made me think of changing my mind. All those chimneys belching out black soot and gasses from coal mines, iron foundries, steelworks, and brickworks, left me slightly depressed. Until 1840 there had been green fields there, but for the whole of the reign of Queen Victoria there was a blanket of harmful smoke and soot. The Clean Air Act had just been passed in 1956, recommending coke to be used and not coal, along with electricity and gas. The Government had been persuaded to take action when 12,000 died because of the smog in London four years earlier.

Luckily, I met Mick Archer, Halesowen's Chief Public Health Inspector, while I played some cricket matches for Halesowen CC, and he was the ideal mentor to help me with my thesis on clean air. Clem Jones thought it was a good idea as well, and he gave me time off to see the biggest oil refinery in Europe at Fawley on Southampton Water, and another research centre in Greenwich. As a result, my thesis was accepted in 1959, and I moved on to work briefly for the *Eastern Daily Press* and *Norwich Evening News* that summer. It was a relief to breathe unpolluted air.

For most of the summer the NUJ were on strike, and I managed to play a large number of cricket matches for the YMCA and the Norwich Barleycorns. Norwich is known as "The Fine City", and it is. I relished living in the YMCA, which had a cricket net and was walking distance from the newspaper offices. But it was too far from all the action in London, and a fellow sportswriter tipped me off that the Press Association had a vacancy in their offices in London.

I wrote to Norman Preston, who was also editor of the *Wisden Almanack* and ran the Pardons's Cricket Agency, and he fixed up an interview for me on the 5th floor at 85 Fleet Street. Two other directors – Harry Gee (Football) and Ebe Eden (Rugby) – joined in to quiz me, and I told Ebe (short for Ebenezer; a Hebrew name), "I'm not interested in rugby because it is dangerous to health." Norman agreed.

They gave me the job, and the following winter I gained invaluable experience at First and Second Division football matches and FA Cup ties. At the end of the matches, right on the whistle, I would find a telephone and pass on the score and a hundred or so words to the PA serving all the newspapers in the country. It demanded 100% accuracy. Anyone who made a mistake could be fired.

I loved going to White Hart Lane. Tottenham Hotspur were building one of the finest club sides in Europe, and under the floodlights the atmosphere was electric. My allocated seat was right behind where their manager Bill Nicholson

(1919-2004), had just taken over, sat. He used to make notes in a notepad, and as his writing was very legible, sometimes I could make out a few words.

Bill was a tough taskmaster who rarely gave praise. Jimmy Greaves used to repeat a story about scoring a hat trick in one match, and as Bill came into the dressing room he said, "You should have scored five."

Jim replied, "Blimey, we won, didn't we?"

Close to the end of 1959-60, I was at another Spurs game and having a cup of tea and a sausage roll in the Oak Room at half time, when Laurie Pignon, the tennis and football correspondent of the *Daily Sketch*, was complaining about the volume of work he had to do. He said in a loud voice, "We need to sign up a young whippersnapper to take the strain."

Laurie had been captured at Dunkirk and, along with his colleagues, lined up and about to be shot by an SS squad when the commander changed his mind. Instead, he was told to dig coal in mines in Silesia, and Laurie and a friend survived on stale bread and water for five years. "I hate Germans," he always said.

At White Hart Lane, I was first out of the door and headed to the telephone room and rang Solly Chandler, the sports editor of the *Sketch*. I told him what Laurie had said and added, "I'm the right man to be a whippersnapper!" Solomon – another Hebrew name – made his name by breaking the story in the *Daily Express* about Guy Burgess and Donald Maclean defecting to Russia as spies for the KGB. He was a newsman, not a sporting type.

He seemed keen to see me, so I said, "I've got a day off tomorrow. I could see you then." I turned up on time at 9.50am and pulled out my certificates, the diploma, and my Pitman's and typewriting details to show him.

"Not interested in that," he said. "The key question is, who do you know?"

I reeled off a lot of names of people I'd seen at clubs, some of whom I'd spoken to – Bill Nicholson, Alf Ramsey,

Sir Stanley Rous, Walter Winterbottom, Billy Wright, Danny Blanchflower, Colin Cowdrey, Fred Trueman, Jim Laker...

He interrupted, "Wow, when could you start?"

I asked about the weekly salary he had in mind, and when he spelled it out, I told him, "That is the same wage I'm on at the PA."

"Okay, another ten bob to make it a fiver," he said.

Rather foolishly, I said, "I'll have to think it over and let you know." He was taken aback: what a cheek!

Next morning I called him, and before I'd agreed, he said, "I've increased it to six pounds fifty, plus expenses." That was more like it!

I said, "Thanks very much."

A month later, my first job was reporting on the championship-winning side Yorkshire against Middlesex at Lord's in the opening game of the season. With a small staff, I had the chance to write plenty of stories.

Solly wanted to use Rex Brian as the by-line for my writings, because he was a fan of the actor Rex Harrison, who had six marriages. And if I had failed, he could sign up another anonymous whippersnapper.

After I had had a couple of scoops, I told him, "It's about time you used my name!"

He agreed. "How do you pronounce your surname?"

I said, "It comes from Normandy, in a small village near Caen, Scoville, and the Comte came over with William the Conqueror in 1066. In the Isle of Wight, they say Scuvvle. In Belgravia, it's Sco-vell."

Next day, my by-line – in bold type – was "By Brian Scovell, rhymes with Shovel!" That was kept for a month before Shovel was dropped.

I had 11 happy years with the *Sketch* before it was swallowed up by the vastly richer *Daily Mail* in 1971. I still have a picture in my study, taken on the night the staff was summoned for a meeting to know who had been sacked or retained. The managing editor offered to give the letter then or receive it by post next day. I voted for helping the Royal Mail.

Next morning, I was in the bath when Audrey brought my letter. I opened it. I stayed – for another 29 years. I think the deciding factor was that David English had been editor of the *Sketch*, and Lord Vere Harmsworth preferred him as editor of the *Mail*, and I got on well with him.

David was knighted and was a great, enthusiastic newsman. I went to his funeral at St Mary's in Trafalgar Square, attended by a capacity of 800 people, including Margaret Thatcher and several Cabinet Ministers. It was rudely interrupted by members of Stonewall demonstrating against Sir David's policy of reporting on homosexuality. They were ushered out, still shouting.

BORIS NOT IN THE
SAME CLASS AS WINNY

Winston Churchill's speeches in WW2 roused the whole nation, promising that we would eventually overcome Hitler and his insane acolytes. In the same way, the majority of Germans were mesmerised by the rantings of Hitler. Words win battles and arguments, and Boris has always strived to copy Churchill, but has fallen short in the verbals. However, on the final day of the final Brexit deadline, he successfully bartered with the 64-year-old EU President Ursula Von Den Leyen – the first woman to hold the post. They are of similar age and first met in their twenties. He was working in Brussels as a foreign correspondent for the *Sunday Telegraph*; she was born and lived there for 13 years, while her father Ernst Albrecht, a high-up diplomat, was employed by the EU. Ernst and his wife had seven children, and Ursula and her husband Heiko, a physician, have the same number.

The slim, personable Ursula had a year studying at the London School of Economics, worked as a doctor in the USA, speaks German, good English and French, and – lucky for the British Tory Government – she is an internationalist who could see the whole picture where previous EU negotiators were blinkered.

However, she made a crucial mistake by trying to force Britain to transfer their vaccines to bail out European countries, and eventually had to give way. Her previous record of making clangers during her time as German Minister of Defence was also brought up, and her reputation dipped alarmingly.

We look to the USA to give the world a Churchill – a Franklin Delano Roosevelt (1882-1945), or a John Fitzgerald Kennedy (1917-1963) – and we looked in vain at the narcissistic Trump, who was the first President to be charged with inciting a riot, at Washington's Capitol. And the Democrat Joe Biden made a promising start as a nice guy before he started to nod off.

Remember what Roosevelt said in the 1929 Depression? "This great nation will revive and prosper, and the only thing we have to fear is fear itself." He contracted polio at the age of 39, and had to be in a wheelchair for the rest of his life.

When he became President, Kennedy said, "Ask not what your country can do for you; ask what you can do for your country."

Like Biden, Roosevelt and Kennedy were Democrats. Joseph Robinette Biden Jnr – born in 1942 in Scranton, Pennsylvania, son of a car salesman – overcame his stutter some time ago by reciting poetry. In his first speech as President-elect, which lasted 22 minutes, he celebrated the popular vote of 75m for him to Trump's 71m.

He faltered only once, when he said 230 million Americans died from Covid-19, but he quickly corrected it to 230,000 without being prompted. I thought his inaugural speech outshone Barack Obama's and even Bill Clinton's, and it was much more appealing to a worldwide audience, stressing decency, family values, and healing the divide. It was far better than the one of Richard Nixon, the two George Bushes, Jimmy Carter, Dwight Eisenhower, Gerald Ford, Harry Truman, and Lyndon Johnson. I particularly liked Joe's tribute to his wife Jill and his family. He came over as very likeable man, without being divisive.

Kamala Harris, the first black Vice President – clad in all-white to celebrate the hundred-year anniversary of suffragettes winning the right to vote in the USA – came over as far superior to the wooden-faced, expensively dressed Melania

Trump, who was born in 1970 in Slovenia, and is 5ft 10 inches tall. Kamala's diction was faultless, as a former Attorney-General and Senator in California, which has a high percentage of weirdos. Her father was Jamaican, and her mother came from India.

But her rating fell to 28% when she was asked why she had failed to visit the migrants at the Mexican border, and said, "So what? I've not been to Europe." Ugh!

Joe has celebrated his seventy-ninth birthday, outstripping Ronnie Reagan as the oldest man to hold the office, and he wants a second term. He has led an abstemious life – he jogs at a sedate 5mph, which is not surprising, as in 1988 doctors managed to save him from a life-threatening aneurysm.

Only one of the 46 US Presidents was black – Barack Obama. The others were all white, mostly descended from migrants from the British Isles who sought a better life in America. JFK was descended from Ireland, and Joe Biden joked that he came from the Emerald Isle, but some experts claimed that he is descended from an English family who were stationed in that ghastly place Nagpur in India. A professor in King's College traced a link with a ship's captain named Christopher Biden, who died from wounds sustained in the Indian Mutiny in Chennai in 1858, aged 68. Another American professor soon debunked the idea. An odd fact is that Biden is only the second Roman Catholic President.

In 1989, I went to report on the Nehru Cup – a cricket competition to celebrate the centenary of Jawaharlal Nehru (1889-1964), the first President of India. The aircraft, occupied by six groups of the world's best cricketers and media men, was taxiing along from a side runway in the Nagpur Airport when another aircraft, which had just touched down on the main runway, began careering straight at us. The pilot, who was celebrating his 70th birthday, slammed on the brakes and everyone was hurled forward. Luckily no-one was injured – just shocked.

As he walked down the aisle after the plane had screeched to a halt, he said, "Everything is under control." Sick bags were handed out, and some were used.

We spent five days in Nagpur, and we vowed we would never go back. Pakistan beat the West Indies in the Final at a full house Eden Gardens (capacity 70,000), and Imran Khan, later President of Pakistan, was Man of the Match in his final One Day International. Next day, the English press lost to the Indian press, watched by seven spectators.

When the elections were held in the Punjab in 2022, Khan's party won 15 out of 20 seats, so he still has a chance of regaining his premiership.

WINNING A CLOSE CALL

When the Republican candidate Donald Trump claimed he'd won America's general election, I made a similar claim the day after. I told Tino, my domestic repair man, "I'll win my latest PCN appeal without helping from the Supreme Court of Justice!"

At the end of October, I parked round the corner overnight on a yellow line (permissible for Blue Badge holders) and a place I normally use when the free spaces are occupied. And I was astonished to find a PCN!

I emailed this to Bromley Parking GHQ:

"We only have two parking spaces in my narrow drive in Widmore Road, and my daughter Louise parks her vehicle and wanted to use it. I moved mine and parked at Murray Avenue overnight to allow her car to drive off, but next morning I learned her car couldn't start and she called the AA. Afterwards, I went to collect my car – which I do quite often in this predicament – and a PCN was placed on my windscreen clearly displaying my Blue Disabled Badge. The single yellow line enables me to park there, and I've always done that. Have new restrictions been brought into that part of Bromley? There is no signage throughout Murray Ave, and there are designated free parking spaces, which I normally use near the open space adjoining Widmore Road. On this occasion, they were all filled.

"I am appealing against this charge: 'parked in a restricted street during prescribed hours.' I've examined the photos, and the explanation of my car being slightly off the yellow line is that when I reverse, my dashboard shows an indication of it being out of sync. In view of the facts, I think I am being owed an apology from CEO BY141.'"

An adjudicator would have quickly dismissed the case, because I was booked at 9.47am and, though I had parked overnight, my three hours would have expired at 10am so I'd have been saved by the bell!

Forty-one days later, a letter arrived in the Christmas mail from Sarah Fox, of Bromley Parking Department, saying, "Having considered the contents of your letter, we have decided to close the case and no further action will be taken." A nice pressy to end a troubled year!

A FINAL, FINAL THOUGHT

The troubled year of 2020 ended with Boris telling us that Brexit had been signed and sealed on Christmas Day, which coincided with the 20th anniversary of Audrey's death. It was a sunny day of love and happy reflection, and we were still alive. I was one of the first lucky ones who had the Covid vaccine on December 16.

I always thought Brexit would happen, because Germany, France, and Britain were the main subscribers to the EU budget, and Germany and France would lose more than Britain. The other countries pay nominal contributions and have to be subsidised. The day before, a small parcel was wrongly delivered to my house, so I took it to Liz next door. She said, "I've just been on the telephone to the Post Office complaining I hadn't received it." It was a pleasure to hand it to her with my stick, which I use to put a sock on my right, stiff leg. It brought a welcome laugh.

While I was typing, an advert was shown on TV saying the Royal Mail were giving advice about sending parcels. With so many people housebound, they switched to buy online, and over the Christmas holiday period I received only one letter in three weeks. I asked for the reason and was told the majority of staff was part time, working in three shifts each day in the Bromley main Post Office, and they were swamped by parcels which were given precedence. So letters and cards were piled up. Some full-timers had contracted Covid-19, and others were on holiday. Ridiculously, anyone not having used their holiday entitlement had to take it by the end of the year, otherwise it would be cancelled.

My good friends, Dr David Davies and his wife Susan, living in Islip, posted their Xmas card in the first week in December, and it arrived on January 9.

When Audrey died, Susan wrote a very true letter which we treasure, including these words: "She was loved so much by many people – life will be less without her vibrancy, warmth, generosity of spirit, and enthusiasm. For me, Audrey was that very rare and special person, a kind and generous friend who lit up one's own life with her wonderful personality and beauty."

In the night, I usually wake up around 3-4am and often think about Audrey in happy circumstances, and cricket tours to exotic places. This time, it concerned cricket only. I was imagining I was reporting on the greatest finale of any Lord's Test match and trying to get a scoop. Cricket has always been my second love.

On Christmas Eve, a retired Australian doctor Mike Jay called. Mike was a retired cricketer from Adelaide, who played for my wandering cricket club the Woodpeckers in two seasons when he was guesting at a London hospital. I looked on him as the most talented all-rounder of our club, like a Keith Miller.

He was also a star of Australian Rules – a rougher sport than rugby – and now has a dodgy knee, like Compo's.

Denis Compton set me off as a cricketer. And Keith "Nugget" Miller – the all-time Australian all-rounder and war hero who piloted Mosquitos in WW2, and who coined the phrase about pressure: "Pressure is up your backside with a Messerschmitt behind you" – he always rang Compo during Christmas time for a cheery talk, until cancer caught up with him in 2004. Compo predeceased him in 1997. If I hadn't listened to Jim Swanton on my portable radio, I wouldn't have gone in for any sport.

At breakfast on Christmas Day, my mobile rang. It was Gavin ringing from Tauranga in the North Island of New Zealand, where he was in charge of the TV coverage of the

New Zealand v Pakistan Test match. Thirty-four-year-old Neil Wagner, New Zealand's left arm fast medium bowler, bowled 49 overs in the second Test match against Pakistan with two fractured toes – arguably the first to do it. He had 12 injections to deaden the pain and took four wickets for 109 runs. He said, "I hate injections, but I had to do it."

Wagner played for three English counties – Northants, Lancashire, and Essex. He was born in Pretoria and educated at an Afrikaans school, but and transferred to New Zealand in 2008 and is known as "The Workhouse". He's a tough cookie!

Throughout the lockdowns I watched an average of ten to 15 live football matches each week on Sky and BT, and regularly saw players throwing themselves to the ground holding their head, their back or leg, trying to "earn" a free kick or a penalty. Jack Grealish, of England and Aston Villa, was the most fouled player in the 2019-20 season and set a Premiership record of 167; in the following season, he must have set another record of dodgy tumbles. He had a habit of using half size shin pads and socks and risked having more injuries than the average. Normally referees tell players wearing the small versions to go off to change into the customary attire, but £100,000 a week Grealish is an exception.

At the end of 2020, he was suspended from driving for nine months and fined £82,499 for crashing his car. He also breached the Covid-19 regulations. On another occasion, he was attacked during a match by a Birmingham City fan named Paul Mitchell, who was sentenced to 14 weeks. Grealish later signed a new long-term contract with Aston Villa, but it proved to be short-lived because Manchester City snaffled him.

Instead of spending time on piffling cases of supposed racism, the football authorities should penalise the divers and those who charge into opponents with the so-called "professional foul". Two shocking cases happened in the final week of the year. Karen Carney, England's second most capped woman with 144 appearances, now an Amazon Prime pundit, was found guilty of inappropriate use of words by saying, "I actually think they (Leeds) got promotion because of Covid, in terms of it gave them a bit of respite." She made the remarks on the Leeds United official Twitter account and was hit by an avalanche of abuse. Leeds owner Andrea Radrizzani defended her, but the FA came down with an iron fist. She soon cancelled her Twitter account.

The other case concerned Manchester United's Edinson Cavani, the Uruguayan striker on loan from PSG, who tweeted the words "*Gracias negrito*" to a friend. In South America, the term is looked on with affection. But instead of reprimanding him and giving him a lecture, he was fined a whopping £100,000 and suspended for three matches – despite the union of Uruguayan footballers calling for the ludicrous sentence to be rescinded.

In 1950, the Wisconsin US Senator Joseph McCarthy announced he had a list of 200 Communist sympathisers in the US Government, as well as Hollywood stars, playwrights, and authors, and he claimed they needed to be rooted out. It was the period of the Cold War with Russia, and it developed into a vicious witch hunt. Fortunately, McCarthy failed to provide any evidence and died in 1957. His name is still remembered today.

Are we overdoing the issue of racism? As a good friend of Lord Learie, I soon learnt the evil facts of racism. I am sure he wouldn't condemn either Carney or Cavani, because he was a very fair person with a wonderful sense of humour. Back living in Ventnor following my hospital stays after WW2 ended, I heard about only one black person in the town – an American GI soldier who met a girl and, after a whirlwind romance, took her to the USA and they were married. He wasn't abused but accepted.

Now we have gone too far in accusing people of being racist at the expense of humour. The disgraced former Pakistan leg spin bowler Azeem Rafiq posed as an honest whistle-blower until he failed to say at the start that he had previously tweeted about Jews and had made lewd comments several years before to a 16-year-old girl on a plane. Michael Vaughan's career was nearly ruined as a pundit. Soon David 'Bumble' Lloyd was sacked by Sky.

In the 2021-2 Ashes series, the Aussies were still using the word "Poms" to refer to Joe Root's players. Is that racist? Poms originated from Englishmen who were sent to Australia for menial "offenses" like stealing sheep, and the locals were known as prisoners of Her Majesty.

An exceptional footballer sadly died on the eve of Lockdown 3 – Colin Bell of Bury and Manchester City, where he had a reputation for being the fittest, nicest, and quietest star at Maine Road and England. Son of a Durham miner, his mother died of cancer when "Nijinsky" - named after the Derby winner renowned for outrunning the rest of the field – was just one year old. With only a sister to play with, he used to kick tennis balls against walls and doors, giving him a head start on other boys. Trevor Brooking was a tennis ball practitioner as well, and I ghosted his first autobiography, in which he said, "It's essential to master the ball before taking part in games."

I had plenty of tennis balls to knock about in my youth, but living in hilly Ventnor meant there were lots of drains, so too many of mine went down into the sewers and couldn't be retrieved. That's my excuse. Trevor was never booked, and Colin Bell had a similar temperament- two great footballing masters.

WE WERE THE LUCKY ONES

On a rare day off in Covid-19-free New Zealand, Gavin emailed: "I've been playing cricket on a beach, and I bashed it around and hurled the ball at a great pace." Enthusiasm is the key part of the DND of any athlete, and he has it in abundance.

He thanked Audrey and me for having had a happy 35-year marriage and raising him and his sister Louise, who both turned out to be good and talented citizens.

One of the major problems of the civilized world is that a large number of marriages break down, and in so many cases children are brought up by one parent. We were one of the lucky ones.

PS: THE DUKE'S RANGE ROVER
IS A VICTIM OF PCN

Late in February 2021, the 99-year-old Duke of Edinburgh
was admitted to the King Edward VII Hospital for an
undisclosed infection. And two months later, I contacted
bullous pemphigoid – a rampant skin infection. For the rest of
the year, I was housebound and was treated in four hospitals.
One was in a tiny dementia ward of four beds, and I found it
difficult to sleep. I suggested to my consultant that I should
discharge myself, and he agreed.

Despite taking up to 15 pills a day, the blisters in
various places, including my private parts, were winning. It
was awful!

On April 4, a zealous parking warden stuck a PCN on a
Range Rover, owned by the royal family, which was parked on
a yellow line. The driver was a protection officer who had
allegedly spent two hours inside before coming out.

I had one of my hip replacements at the King Edward VII
Hospital, which was founded by Agnes and Fanny Keyser in
1899 as a charity for wounded soldiers from the Second Boer
War. It boasts having the highest nurse ratio per patient in
private hospitals in the UK. It has 58 small wards, and I
counted 28 different nationalities among the staff during my
five days. I found it very educational, learning about different
countries and their love of cricket. Four hours after the
operation, I was back on my feet, aided by crutches.

After being discharged, one of my upper left side teeth was
very loose. I saw my long-time dentist Sean Buckley, in Tweedy
Road, and he said it had been caused through having to
remove a piece of equipment suddenly from the throat.

"If the patient's eyelid starts to become blue, it could be dangerous," he said.

I wrote to the anaesthetist who had been responsible and he apologised and returned my cheque for £259. Must have been a cricketer who "walked"!

Earlier, Prince Philip had been transferred to Bart's Hospital's renowned heart unit for more minor surgery – to open an artery, one suspects. He had previously had a stent inserted. In 1997, I had two stents put in, and they are still working well, boosted by a pacemaker.

The closest I've been to Prince Philip was when I sat ten yards away, facing the wrong direction, at the annual Forty Club dinner in the Long Room at Lord's in 2013. He had been their patron since 1961 – one of the 800 or so organisations with which he was connected.

As an official and editor, I normally went to the VIP pre-drinks hour, but on that occasion I was excluded. Perhaps someone thought being a friend of Nigel Dempster, I might give a scoop to the *Daily Mail* diary about the Duke's possible indiscretions. He didn't make any gaffes in his brief, amusing speech while presenting the Forty Club Trophy, and he was given a standing ovation. The Prince still had his keen sense of humour.

The Forty Club ordered a number of Centenarians' ties to send to Buckingham Palace but the Duke died on April 9, 72 days too soon, otherwise he would have joined with another member, Lt Commander John Manners, who died at 104 as England's oldest first-class cricketer.

Sophie, Countess of Wessex, who is married to Prince Edward, was with Prince Philip at Windsor Castle when he died, and she said poignantly, "It was so gentle. It was just like somebody took his hand and off he went. Very, very peaceful, and that's all you want for somebody, isn't it?"

Several years before, I was at Marcham Green – a village in Essex which boasts the biggest cricket square of English villages – and was writing an article about the Forty Club's match for their Yearbook. David Humphries, whose trade was selling high class maps, kept hitting sixes into the ponds on either side of the square, and eventually there were no more Dukes balls left (Dukes was the name given by their maker Dilip Jajodia.

Another player, Tom Cartwright, a solicitor, found a fishing net and retrieved one of the balls, and Humphries reached his century. When the article was completed, I put a strap on the top of it saying, "Fishing for Duke's Balls in Deepest Hertfordshire.'

Barry Aitken, the Hon. Secretary of the Forty Club, always sent a copy of the annual Yearbook to Prince Philip, and he replied that he thought it was very funny. Not now, with wokers on the march!

Another prime example of his humour was when a TV interviewer asked him, "With your marriage so successful, you must regret that some of your family had failed marriages?" He replied, "Should they be strangled at birth?"

On another occasion, he visited a care home in Bromley, where our family have lived since 1978, and a carer had wrapped the patient with tinfoil. He joked, "Are you oven ready?"

Discharged from the King Edward VII Hospital and back at Windsor Castle, the royal family and their advisors were hit by various insinuations from the exiled Prince Harry and his glamorous wife Meghan, in the sycophantic Oprah Winfrey interview.

We never found out whether the parking attendant who booked the Range Rover outside of the King Edward VII hospital was let off.

My doctor thought it wasn't from Covid-19, as I'd had my two jabs over Christmas, but luckily my daughter Louise spotted the NHS notices about bullous pemphigoid.

One of my happiest cricketing days occurred on July 15, 1953, when I first went on a cricket tour for Newport Cricket Club in Devon, aged 17. Bowling Chinamen, I had figures of 13 overs, three maidens, five wickets for 44 against the

Dartmouth Naval College, where the Prince was voted the Best Cadet in 1938-9 before he joined the Royal Navy. In 1947, he was introduced there to Elizabeth, his future wife, by the impressively Commanding Officer, later Admiral, Sir Frederick Dalrymple-Hamilton. The royal marriage lasted 73 years but couldn't have been happier than mine of 35 years with the beautiful, serene Audrey – and we had less trouble!

PRESS BOXES WHERE
I HAVE BEEN SICK

The football-watching public think our football writers have a parking space outside the ground. Don't believe it. I've been to more than a thousand grounds in 92 countries, and less than 10% give free passes. The majority of sportswriters have to park a mile or so away from the ground to reduce the likelihood of their vehicles being stolen or damaged, and I haven't been booked near a ground.

The funniest incident happened at Withdean Sports Complex, off the A23, when Brighton FC were waiting to move to Falmer's spanking new ground next to Brighton University. I parked early on a cold day and sat in the temporary press box behind two broadcasters. After ten minutes, I suddenly sicked up the contents of my stomach, which landed on their heads. They took in good spirits and continued their commentaries while wiping off the mess with hankies. Two St John's Ambulance men arrived and persuaded me to go to the treatment room, so we marched round the touchline, and they put me on a bed in the portable medical centre.

Suddenly there was a scream: a Brighton player had broken his leg. The St John's ambulance men left to treat the stricken footballer, leaving me to my own devices. Twenty minutes later, I was given permission to resume sitting in the press box. The broadcasters gallantly stayed in their places... and put on their hats as a precaution. Afterwards, Steve Coppell, the erudite Brighton manager, joked about bringing a spittoon next time.

My first visit to Kenilworth Road – Luton's cramped ground – provided a shock. It was 1962, and there was no sign of luxury. One of the local reporters showed me how to reach the smelly, male urinals. When I finished, he pointed to a gap in the ceiling and he said, "That's the way to the press box." He showed me how to climb without being injured.

Cricket clubs have better facilities, and I tell football people they should spend more on press boxes than duff players. I was the Football Writers' Association Chairman and Cricket Writers' Club official in charge of facilities for 40 years, and other than Tottenham's splendid new ground, I would say that Lord's, the Oval, Edgbaston, Ageas Bowl, Old Trafford, and Trent Bridge, are vastly superior. You're not sick, and the five counties provide car park passes.

THE ONE AND ONLY
UFFA FOX, OBE

In 1949, Prince Phillip was introduced to the quaintly named Uffa Fox – the eccentric, rather coarse yachtsman, and naval designer of boats in Cowes – and they became loyal friends. Today, he might have had a criminal record after he took a group of sea scouts, without their parents' permission, up the Seine nearly to Paris. He had told them they would only sail in the Solent.

Uffa was born in East Cowes in 1898 and grew up in Puckaster Cove, a tiny village near Niton on the south tip of the Isle of Wight, where my father was born. Percy worked in Uffa's boat yard at Cowes for several years, and my brother Allan worked there as well. I well remember Percy saying that "his swearing might upset most people".

Philip often stayed with Uffa and taught him to sail. The rocky coastline almost killed King Charles II in 1675, when his small vessel broke up in a ferocious storm before he was rescued. Marconi also started his radio telegraphy experiments there, and the well-known nude model Pamela Green was a resident. In WW2, German aircraft dropped a bomb on St Catherine's Lighthouse, but it was repaired and back in action within days. Puckaster has a reputation for breeding bees and rare plants.

Another good friend of the Prince around that time was Max Aitken, the Canadian owner of the *Daily Express*, who became Lord Beaverbrook and was Minister for Aircraft Production during WW2. Max wasn't liked by most people, but he got on with Churchill and was credited for providing enough Spitfires and Hurricanes to win the Battle of Britain.

Uffa designed the Flying Fifteen – a speedy yacht – and several pioneering yachts, and he took Philip out in them, daring to take more risks than other yachtsmen. Once, both of them were flung into the sea while trying to turn round a buoy. A yacht named *Coweslip* was given as a present to the Prince by the grateful people of Cowes. The royal children were sometimes taken to Cowes Week, but they soon lost interest in sailing. Before the Prince's funeral, Sophie released a picture taken of Princess Anne in 1970, in which her face showed obvious dissatisfaction.

Uffa was reputed to have started playing cricket on an exposed sand bank in the Solent at Christmas time, although he wasn't a good player. But the newspapers used pictures of it after the Boxing Day gimmicky "match". It is not known whether Prince Philip took part.

Uffa married three times, and his third wife Yvonne Bernard was French who spoke no English, and Uffa spoke no French! Did they use sign language? He owned a 300-year-old, gaudily painted Commodore House overlooking Cowes harbour, and he fitted lifts to anticipate his old age. But he died in 1972 and didn't use them. His packed memorial service was attended by the Prince in the St. Martin's Fields in Trafalgar Square.

Due to Covid, Prince Philip's funeral was restricted to only 30 mourners in St. George's Hall in Windsor Castle on a bright sunny day on April 17, 2021, and he and Uffa would have laughed about Philip being ignored. But half the population watched on TV or listened on their radios to honour the most revered man in the history of Great Britain – certainly the funniest. Remarkably, I woke up at 6.40am to see BBC Breakfast's programme and saw a shot of the craggy, tousled hair features of Uffa Fox in Philip's carriage, designed for his latest sport – carriage riding – on one of the Island's beaches.

In the previous week I had this letter printed in the *Daily Mail*'s letter page: "Part of Prince Philip's Fund should be spent on statues with him and Her Majesty together outside

Buckingham Palace, in front of Queen Victoria's memorial. It would remind future generations of their love for each other and his wonderful sense of humour, which is now under attack."

Some others, mainly politicians, wanted a statue of the Prince on the fourth plinth in Trafalgar or in Great Westminster Hall, but thousands of tourists prefer going to see Buckingham Palace. The royal family's advisors asked the public for charitable donations in preference to buying flowers, which would cause unnecessary litter.

In today's rapidly changing attitudes, we will never see a Prince Philip or an Uffa singing his sea shanties again – regrettably. Humour of that type has been replaced by American humour, as experienced by my friends Michael Vaughan, David 'Bumble' Lloyd, David Gower, and a host of Sky, BBC, ITV, and others – bowled out by the wokes.

While ending this book (May 1st), it will be a year since I had bullous pemphigoid, leaving me very weak, and finally I caught Covid. More than a hundred doctors, carers, district nurses, ambulance staff, porters, and the staff of five hospitals have worked on me, and I can only thank them along with my magnificent daughter, Louise.

Our first doctor, the German Carl Prausnitz who was a famous expert in immunology, might have found an answer had he lived now.

Lightning Source UK Ltd.
Milton Keynes UK
UKHW011856041222
413331UK00001B/72

9 781803 813165